A love of ships

A love of ships

by G A B King

 KENNETH MASON

For Cath

Published by Kenneth Mason
North Street, Emsworth, Hampshire PO10 7DQ

© G A B King 1991

British Library Cataloguing in Publication Data
King, George
    A love of ships.
    1. Great Britain. Merchant shipping, history. Biographies
    I. Title
    387.5092

    ISBN 0-85937-358-4

Designed and printed in Great Britain

Acknowledgements

TO WRITE ONE'S MEMOIRS is a vanity, but sometimes a vanity with a purpose. My grandfather, Tom King, was a wonderful story-teller who brought alive for me the late-Victorian and Edwardian years in a douce coastal town in south-west Scotland. When he died I deeply regretted that he had never committed his anecdotes to paper. I cannot speculate on how my grandson, Alexander, will view these reminiscences for he is still too young to have an opinion; but I should like him to know, some day, that he was in my thoughts as I laboured.

Without the encouragement and support of the Marine Society this book would not have seen the light of day and I acknowledge my debt of gratitude to that splendid maritime charity with which I have been involved for a lifetime, first as a student and beneficiary of its great library service, later as a contributor and ultimately as a member of its Court. I am particularly indebted to the present chairman, Mr J G Davis, the general secretary, Lieut Commander Richard Frampton, and Mr Michael Grey, a member of the Court who read the original manuscript and gave me invaluable advice. I am grateful, too, to Mr Roderick Kennedy and Mr Charles Barr of the British Petroleum Company plc. The first, a professional journalist, read the manuscript and made many helpful suggestions. The second provided most of the ship photographs from the comprehensive pictorial archives maintained by his department. In this respect I gratefully acknowledge the British Petroleum Company plc.

But my greatest debt is to the Cath of this book. Throughout our early married life she endured without complaint the partings and the loneliness which are the lot of all sailors' wives. She brought up our son, Geoffrey, single-handed and in my view made a splendid job of it. Later, she and I learned together a whole new repertoire of performance to fit the life into which we had been thrust, and she did it superbly well. She has always been my greatest support – and sometimes the most devastatingly-honest critic, infuriatingly correct in her judgements. Without her there would have been no life worthy of a memoir.

Contents

Illustrations

Foreword by Admiral of the Fleet Lord Lewin

George King and I have led parallel lives, he with the Merchant Navy and I with the Grey Funnel Line. It is a privilege indeed, as a Royal Navy sailor, to have been asked to write a foreword to this very personal account of the life of a distinguished Master Mariner. In those of us who experienced the never-ending drama and tragedy of war time convoy was born an enduring respect and admiration for the merchant seaman. When Apprentice King was sailing the seas in a virtually defenceless merchant ship, delivering the sinews of war to distant battlefields and returning with the supplies that sustained the home front – and being sunk by a U-boat for his pains – I was serving in a thirty-six knot destroyer, bristling with guns. Far too often we were enraged with frustration when we failed to protect the merchant ships in our charge; the men who crewed those ships were the real heroes of the war at sea.

The war over, George King turned to tankers, those ubiquitous ships that transport about the world the source of energy on which our prosperity depends, so little appreciated by many of the general public who see them only as a threat to our environment. We must have been in the Gulf together in 1951 when the Royal Navy was frustrated again in its inability to prevent Mossadeq's nationalisation of the Anglo-Iranian Oil Company, an act that I have always seen as the beginning of the end of the predominant British influence in that important area.

Those who are lucky enough to have the opportunity to pass on their experience by training the young gain much in return, and George's time in *HMS Conway* was no exception, although losing the ship by stranding was an episode he would no doubt willingly have missed! Thence to admininstration, and the problems encountered in the offices of the BP Tanker Company bear much resemblance to those of the Admiralty, but it is evident that in both the important factor is that people come first, as in any successful enterprise.

It is clear from this book that George King's association with the sea has been more a dedication than a career, he has contributed so much to maritime matters and continues to do so. His love of the sea and ships runs through every page, and that is a sentiment that unites all true sailors.

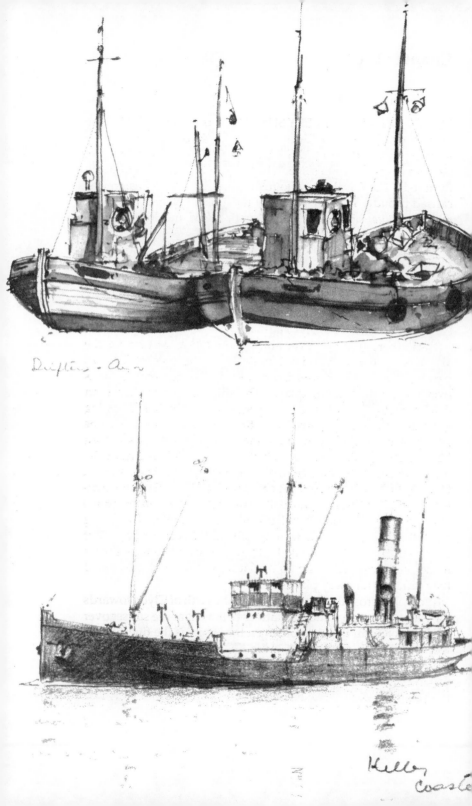

Drifters Aground

Kelly Coaster

Chapter 1

LONG AGO, WHEN EVERY SUMMER was golden, I fell in love with ships.   In 1935 that was not difficult for a boy of ten in the town of Ayr.   The sun did not then set upon the British Empire strung along trade routes over which the Red Ensign ubiquitously fluttered.   The Royal Navy flourished and the White Ensign was carried proudly to every corner of the globe.   Names like *Mauretania, Aquitania, Olympic* and *Majestic, Hood* and *Repulse* were common currency.   In these islands vast fishing fleets sailed from Aberdeen and Hull, from Grimsby and Lowestoft, from Fleetwood and the West of Scotland.   Sir Thomas Lipton and Tommy Sopwith were household names and every summer the Firth of Clyde was speckled with the sails of a thousand yachts.   In any case, it took only ten minutes, on a second-hand bicycle, from Newton Park School to Ayr Harbour.

It was there that the fever entered the blood, at first for the artefacts, for the craft, and not for the sea.   The smell of fish was part of it, as drifters and seine-netters discharged their baskets over the South Harbour quay.   The ship sounds of sheave on derrick, rattling winch and hissing steam, the mewing of herring gulls and the joking laughter of the fishermen touched some ancestral nerve.   A fair prize for a small predator was half-a-dozen herring strung together through the gills and filched from the quayside under the indulgent, Nelsonian eye of the boat skipper. Over at the North Harbour the ships were bigger.   Kelly coasters loaded coal for Belfast and Baltic traders discharged pit props along the jetty.   The air was full of coal dust and the smell of frying bacon and the little ships were mostly battered and rusty.   But they were ships.   They floated.   They strained at their moorings in the gentle swell coursing up the harbour. They were alive, and they sailed to far away places.

Ayr looks across the southern part of the Firth of Clyde towards the island of Arran – and the natives believe that the sunset over Arran, seen from the Low Green on the shore, is the finest in the world.   To the south-west, Ailsa Craig sits up like a purple haystack and the Firth itself stretches off into the north-west distance towards the Kyles of Bute and the Cowal Hills encircling the Tail o' the Bank.   The Firth of Clyde is a noble waterway and in the 1930s it was a major sea lane with the port of Glasgow at its head.   Clyde-built meant something then and, after years of rusting on the stocks, the *Queen Mary* was nearing completion. She was to become perhaps the best-loved great ship in the Clyde tradition, but for many conservative small boys she was seriously flawed for she had but three funnels when a proper, self-respecting transatlantic liner ought to have four. Great shipping companies occupied offices in and around Bothwell Street in Glasgow - the Anchor Line, Ellerman's City Line, the Donaldson Line, 'Paddy' Henderson, Canadian Pacific, 'Hungry' Hogarth, Denholm. Their ships - liners, cargo ships, tramps, tankers - rang 'Full Away' off Toward Point and headed for America, South Africa, India, Australia, China, Japan, the world - and made their homeward approach coming over the south-western horizon, past Paddy's Milestone, before shaping up for the pilot station south of the Cumbraes. In summer the Firth was alive with excursion steamers of the railway companies, for going 'doon the watter' was still a Clydeside thing to do.   Fast turbine steamers and elegant, if mostly old-fashioned, paddle steamers weaved their way between the white sails of yachts.   Ayr was at the southern-most edge of all this maritime activity but it would have been difficult for a small boy, sensitive to the world of sea and ships, not to have been aware of it.

My introduction to the sea, nevertheless, had happened long before.   In Buenos Aires, in early 1926, my mother carried her nine-month old first-born on board the *Highland Pride*, an old Nelson Line ship, for the homeward voyage to London.   Born in the Argentine in 1901, first child of an English couple, she had been sent home to school in England in 1913, spent the war in Southsea and, in 1919, returned to her parents' home in Buenos Aires.   My father, a Scottish bank clerk, went out to the Argentine in 1920 to work.   There my mother and he met and were married on their 23rd birthday - they were born on the same day, July 18, 1901 - and their first child arrived nine months and nine days afterwards, which I suppose is what is liable to happen to ardent young people.   Exactly why Tom King was returning to Scotland after only five years in the Argentine has never been wholly clear to me. He was a charming, gregarious young man who played rugby and golf and tennis very competently and socialised most heartily.   He was said to have danced superbly but he also played the horses and played them rather badly.   Perhaps it was a mistake for him to have displayed such a convivial style, for a Scottish bank clerk, sent abroad to make his fortune, was probably expected to be dour, and unimpeachable. That was not my father's way and my mother, a quiet soul when she was young, a 'mouse' with the heart of a lioness, put up with much during her married life. For whatever reason, Tom and Isabel King were homeward bound for London and eventually his parents' modest house in Ayr. The voyage was said to have been uneventful. I do not remember it but, long after, I established that the *Highland Pride,* the first ship in which I ever embarked - but not my own first ship which is something special and another story altogether - was no great beauty. A grey-painted cargo liner with accommodation for a number of passengers her general appearance seems to me to have been unimpressive. Perhaps she was one of the sad ships for she came to an inglorious end a year or two later when she ran aground in the approaches to Vigo Bay and broke her back. By that time I was a junior citizen of Ayr and had a younger brother, Terence, the first sight of whom prompted me to remark, 'It's got eyes. It's got a nose. It's got a mouth.' - not profound, but they must have seemed remarkable phenomena to an observant year-and-a-half old.

Percy John Bartholomew, my mother's father, started life as a marine engineer in Portsmouth, served at sea in the Nelson and Royal Mail Lines and then obtained an appointment ashore in Buenos Aires in the late 1890s. My mother believed that he had reached the rank of chief engineer by that time. If so he must have been precocious for he could hardly have been 30 years of age when he and his wife, Nellie Palmer from Weymouth, took up residence in the Buenos Aires suburb of Quilmes. When I first became aware of him he was a tall, austere, silver-haired man in

Highland Pride

his 60s whom we knew as Grandpa Barty and treated with cautious respect. I am sure he loved his three daughters and his grandchildren dearly and this was sometimes evident; but I never overcame the feeling that I had to gang warily in his presence. For me his most endearing attribute was that he knew about ships, and I think it pleased him to be asked. Not that every moment of my childhood was spent in a love affair with ships. Far from it. Most of the time it was concerned with other matters and particularly in keeping out of trouble. Thus, Grandpa Bartholomew was to be respected. Grandma Barty, on the other hand, was wholly lovable. She was not much more than five feet tall, wobbled when she laughed and laughed a lot. She would have given us anything we asked but she had little opportunity for such indulgence since she and my grandfather paid only occasional visits to England until they finally retired, in 1935, to a small house in Sussex.

Our family relationships - ultimately there were four of us for Terry was followed by Thelma born in 1929 and Eileen three years later - were much closer with my father's family who were there to hand and a part of our everyday life. Old Tom King, my paternal grandfather, and his wife, Nicholas Brown, were as Scottish peasant as the Bartholomews were English petit bourgeois. Grandpa King, fourth or fifth child of a master joiner, had been a postman (or letter-carrier according to his marriage certificate) in Ayr. Some time in the early 1890s he married the parlour maid from a big house in the elegant south part of the town. She was the daughter of an Ayrshire shepherd and retained her country ways and wisdom all the days of her life. Tom was a small-town card, bald and bespectacled, with a white moustache, a short pipe constantly in his mouth, slightly bowed legs, standing about five feet four and possessed of a twinkling sense of humour. He was a very competent handyman and an excellent maker of toy swords and shields, given to whistling psalm tunes or singing music-hall songs as he worked, an infuriating habit I have apparently inherited. Photographs of Rudyard Kipling remind me of him - it must be a late Victorian type. My grandmother was fanatically opposed to the demon drink. Tom enjoyed it and, despite this fundamental difference in viewpoint, they had three of a family - Isabella, known as Isa, born in 1895; Margaret, called Tot all her life and two years younger than Isa, amd my father, Tom, the apple of his mother's eye and the inheritor of his father's charm, humour and taste for the good life.

Grandma and Grandpa King lived in a small, solid, red-sandstone, terrace house in Marchfield Road on the northern boundary of Ayr Burgh and the edge of the neighbouring small town of Prestwick. In those days Prestwick Toll, where Marchfield Road joined the main road, was the northern terminus of the tramcar service which ran through the centre of Ayr ending south of the town at Doonfoot and at Burn's Monument, near the poet's cottage. It was upon this terrace house, grandly called 'Aralia', that my mother and father descended when they disembarked from the *Highland Pride* in London. There they had to stay, with my grandparents and my aunts and first one and then two infant boys, for several years until they were in a position to rent their own bungalow in neighbouring Prestwick. I remember the house, vaguely for the most part but crystal-clear in a few details - the wag-i'-the-wa' clock in the kitchen, the shape of the scullery where Grandma King, an excellent cook and an even better baker, seemed to be perpetually engaged, her arms flour to the elbows, the 'recess' bed in its own tiny alcove off the kitchen, the iron range polished and blackened every day, mahogany Victorian furniture in the front room used only on Sundays and holidays, a butterfly collection in a heavy gilt frame, a view from the back bedroom into a walled garden which seemed enormous but could not have been more than 20 yards long and 10 wide. It was small, over-crowded and unpretentious; but it was spotless, warm and welcoming and, even though best house coal cost at least a shilling a hundredweight, the fire in the black kitchen range constantly flamed high in the chimney. It was the home I liked best during the first 10 years of my life for we always seemed to return to it in the intervals between my parents' occupation of a series of flats and houses belonging to other people. Perhaps our life need not have been like that but the years between the General Strike and the mid-1930s were difficult and dangerous for many. Small boys do not readily understand such things, especially when they are well protected. Only gradually did I come to realise that the path along which my mother and father embarked in 1924 had proved far from easy.

The great protecting arm about us children was the family. My mother, a fair-haired young woman slim almost to the point of emaciation, was stoical and determined against the odds that marriage and sojourn in a strange land threw at her. In some subtle way, as we grew older, we knew she was different from other mothers - and, of course, she was. She spoke in what I would later recognize as a standard received accent which was natural to her. Her style and her methods were those of southern England overlaid with the experience of the expatriate's life in Argentina. This contrasted profoundly with the douce Scottish people by whom she was surrounded and who must have seemed alien to her at first. But she became the darling of her husband's family and to the ends of all their lives Isabel was treated as another daughter or sister and never, under any circumstances, as a stranger. And in an odd tribute to that family she became more Scottish as she grew older outliving all the Kings and ending her days in the town she had come to as a young woman more than 50 years before.

My father was an altogether different character. The youngest of three, and the only boy in a comfortable working-class household, he might have been a little spoiled as a child. He was certainly well protected, and he was also bright. He did well at Ayr Academy (and had his nose broken playing rugby). At 17 he entered the Royal Bank of Scotland as a junior and less than four years later he and several others, mostly a year or two older, sailed for the River Plate to seek their fortune. It was typical of aspiring young Scots of his generation for whom opportunities at home, just after the Great War, were so much less than seemed to beckon from Shanghai, Bombay, Buenos Aires or Toronto. The destination was mostly a matter of chance or where friends had already beaten a path; but the pattern was the same and many, perhaps most, found their modest fortunes and lived their lives of service running railroads, banks, plantations, oil fields or sawmills. I don't know what happened to my father's fortune – perhaps the horses got it – but his early experience turned the provincial Scots boy into a rather cosmopolitan individual with a gift for languages. In the late 20s that must have been of some value and, for several years after their return from Argentina, he was employed by J & P Coats' Central Agency, representing them in quite a junior capacity in Paris, Algiers and the Canary Islands. But he fell foul of the system and from the early 30s moved from one barely-satisfactory job to another selling, first, insurance and then reconstituted stone and building material for the civil engineering industry. As a companion he was wonderful. Young enough to understand children, and energetic enough to be able to tire them out before they did him, he seemed an ideal father when we were small.   He was a superb story-teller and his home-comings, especially from abroad, were great events.   He knew about the good life. He enjoyed living it when it was within his grasp but all his life he never quite managed to acquire the means to live in the manner to which he aspired.   He was a product of his background, his times and his character - as are we all.   The background was sound enough, but the times were unpropitious and, although the ball bounced right for him now and then, he always seemed to kick it into touch without gaining any ground. His life was one of wasted opportunity; but I doubt if he would have thanked anyone for feeling sad on his behalf because he was, for the most part, a cheerful, ebullient and outgoing individual who kept his frustrations to himself. After 16 years of marriage he and my mother separated in 1940 when he was serving in the Army and I saw him only once or twice between that time and his comparatively early death from cancer in 1968.

Two of the most significant figures throughout our childhood and, indeed, the whole of our lives were our aunts, Tot and Isa - always said in that order although Isa was the elder. They never married. Isa went into the counting house of a solid, prosperous boot and shoe manufacturing company in Ayr in 1909 and retired from it 60 years later in her mid-70s. She was the sheet-anchor of her parents' family - a small, busy person with wispy auburn hair, spectacles, a blunt nose like her father, a rifleman's quick stride and a formidable sense of responsibility. She was religious but light-hearted about it and never seriously proselytised although she enrolled Terry and me in an organisation called the Guild of Honour when we were too young to protest. At 14, as first in her year, she had been the Dux Medallist of Newtonhead School and, had her year been five or six decades later, she would have become an educated woman for she had a clear mind and an infinite capacity for work. Of all my relations she was the one I most admired.   Her sister Tot on the other hand was, like my father, charming, quite handsome but vaguely irresponsible with money, although she never had much to be irresponsible with. She was a romantic and had numerous suitors for her youthful hand. But she was selective and, in any case, increasingly ran the household as my grandmother became more of an invalid after developing heart trouble. Under Tot the house was run as impeccably as it had been by her mother.   Probably as a result of her mother's experience and influence she laid a most attractive table. Tot was intermittently at war with her father especially when he had taken a drink too many. But they were devoted and her life was spent - one is tempted to say sacrificed - in the service of her mother, father and sister. Sacrifice is the last word she would have used herself because she would not have seen it like that. She thought all her nieces and nephews were wonderful, but she had a particular affection for my sister, Thelma. Those two good, amiable, hard-working, loving and lovable women are part of my heritage. I cherish their memory for, in the sometimes difficult conditions of my own early life, they were part of the solid base which ensured that it did not seem difficult to me at the time.

My brother John Terence, called Terry except when he was in trouble with his mother who then addressed him rather stiffly as 'Terence!', although 18 months younger than I, must have grown faster or been gifted with a different set of genes for we tended to be taken for twins although he was a finer and more handsome specimen. At about the age of 10 he bore a striking resemblance to the boy actor Freddy Bartholomew - not surprising since our mother and the actor's father were first cousins. This did not impress Terry much and it was possible to raise his ire by calling him Little Lord Fauntleroy. In our early days we were inseparable although we fought like puppies in a litter. As small schoolboys we were known to break off fighting each other in order to promote our common defence, back to back, when taken on by other young hooligans. Terry was a dependable companion and an excellent foil. There was the added advantage, for me, that he drew the fire more than half the time for he was so innocent that it was always he who was caught. As a small boy I thought this an admirable arrangement although I did recognize that it was less than fair.

The two girls, Thelma, an engaging infant with a lisp and what used to be called a peek-a-boo bang - a King, and Eileen, an elfin child with straight ash-blonde hair and fine bones - a Bartholomew, had arrived some years after the boys. In a similar way they grew up together although their relationship with one another may have been less close since there was a gap of three years between them and they could never have been mistaken for twins as we were. In theory the boys were the guardians of the girls but the stewardship was far from exemplary. Told to push a low pram bearing an infant requiring fresh air our reaction was to duck under the handlebar as soon as we were out of sight, grasp the

18

sides of the pram and push it at the highest possible speed making raspberry noises as if the pram were a police car. The infant got fresh air and either a thrill or a fright, boredom was avoided and we never lost a sister yet.

Some time before we reached this stage of irresponsibility we had passed through life's second toll-gate, learning to compete and co-operate with our peers at school. Ayr Academy, the great school of the town and county, traces its origins to the mid-13th century. My father attended it before the Great War and in 1930 I was enrolled, followed a year later by Terry. It was a magnificent school but of my days in it at that time I remember only making patterns with tiny coloured cubes which had to be set into a wooden, honeycomb frame, decorating Woolworth glass tumblers with stylised pictures of flowers and doing it very messily, and repeating *a, b, c* as an immensely tall lady pointed to symbols on a blackboard. I lasted at Ayr Academy little more than a year and my brother only a term for it was a fee-paying school in those days and our father suffered one of his periodic eclipses. I do remember how solicitous he was in telling us that we should have to leave and attend a humbler establishment which cost less. Newton Park Higher Grade School was run by the Education Authority and, in fact, cost nothing. Housed in an impressive Victorian red-sandstone building, which would have looked even more impressive without the industrial grime clinging to its stone-work, it lay about midway between the centre of town and Prestwick. On the west side it was bounded by several streets of small detached and semi-detached bungalows and terrace houses, neat and tidy for the most part and with about two yards of garden between the front door and the pavement from which each was separated by cast-iron railings set into low stone walls. To the south there were some small factories and Somerset Park, the ground of Ayr United, the local football club. To the east, immediately opposite the front of the school, stood a foundry and die-stamping works. This grimy group of buildings was flanked to north and east by council estates, the hinterland from which many of Newton Park's pupils were drawn. The school building stood in a playground surfaced in fine, dark-grey clinker which was no doubt a great economy in the centre of a coal-mining district but raised clouds of dust in dry weather and was unmentionable in wet. There was an entrance at one end of the school for girls and another at the opposite end for boys, the playground being divided by a high wall surmounted by the ubiquitous iron railings to ensure proper segregation of the sexes during breaks. It was not Ayr Academy.

Inside, the odour of carbolic, gym shoes and high endeavour was overpowering. The ground floor had a central corridor extending the length of the longer axis of the building and joining the girls' and boys' entrances. On each side of this green and cream-painted thoroughfare were four or five classrooms the corridor walls of which consisted of yellow-varnished pine panels to a height of about four feet surmounted by windows of ribbed glass. Similar panels separated each room from the next. All the rooms were the same, perhaps 20 feet wide and 30 feet long with a raised dais for the teacher's desk just inside the door and a blackboard on the wall behind. We sat at twin, metal-framed, wooden desks which incorporated a tilting bench seat. It was the classic, simple, elementary schoolroom of the first half of the 20th century and must be woven into the experience of generations of us. And, whatever Newton Park lacked in aesthetic appeal, it made up for in its commitment to elementary but fundamental learning. The headmaster was a dark-avisaged man called Lewis, a Welshman as was established for us when one enthusiastic end-of-term volunteer offered to sing 'Taffy was a Welshman, Taffy was a thief' as his contribution and had to be dissuaded. I cannot imagine how many staff there were and I remember only two of them, the first, Mrs MacArthur, with almost total recall. She was a ginger-haired Boadicea of a woman who dressed in simple long-sleeved blouses, tweed skirts, lisle stockings and sensible shoes. She had strong, well-shaped calves and stood four-square like one of Horatius' men defending the bridge. Her spectacles tended to slip down her nose as her enthusiasm or anger developed. She was tough. She was dangerous. But she was inspired and I have often thought that there is a generation of now-ageing men and women who passed through her hands and have owed her an immense debt of gratitude all their days – a Miss Jean Brody in her own right. She taught our class of 30 boys and girls from 1933 to 1936. On January 20, 1935, the day old King George V died, she spoke about his death after assembly and prayers. Her eyes filled with tears as she said, 'You know, to older people, it's like losing a father,' and then quietly broke down. A banal statement to sophisticated adults, but the words and the public disintegration of a very strong lady spoke profoundly to 10-year olds and took them one more step into a tougher world. When Mrs MacArthur had done her best for us we were passed on, for a final year's polishing, to the tender mercies of a balding, self-contained disciplinarian called McBain who stood no more nonsense than the good dame had done but made no fuss about it, the mailed fist being concealed in a conspicuous velvet glove which, nevertheless, transmitted the message.

Discipline at Newton Park was strict and no-one set out to suggest that school should be fun. Nevertheless, it was enjoyable despite the rigid control and especially so for the brighter ones who were not only praised publicly for success but encouraged to help their slower-moving colleagues - a recipe for conceit, but no damned nonsense about elitism being unacceptable. Reading, writing, arithmetic, scripture, history, geography, nature study and physical training just about encompassed the curriculum and play was confined to 10 minutes in the forenoon, five in the afternoon and as much as you liked after four o'clock provided your homework was done for the following day. Reading started with thin primers bound in russet-coloured linen, printed in bold type and illustrated by some long-dead Victorian or Edwardian artist. Dan was perpetually a good boy, Ted a smart lad and the cat sat a lot on the mat. The system must have worked well enough and produced quick results because the first newspaper I ever remember managing to read for myself - at least the headlines - covered the R101 disaster in October 1930 when we were still doing *a, b, c* at Ayr Academy – where the system of teaching was the same – and trying to decipher simple, single-syllable words. As we progressed at Newton Park we were allowed to take home the next book when we had completed the current one, but only as a special treat. Later, at the age of seven or eight, we could borrow one book at a time from the class library kept in a cupboard behind the teacher's desk. This kept us going until we were old enough to be given a ticket at the Carnegie Library in the town where the choice seemed to be infinite and the quality so much better. By the time we were 10 or so books like *The Pilgrim's Progress* and *Hereward the Wake* were given as prizes although I doubt if they were read because there was so much of Richmal Crompton to be got through. But we had moved some way from the semi-wild little animals we had been but a few years before. We started writing by learning the simple, printed Roman alphabet but, as soon as that had been mastered, we were weaned onto cursive 'joined-up' writing which had to be immaculate copper-plate or your knuckles were rattled with a ruler.   Writing was done into a blue-covered, lined exercise book code-numbered J4 I think.   Each set of two principal lines was supported by feint-ruled lines above and below for the tops and bottoms of the loops.   Mrs McArthur dictated. We wrote. At first it was done in pencil and the teacher's pet of the day was given the preparatory task of sharpening the pencils with Mrs. MacArthur's own penknife!   Oh, perfect bliss. Later we graduated to pens - brown-varnished holders invariably nibbled soft and bone-white at the ends and fitted with sharp, bronze-tinted nibs - not the Pickwick, the Owl and the Waverley pen but a distant relative which came cheaper by the gross.   Ink was contained in small white porcelain pots set into holes in the desks and sometimes used for murdering tadpoles.   Small screws of blotting paper - I seem to remember we had to provide our own blotting paper - were sometimes stuffed into the inkwells by the rougher element and caused consternation when the responsible monitor or nominated helper went round with a large brown bottle to replenish the pots.   Preparing for ink writing was lengthy and hazardous.   The actual writing was carried out with 30 pink tongue-tips protruding from 30 pairs of rose-bud lips, the only sounds being heavy breathing and the scratching of the nibs, emphasised now and then by a tiny expletive belying the apparent innocence of the toiler whose nib had just become stuck in the paper or got crossed and spattered his laboriously-executed work. I find it inexplicable that, at the age of 10, I won a prize for this copper-plate writing in ink.   By the time I was 13 my writing was infinitely faster but quite illegible, although neatly-enough placed upon the page.   Thus it has remained, in its unrestructured state, for 50 years.   Later generations seem to have been taught a very legible italic script but now, perhaps, only those who can dominate a word-processor will be able to put words together at all.

Arithmetic was another stimulating mental exercise for developing young brains.   The Scots pride themselves, among many other things, on being above-averagely numerate, but on what basis I am not clear.   Certainly, we learned early in life the speed at which a water tank filled through faucets A and B while the skulking waste-pipe C was simultaneously emptying it.   Money sums were of crucial concern and we early learned the importance of this in Scottish history because of the origins of the Bank of England.   Simple interest was disposed of in a relatively short time and we moved on to compound interest which was obviously more lucrative and would be of greater value to those of us who ultimately became clerks in the counting houses of commercial enterprises. Before the down was on our upper lips we used terms like, 'differential calculus', 'integer' and 'to the base ten' with huge confidence and total ignorance. They sounded impressive and we did relish the conundrum about the velocity of the fly and the oncoming railway train at the moment of impact. The square root of minus one came later when we had graduated to a more senior school; but after five or six years at Newton Park we were unquestionably numerate, which was what the system was supposed to make us. Although we started learning the multiplication tables up to 12 by rote, everything else was taught from first principles and one has to say, with hindsight, that it was not a bad way to learn.

Religious knowledge was covered in a morning period once or twice a week and only served to remind most of us that we went to Sunday School as well and had to remember the catechism in case Mrs MacArthur asked us - unfairly - to repeat it during the week. She was more formidable by far than any young Christian amateur doing his parish duty on Sunday afternoon. History, on the other hand, was dealt with seriously and taught in the most chauvinist and partisan way. The facts of history were sacred - kings and queens and battles and dates. The most important battle in the history of the known world had been fought in 1314 at Bannockburn near Stirling where Robert the Bruce, of spider fame, had trounced the hated English. I was not too sure, sometimes, about the hated English. My mother was one of them. But I accepted the concensus because I was one of the boys and the need to belong, the tribal urge, starts very early in life. In one way or another 'tribalism' became a significant part of my own life and work, but I think I recovered from the Scottish chauvinist phase fairly rapidly. *1066 and All That*, thrust into my hands by my father, put things in a better perspective and he had a gift for story-telling about the past which kindled the flame of imagination. Geography lessons, at least for me, were self-igniting. Very early in life I became fascinated by maps and place names. England, 60 miles to the south, was a foreign land where people spoke the same language in a different, fol-de-rol accent. But beyond England there were other places more and more exotic, like France and Tibet and the Rocky Mountains and Siberia and Tahiti. To begin with one had no conception of how those fabulous places lay in relation to one another and school geography lessons did little to encourage romantic views of the world. The rivers of Scotland, the mountains and their heights, the chief towns and their industries, just about exhausted the curriculum. But geography - the beautiful world - spoke for itself, and the *Children's Encyclopaedia* opened the door to romance. I was captivated by the magic in the phrase, 'Over the Hills and Far Away', and it still sends a frisson of anticipation through me.

With one or two notable exceptions, I can scarcely recall my school fellows. Jimmy Fullarton was my 'horse' when we fought like jousting knights in the playground. This was because he was four feet six and I was three feet ten. He must have been a decent fellow for he never complained and there was never any suggestion of reversing our roles. Robert S Blain was a clever chap perfectly justified in calling himself Robert Speedy Brain; but Charlie Chambers, known as 'Chanty' which is vernacular Scots for a chamber pot, was greatly respected for his diversionary behaviour in class. There is always a class buffoon whose need for applause and the acclaim of his fellows overcomes his natural instinct for self-preservation. Such an one was Chanty. He was the boy likely to be caught with a comic under his reading book, or who had just fired an ink pellet when Mrs MacArthur re-entered the room, or who claimed, when we were learning to use rulers, that he had the longest willie in the class and would prove it, when the teacher's back was turned, if someone would loan him a ruler! He lived in the council estate and was somewhere in the middle of a very large family. When he returned to school after being sick his mother would send a note written on the first scrap of paper to hand regardless of whether it had been used previously to wrap sausages or fish. Chanty always wore large boots with heel and toe caps and triple nails in the soles. The boots tended to flap open because he was well advanced in years before he mastered the tying of laces. But he was an amiable soul with tousled yellow hair, a wide grin, a milk-and-roses complexion and a smear of jam from his breakfast at the corners of his mouth. I expect he is still about somewhere for he was one of the world's cheerful survivors. I admired him - not least for having the biggest willie in the class, at least among those few which were measured.

With the exception of three, the girls are even more indistinct. Sheila Wilson and Sheila Gibb were bosom companions, the first a Shirley Temple type, the second a cut-down Deanna Durban without the voice. I was in love with both alternately and then simultaneously for a brief while; but girls were not then a serious preoccupation and out of school one only met them at Christmas parties - invariably their parties since the parents of boys never seemed to give any. The third memorable young lady from that far-off time was a tall, willowy blonde with glasses called Cecilia Hewitson. She was an innocent and not very good at sums but she was grateful for friendship. She was put in my care for a term or two in the arithmetic class and this cemented some kind of a relationship. Mrs MacArthur's method of control at this time was to set a number of problems, say 10, and wait for the smart alicks to signal that they had finished. She then scrutinised the work and, if it was correct, the pupil was told to sit, not on the seat but up on the desk, to work the second set of problems. Successful completion meant standing up to do the third set of problems after which one was encouraged to help one's nominated charge. Cecilia was mine and she was hard going. She could barely count but she was a gentle soul whom I greatly liked. I saw her last when we were both about 17. She was an assistant in a chemist's shop in Ayr and I was on leave during the war. She spotted me looking in her window while waiting for a bus and rushed out to greet me as if I were her brother. I was hugely flattered just to be recognized and decided we must have developed some kind of rapport when we were jointly struggling with the Highest Common Factor and the Lowest Common Denominator.

But, though school was no great burden to a happy extrovert, real life was lived outside of school. At 10 minutes to four every afternoon we all burst through the door like peanuts out of a packet, formed into groups and repaired, sometimes, to a field behind the Stamping Works to watch a fight between two bitter enemies - or, once or twice in a lifetime, to be part of the fight. And then we gradually dispersed homewards. Whatever mental and physical skills school developed in us it was outside that we extended them. We learned to ride bicycles, to swear when there were no adults about, to play football and cricket, to swim in summer, to disappear just before errands had to be run and to materialise again just as food was placed upon the table. We learned to wash our hands and faces before eating - if we had to. We learned what you could get away with and with whom. We learned about pecking order; but couldn't have understood the term. We became small gangsters, forever gathering together in groups with special initiation rites, secret signs, messages passed in invisible ink and no purpose served except to cement our membership of a peer group. We inherited games from our seniors. 'Releave'o' was a favourite, although some mistakenly called it 'Release'o'. Another was a particularly rough and physical game, common in Scotland, and known to us as 'Dunch Cock'a Roostie'. It involved a great deal of leap-frog over several bent backs in the vicinity of a wall with the sole aim of crashing down so heavily that the chain of bodies was broken. We built vehicles from pram-wheels and wooden soap boxes, called them 'bogeys' or, sometimes 'rookamashooks', and raced them down hills to the peril of the citizens who shouted at us, waved sticks and clipped our ears if they could get close enough. In fact, our ears took a lot of clipping from teachers, parents, adult relatives, shopkeepers who thought we might be stealing apples, and other large persons in authority. Terry and I became enthusiastic Wolf Cubs but, a short while after I was promoted to the Scouts, I was rusticated for persisting in calling a boy Soapyhead despite several warnings. Had he had the wit to punch me on the nose I would have held my tongue and probably remained a Scout for much longer. Though they were figures of supreme authority, we did not exactly hate policemen; but we feared and respected them, and breaking a street lamp or a window with a cricket ball was recognized as the kind of accident out of which a bobby would make a capital crime. In season we bought small tops and whips made from a stick of soft-wood with a hole drilled transversely in one end through which a leather thong was threaded. The upper surface of the top was decorated in individual patterns using sticks of coloured chalk costing a ha'penny for a packet containing an assortment of five pastel colours. When the top was spun the effect was like looking into a kaleidoscope - well, it bore a faint resemblance to that, and it amused us. Marbles came in due season and the girls took to skipping ropes. Even in winter we were allowed out to play for perhaps an hour after tea. We tended to gather round a lamp-post which was probably the den for the game of 'Releave'o', abandoned as darkness fell. And then, one by one, we were called home to bed.

In those days all children - or all the children I knew - seemed to spend a great deal of time with their noses in books. Like most, I read voraciously and indiscriminately. The fairy tales of Grimm and Hans Andersen were interspersed with comic annuals and the *Boy's Best Book of Ships*. On the way, we absorbed all the children's classics by some form of osmosis and I was fascinated by the tales of Greece and Rome which occupied the latter part of every volume of Arthur Mee's *Children's Knowledge*. The boys' papers current then were the *Adventure, Rover, Wizard, Hotspur* and *Skipper*, each published on a different day of the week. We all bought one journal, when we could afford it, and then arranged complicated swops. The *Boys' Own Paper* and the *Gem* were not highly regarded in our circle, but a publication called *Film Fun* was. The memory of wet days indoors, or long winter evenings curled up in a corner or stretched out with a book in front of a blazing fire, is tender. It is where our dreams began.

Young as we were, I am sure we discerned very quickly the pattern of the year. In Scotland, Christmas, except for children, was not the event it was in England and seems to be everywhere now. New Year - Hogmanay and Ne'erday - had far more impact. In our household, in which alcohol was frowned upon by the women but indulged in by the men, the New Year celebration was the occasion for some relaxation of attitude. Women and children managed very well on non-alcoholic ginger wine accompanied by shortbread and a particular Scottish treat called Black Bun which seemed to me to consist of compressed raisins and other fruits heavily fortified with brandy and encased in thin, short pastry. New Year safely over, the next problem for children was the return to school, for the Spring term was a hard-working one with little outside diversion except for the Saturday matinee at 'the pictures' where Tom Mix, to me the original White Hat, leapt off balconies two floors up to land astride in the saddle - even at nine, and well before the age of puberty, I groaned at the idea - and Tailspin Tommy crashed his flimsy biplane at the end of every episode to be left hanging onto a bush sprouting from the face of a 200 ft cliff. These were rowdy sessions during which male and female attendants with long torches were as hard-pressed to keep order as warders in a riot jail. It was not unknown for some ruffian to provoke a fight with the boy in front of him by suddenly removing the chewing gum from his mouth and sticking the wad firmly into his victim's hair. There is only one way to remove chewing gum from the hair and that leaves the recipient with an amateurish-looking cut.

Easter arrived in about 15 months and, with the changing

season, we were allowed into sandals and gym shoes. What a happy release – especially into gym shoes. I have to remind myself of this when tempted to sneer, 50 years on, at the ubiquitous training shoe. On the morning of King George V1's coronation, in May 1937, I can remember stamping along a sunlit pavement, ecstatic at having the day off school, knocking puffs of white dust off my newly-blancoed gym shoes and certain that the free feel of gym shoes was every bit as satisfying as anything to do with coronations. But the early summer brought its own difficulties too, for that was exam time and examinations were taken just as seriously by nine- and 10-year olds as they ought to be by undergraduates. Promotion to the next class depended upon performance which became even more important in one's final year when selection for the next level of schooling took place. The pyramid narrowed: competition was fierce, at least among the serious aspirants. It is my belief that these were not numerous, however, for most children seemed to have accepted a modest level of aspiration and achievement by the age of 11. Perhaps the system was not as inspiring as I would make myself believe.

The end of June heralded the Great Release, the summer holidays, eight weeks of casually-dressed freedom where every golden day was an opportunity for adventure. In the West of Scotland half of the days at least must have been silver with rain and grey with boredom but it does not seem like that in retrospect. We swam in the sea and we believed, earnestly, that the water temperature at the southern end of Ayr Bay was higher, at 56°F, than it was at the northern end in the vicinity of Troon, a snobbish little town full of retired Glasgow bankers who played golf. We raced bogeys. We learnt circus tricks on bicycles which, almost without exception, we had acquired second-hand for sums not greater than 10s obtained by running errands and looking pathetically at visiting relatives. We seldom went anywhere on holiday. We lived in a town that was itself a holiday resort so did not need to go away, it was said. In any case our parents could not afford expensive excursions. Sometimes that hurt even a small boy - not the denial of a holiday trip but the knowledge that we couldn't afford it.

There were two years, however, in those memorable 30s, when the summer pattern was broken. In 1935 Grandma and Grandpa Bartholomew came home from the Argentine to retire and, the following year, bought a house in the village of Shripney a mile or two inland from Bognor Regis. When school broke up we were piled into my father's Morris Minor, registration number CS 7787, one Saturday morning and set out for Sussex. Two adults and four children in a very small car must have been a tight squeeze but I remember only the excitement of the journey and the glamour of crossing the border, at last, into England. Some 500 miles through the heart of England in 1936 was a different proposition from the same journey today but my father achieved it between six in the morning and 10 at night, except for the last 100 yards. At that distance short of our destination he decided that he was lost and we would have to wait for daylight. We slept uncomfortably in the car until 0530 when he reconnoitred and found the house round the next bend, hidden by a great elm tree overhanging the road. It was the start of one of the most idyllic times of my life.

At 11 I was sufficiently perceptive to appreciate the difference between Ayrshire, a rich farming county, and Sussex, a lush and beautiful English pasture. There was a farm a quarter of a mile away, near what was then the centre of the village of Shripney. Terry, who had a great love of horses, and I spent a lot of time in the first few days hanging about the farm waiting to be noticed. We made ourselves useful when opportunity arose and before long had become two small, insignificant and unpaid members of the labour force. The foreman was a Gary Cooper of a man called Browning. He walked with a limp, a romantic – to me – reminder of his service in the Sussex Yeomanry on the Western Front during the Great War – 'You can tell them all that they know damn-all in Sussex by the sea.' Mr Browning lived in a thatched cottage near the farm with his softly-spoken wife, several beautiful adolescent daughters and a son called Neville who was Terry's age and could match him in cunning if not audacity. Neville Browning and Terry had an argument one day about some plums they were stealing from a tree overhanging the lane. The plums were being carried, by Terry, in Neville's school cap. The argument reached its climax when Terry suddenly exclaimed, 'Oh bugger Neville Browning!', squashed the cap and its contents into a juicy mess and handed the headgear back to its owner.

The farm had a blue and orange Fordson tractor and the smell of kerosine exhaust - I would learn to call it tractor vapourising oil many years later - is powerfully evocative of that glorious summer. The smell of horses, too, for the farm had two Shire geldings and a mare, Colonel, Captain and Blossom. It was then that I first helped with hay-making and with the harvesting of wheat, oats and barley by methods long-since out of use. The whirring sound of a horse-drawn mowing machine, the scent of new mown hay, field mice and young rabbits scurrying away from the reaper as the island of uncut grass became smaller and smaller, the yelping of an over-excited terrier, bread and cheese and tea from a blue enamel billy-can under the shade of a tree, the sights and sounds and scents of hedgerows. Summer in England. In 1936 it was imprinted on my mind forever and, four years later, I knew without being told what the Battle of Britain was about.

That summer was significant in other, far more important ways. Joe Louis became heavy-weight champion of the world; the German airship *Hindenburg* flew low over the Sussex Downs and was said to have been photographing Portsmouth Harbour; the Italian Army overwhelmed Abyssinia; the Spanish Civil War began; the Germans occupied the Rhineland, and even schoolboys began to be aware of the idea of war. On a Saturday in late August our father came back south to pick us up arriving at six on Sunday morning. He had breakfast and slept for an hour or two and in the middle of the forenoon we started back for Ayr. Night fell with us still somewhere in Lancashire and, over one stretch of the road, we passed what seemed like 40 or 50 roadsigns indicating the route to a place called Chorley. I developed then a horror of that innocent northern town and have managed to avoid it throughout an entire lifetime. I have no idea how my father felt – he was a robust male of 35, but it had been a long drive each way. By the end of the journey, however, I was hallucinating with weariness and tried to convince everyone that I could see the sea when we were still 20 miles inland on the moors above Cumnock. It was the end of the idyll.

Two years later, in 1938, the pattern was again broken when Terry and I had a great treat for our summer holiday. We were given a fortnight's run-about ticket on the *Duchess of Hamilton*, the LMS steamer then based every summer in Ayr. This permitted us to embark on all the day and evening cruises the steamer made during the two weeks, or to change to any other ship operated by LMS, LNER or Williamson Buchanan. We thus had a roving commission and, with several school friends, mastered the time-tables so that we knew exactly where connections could be made throughout the day leaving us well-positioned to rejoin the *Duchess of Hamilton* on her final leg back to Ayr. There was much competition to see who could board the greatest number of steamers in one day. Eight was reasonably easy, 10 very good and 12 exceptional with the hazard that one might end up be-nighted at some outlandish spot like Lochranza. I don't think that could have happened often for I never heard of a lost schoolboy from the ship's complement. Although I played the numbers game with the rest once or twice it had little appeal for me. I was wedded to the *Duchess of Hamilton*. She was my ship and I liked long passages to the head of Long Long or Loch Fyne or round Arran to Campbeltown on the Mull of Kintyre. I was fascinated by the feel of the ship, the low-key whine of the turbines, the faint vibration of the deck, the hiss and boil of the sea along the waterline, the turquoise and white of the wake, the seagulls wheeling over the stern, the proud fast progression and the green

Abraham Rydberg

hills sliding past. It was my first real taste of how a ship moves and handles and, from a location out of the wind, inside the coils of a mooring rope on the foredeck, I watched every move with rapt attention, kept a good look-out, ate my heart out to be on the bridge and became familiar with the Firth of Clyde, the Arran hills, the Kyles of Bute and the whole majestic panorama to which the *Duchess of Hamilton* was my key.

Earlier that year the Swedish four-masted barque, *Abraham Rydberg* (it took me 40 years to learn to pronounce it *Aabra'm Reedberg*) berthed in Ayr after a homeward passage from Australia. She stayed only a few days before sailing further up the estuary to discharge her grain cargo but, for that time, she was the wonder of the town. We were despatched from the school art class to see what we could make of her intricacies. Inevitably, I was fascinated but thought, privately and sacreligiously, that no matter how beautiful a great sailing ship looked, it was an out-of-date way to traverse the ocean. A Philistine, I had yet to see a big sailing ship at sea under full canvas and was several years away from the direct experience of steering a coastal schooner under sail. About this time the actor Spencer Tracy and our distant relative, Freddie Bartholomew, played in a film of Rudyard Kipling's *Captains Courageous*. The sea shots of Grand Banks schooners out of Gloucester, Massachusetts were my favourite cinema for a week or two. The little ships were beautiful. At home I tried to draw and understand them and, though the *We're Here* was easier than the *Abraham Rydberg*, she was still a difficult subject for an ignorant lad. By this time I was mentally and emotionally committed and the closest I could get to the real thing was the *Duchess of Hamilton*. Two weeks in the summer was not enough but it was better than nothing - and there was always next year.

After the summer holidays of 1937 I had returned to Ayr Academy having passed out of Newton Park well enough to gain a place. Of course I rejoined all my companions from five or six years before. In the interval they had been taught rather well and the competition was stiff if stimulating. If not exactly displaying signs of genius in my first year at least I managed to keep my head above water and, with the rest, reached second declension Latin nouns, the pen of my aunt in dog French and a less than total understanding of the theorems of Euclid. 1938 was the year of the Empire Exhibition in Glasgow and we enjoyed it greatly on the several occasions we managed to be taken, my particular delight being the ship models in the Palace of Engineering – what else? But it was also the year of the Munich crisis and, while everyone wanted to believe in Mr Chamberlain's 'peace in in our time', few of the grown-ups who revealed their views in our hearing had much faith that it would happen like that. The elder brothers of some of our friends were called up to the Reserve. Every magazine seemed to carry articles persuading its readers that the Germans were not warmongers and that, even if they were, most of their tanks were plywood mock-ups fixed around ordinary motor-cars. It was commonly held that the French army, the biggest in the world and the second best, was more than a match for the Germans, and that the Royal Navy would, if it came to the crunch, take out their pocket battleships three at a time. In all this there was a strong element of wishful thinking and whistling in the dark, and I think that most people knew it.

In the middle of all the rumour of war our family moved. Early that summer my father had found a better-paid job in the neighbouring county of Dumfriesshire. He was given the lease of a small new semi-detached house owned by the company in Lockerbie 12 miles from Dumfries, and we left Ayr behind – with lingering regret on my part and recurrent waves of home-sickness for that tidy grey town in the west. Terry, Thelma and Eileen were sent to school in Lockerbie. I was transferred from Ayr to Dumfries Academy, from one county school to its opposite number. With the move a new phase of life had begun. I had to take my sea fever into the Border hills many a mile from the ocean and ships – but there were to be compensations.

Chapter 2

ANNANDALE IS DIFFERENT COUNTRY from the coastal plain of Ayrshire. The people are different, too - slower of speech, less brash, countrymen whose eyes look to the hills rather than shore dwellers always conscious of the sea. We children had to establish ourselves in another community and that is not done instantly. Boys, in particular, have to walk carefully round each other like dogs, taking in the natives or the stranger in their midst, in order to establish the proper place of each within the tribe. Terry and I spoke differently from the Lockerbie boys; we wore slightly different clothes, and had yet to prove ourselves. Within a few weeks we had achieved that by the time-honoured method of fighting for place. On some pretext we were cornered by superior numbers one summer evening. Exchanged insults led to menacing gestures and finally to attack, by them upon us. The fight took place in a field on the edge of the town not a hundred yards from our house and Terry and I, with pounding hearts, moved back-to-back and set about defending ourselves. Perhaps it was the fierceness of desperation at being outnumbered two-to-one but, within a minute or two, the first enemy was homeward-bound snivelling, another was standing off with flecks of blood near one nostril and Terry and I were tussling on the ground with the other two. My opponent and I realised we were too evenly matched and broke away to continue hurling insults at each other from a safe distance. Terry, on the other hand, had overwhelmed the fourth boy and now sat on his chest jumping up and down until there was a wail of distress.

'You watch him,' shouted my panting opponent, 'he's got asthma.'

Terry was not about to let that stop him, but I was suddenly wary. With only the vaguest idea of what asthma was it occurred to me that the sorry boy might die on the spot. Besides, the first enemy had fled for reinforcements and, out of the corner of my eye, I could see a mother emerging from a doorway. Retreat was inevitable, but it could be done with honour and magnanimity because of the asthma. However, if it were to be done it were better that it be done quickly, or we would become entangled with an enraged parent. We withdrew towards home followed by furious cries of, 'You'd better look out, King. Somebody'll get you.

Mick Callander's a better fighter than you are.'

I was sore troubled. The asthmatic was a boy called Grierson. His cousin, Watson Callander – the 'Mick' of the threat – was a year or two older than I and a hero with the younger fry. By repute he was good at everything - school, sport, country-lore, scouting, using his hands and - sadly - using his fists. I did not know how belligerent he might turn out to be. I did know that he was formidable and that Eric Grierson would put my name, forthwith, on Watson Callander's hit list – - not Terry's name, for he was the junior partner and I should have to answer for both of us. But, for the rest, Terry and I, in one five-minute scuffle, had established what value should be placed upon us and where we stood in the order - not wonderful but certainly not to be tampered with, and better on the side of the locals than as enemies. For weeks I walked in trepidation, waiting for my inevitable encounter with Watson Callander. Late one Saturday afternoon in early autumn I was on my way home from another boy's house in the gathering dusk. Presently I became aware of footsteps overtaking me. A glance over my shoulder confirmed the worst. Nemesis at last – it was Watson Callander. I held my pace and he came alongside. 'Hullo,' he said, in a not-unfriendly tone of voice, 'where've you been?' It was really none of his business and it seemed an odd kind of opening remark, but his tone was not aggressive and discretion seemed to be called for. 'Oh, I've just been to Charlie Davidson's,' said I. 'We were making a model.' Instantly he became enthusiastic. 'Do you make models too?' he said, 'I do.' We walked a further step or two together without there being any question, apparently, of my having to fight him, and then he invited me home. It seemed one way of avoiding the battle to settle precedence – and I knew my place. He was older and the sitting tenant, so off I went with him to his home around the corner. It was a solid little semi-detached cottage built in the local red sandstone and called The Spottes. From that night forward, it became for me a second home and Watson Callander my closest friend outside school until the day he was killed, six years later, flying as navigator of a Grumman Avenger in a torpedo exercise over Morecambe Bay. And we never did fight to establish who was who.

Our home in Ashgrove Terrace was quite the nicest house my parents had ever had. They had managed to take only 12 month leases of all the other places we had occupied in Ayr and Prestwick. Aralia had been the one sure haven, but my grandparents had had to move to somewhere even more modest. Now, all at once, my mother and father had acquired a brand-new house with a tiny garden and a garage for the firm's car. It was paradise and, having become accepted in the young society of Lockerbie, we blossomed. Dumfries Academy, 12 miles away and 45 minutes in a double-decker bus which swept away the overhanging branches of the trees along the way, was a similar school to Ayr Academy. Perhaps it prepared its brightest more with an eye to Edinburgh University than Glasgow, but that would depend upon what the brightest wanted to read. When I started, in September 1938, a new senior school building was opened, a long, two-storey, red sandstone block of commmendable simplicity contrasting with, and yet complementary to, the blackened red stone of the Victorian old school with its central cupola surmounted by a gilded figure of the goddess Minerva. The accommodation in the new building was superb and even coarse adolescents recognized that they were privileged. I certainly did and, although I walked small for a while among a new group of acquaintances, I settled quickly and adopted the colour of the country. Fond as I had been of Ayr, and proud of being an Academy boy, it is Dumfries Academy that I have remembered with greatest affection. Not for pre-war grammar school pupils the agonising of the reluctant English public school boy. We got away from each other every night and at the week-end. We developed no 'crushes' for other boys since there were girls on whom to direct our emotions. The work was earnest but the play was good too and, before the Second World War, such schools could command the best of staff. In retrospect, I believe that Dumfries Academy and the county schools like it enjoyed a golden age in those years and that the quality of teaching and leadership was of the highest. Not that we worshipped every master and mistress in the building, or believed that they were anything other than the 'auld enemy'. But they were good, and some of them were special.

The Rector was a scientist called Alfred Lodge with dark-grey, crinkly hair parted in the centre, a close-trimmed military moustache, heavy horn-rimmed glasses, what seemed to us a rather gravelly English accent and a majestic presence. We saw him at morning assembly. He read the lesson and intoned the prayer. Occasionally, he passed in the corridor, black alpaca gown billowing behind him. But, in all the years I was in the school, I think he spoke to me three times, and one of those occurred when I was sent to be disciplined for a frightful misdemeanour committed several miles away in the village of Lochmaben. The heads of departments were younger than Lodge, no more than 70 or 80 it may have seemed to us; less remote, more approachable, and idiosyncratic as teachers ought to be. Dr Anderson, head of mathematics, was an immensely effective, fair-haired, bespectacled, athletic extrovert from Dundee. Apart from Pythagoras, Euclid and the truth about differential calculus he introduced us to McGonegal, the Dundee bard, and it was from Doctor Anderson's lips that I first heard, 'Think of the poor munition workers working at their benches, many comely men and many comely wenches.' And 'the ships of war were covered in glaur out in the ocean-poshun.'

There was also a long ballad about the Tay Bridge disaster which rhymed occasionally but seldom scanned. Anderson's colleague in charge of the English department was a Dr Robert MacArthur, saturnine, sarcastic, a martyr to sciatica, but gifted, clever and inspiring. Then there was a little, round, butter-ball of a Latin mistress, Miss Howden, known as 'Chucky' because that is the vernacular term for a chicken and the Howden a particular breed of hen. Chucky was prissy, easily flustered and found 17-year-old boys a little difficult although she was more than a match for 13-year-olds. It was generally held that she was besotted with Dr Anderson, a happily married man with a family. Some years later my great school friend, Alec Garven, by then a prefect, a frequent prize-winner, a great nob and almost ready for Glasgow University, was caught at seven o'clock one morning, on top of the old school building, securing Miss Howden's mortar-board and gown to the goddess Minerva. It was said to be in celebration of Empire Day, and intended no insult to the lady – rather the reverse, in fact, as Chucky's was the only mortar board which would fit the Goddess of Learning.

Rugby, soccer and the OTC kept many of us out of mischief for part of the time out of school. The first I played energetically but not well at scrum half. The Corps, affiliated to the local battalion of the King's Own Scottish Borderers, the 'Kosbies', was just as much fun. Living 12 miles away at the other end of an hourly rural bus service did not make attendance at playing field or parade ground easy, but participating was part of being at school and one did not want to miss the experience. Indeed, one or two of us of minor talent added a further after-school activity to the repertoire when we persuaded the junior art master, Robert Lyon, to start a sketch club and give us private tuition in his own studio. Lyon was an accomplished painter and sculptor and I value the memory of those hours in a more relaxed atmosphere than that of a school class-room.

Judy Garland used to sing a song called, *I'm just an in-between.* which expressed the bewilderment of a young adolescent, treated as a little girl one moment and reacting in the next like an immature adult. At 13 or so that is common experience. In 1938 I felt a man when the cadets paraded and I drilled with an ancient Ross rifle almost as tall as myself. I could be frightened enough to worry like an adult when, just occasionally, the menace of Nazi Germany and the prospect of war penetrated my consciousness. On the other hand, I acted with massive immaturity in the horse-play with which we occupied the 45 minutes bus ride to and from school each day. I was also filled with childish delight when my mother and father took us to a cinema matinee in Dumfries one Saturday to see Walt Disney's *Snow White and the Seven Dwarfs*. It was not childish disappointment, however, but something deeper, when I had to accept that there would never be the remotest chance of entering the navy as a cadet at Dartmouth. It would have been unheard of for a boy of my background to do such a thing but, more importantly, my parents could never have afforded it. In any case, I would have been out of my social depth. There was no bitterness in accepting this situation for dawning common-sense made a realist out of a dreamer. It did not ever cross my mind that I could have joined the navy in the ranks. Had the thought occurred to me I would have felt instinctively, if arrogantly, that ratings and petty officers, although admirable chaps, did not really get their hands on the levers and make the system work. Without any justification at all that is what I envisaged, for I carried with me the powerful image of the *Duchess of Hamilton's* bridge and all the other ships' bridges there might be. The siren call of the sea and ships had never really left me after we moved from Ayr. At this time I underwent my first experience of acute home-sickness, but it was not sickness for my home. It was yearning for the sound of waves on a beach, ripples in high summer, crashing breakers when a south-westerly gale blew in from the North Channel in winter. And I so missed the purple backdrop of Arran across the water, my own 'blue remembered hills'. I have spent most of my life going away from home, being away from home, coming back home again, and I have always suffered pangs of home-sickess, of nostalgia for another place, another time. It is as well that such pain has been transitory, deepening one's emotions about people and places and events, but never becoming an obsession – for that would have been unbearable.

Pining for Ayr and the fresh sea coast did not last forever. Gradually, the Border country became as dear to me and even more familiar since, with growing strength and maturity, one was able to range more freely and independently, travel further, fly over the hills and far away. That Border country is really, for me, the 'land of lost content', for there I began to grow out of childhood. It was 1939. War was in the air, frightening but exciting. A year or two before, the film *Things to come* had portrayed the horrors of aerial bombardment and that profoundly impressed me. Behind the false bravado of what the French and ourselves would do to the Germans if it came to war, was the realisation that someone, a lot of people, were going to be hurt in the doing of it. If Alexander Korda's bombers could wreak such havoc on the screen what would Hitler's do to us? Lockerbie was unlikely to be a major target, but there was no doubt in anyone's mind that, if war came, it would not be confined to a Western Front and some bombs on London.

The boys of the town used to swim in a deep pool at the top of a salmon ladder on the Blue Eel stream a mile or two south of Lockerbie. That summer, Watson Callander and I, having read Henry Williamson's *Tarka the Otter*, had become so identified with it that we nominated ourselves The Otters, an exclusive club for those who could dive cleanly and swim under water. There is a special quality about swimming in a freshwater pool in natural surroundings beneath rock overhangs and the thick green foliage above. Laughter and shouts of enjoyment echo in a way quite different from the cool, hollow sounds of a swimming bath or the puny, distant noises faintly heard on a wide and open beach. The Caul was the name of our beautiful pool and I think it must have been somewhere in Sir John Buchanan-Jardine's Castle Milk estate. If so I apologise to his memory now, for I learnt to be a poacher on his salmon stream when, under Watson Callander's tuition, I managed to land a small trout on a wire snare – 'girning' as opposed to 'guddling' which was a different technique involving the bare hand slid slowly under the fish's belly and then whipped swiftly into the air. That summer, at the Caul, I saw death at close quarters for the first time. A younger boy who lived a few houses away from us rushed off to swim in the late afternoon before anyone else was ready.   Alone, he must have got into difficulties and the first arrivals discovered him lying in the bottom of the pool. I can still see the small, white body, inert and greenish beneath the water, face upwards like Millais' Ophelia. We hauled him out, rushed to the nearby farm for help and another boy and I set out, pedalling furiously back to the town to fetch his father. But Ginger MacDonald was dead and I was overwhelmed by the thought that those half-closed eyes we had hauled from the pool would never see again, the parted lips never move. He had gone and there was no returning. It was not my first brush with an awareness of mortality but it was the first time that I had ever set eyes upon someone who had passed through the gate.

Once again, that early summer, Terry and I were allowed to have our cruising holiday on the *Duchess of Hamilton* and the Firth seemed lovelier than ever.   There was a great regatta in July, the local yachts competing for an international trophy known as the Seawanakha Cup. It meant nothing to me but the spectacle of so many sails spread across the Tail o' the Bank was memorable. One cruise took us right up the River Clyde to the vicinity of John Brown's yard at Clydebank where the latest Cunarder was in an advanced stage of construction. The local gossip had it that she was to be called *Queen Elizabeth* and the artists' impressions indicated a further reduction in funnels to two. This upset me a great deal less than my earlier antipathy for the *Queen Mary's* three in contrast to the dear old *Mauretania's* four. But the new ship was too big for my comprehension. It looked like a ship but should have been a building. It seemed almost too much and, with one or two exceptions mostly because of the particular grace of individual ships, I was not impressed by mere size until many years later. Homeward bound that day the *Duchess of Hamilton* slowed down as she passed three warships anchored at the Tail o' the Bank. They were part of a French flotilla on a goodwill visit, painted a darker, bluer grey than the ships of the Home Fleet, low at the stern and with rather small, squat funnels; sinister and probably dangerous but no match in elegance for Tribal-class destroyers and 'J' and 'K' flotilla leaders.   Their very presence, however, was a reminder of the increasing political tension in

Europe and of the unseen but assumed preparations of the military for the battle now tacitly accepted as inevitable. But the battle was not yet joined and for 14 halcyon days I enjoyed my beloved *Duchess* and favourite observation post in the coil of rope on the foredeck. She was a handsome little ship – black hull separated from the bright red boot-topping by a narrow white band, white superstructure, varnished teak wheelhouse, tall thin varnished masts suitable for supporting nothing more serious than wireless aerials and house-flags, and two tall buff funnels with black tops. Her straight sharp stem cleaved the water cleanly and the narrow, fine lines made just enough disturbance to create an impression of speed and purposefulness. There was a rather elegant dining saloon below the after deck but I saw it only from the outside looking in since there was never any likelihood of unaccompanied schoolboys entering it for the 2s6d set lunch. We carried our own sandwiches in a small haversack and drank lemonade when we could afford it, water when we coudn't. In an odd way one experienced, on each day-cruise, a vignette of the emotions with which I was to become familiar later on during voyages of many months: gathering excitement as the life of the berthed ship quickens towards sailing time, distant clanging of bells below decks and on the bridge, slow turning of a capstan with steam faintly hissing, a sudden eruption of smoke from the funnel, orders called in monosyllables in a mysterious jargon, slackening ropes, the rendering round the bitts of the last hawser held tight to swing the bow in and cant out the stern, 'All gone' with a splash of rope in the water and the capstan speeding up to recover the floating end quickly, the throb and vibration of the deck under one's feet as the ship gathers way, and familiar things becoming fainter as the blood stirs to the thought of other worlds to see, steady passage-

• *Duchess of Hamilton*

making with the masts swaying gently against the clouds, ports of call in strange places, surprise that ordinary human beings going about their own affairs should have been on this jetty or that pier all the time the ship had been at sea, realisation that the ship is only the centre of the universe to those on board, everywhere else is the true centre to those who happen to be at everywhere else, end of the outward voyage and the bow turned homeward. Homeward bound. If 'outward bound' are two of the most stirring words in the language, 'homeward bound' must be two of the most comforting. Gathering excitement as the distance to go shortens, land lights, harbour lights, all coming closer and then, suddenly, the twin piers of the harbour entrance sliding past on either bow as the way comes off the ship. Landfall. Home.

Two weeks evaporated like steam from the condenser exhaust. Almost as soon as the great summer adventure had started it was over. In a week or two the autumn term would begin and there was the wrench from Ayr to face and a return to the tranquil Borders. I don't remember looking back at the *Duchess of Hamilton* as we disembarked for the last time. I suppose I must have done, if only out of regret that Terry and I would not be on board the following day and the fun was over. And if I did look back it was the last time I ever saw the ship. She had an active war career in naval hands, returned to the Clyde afterwards and remained in service throughout a good many post-war summers. I cherish her memory for her like will never be seen again.

Some days later and home again in Lockerbie we were getting in our last few swims of the season. It was late August and in another week we should be back at school with no more opportunity to cycle to the Blue Eel. The news was becoming more ominous daily. Danzig and the Polish Corridor and Hitler's latest and most pressing territorial claim in Europe dominated every wireless news bulletin and filled the newspapers, although the *Daily Express* convinced itself, in the last days of peace, that there would be no war. On Friday, September 1, resumption of school having been postponed until the following week because of the crisis, we were cavorting about the Caul when a boy called Buchanan, a patrol leader in the Scouts, came rushing along the bank. 'Come on,' he called, 'all Scouts have to report at the Town Hall. We've got to get ready for evacuees.'

Most of us were Scouts – I had been accepted back in the fold after the Soapyhead episode in Ayr – and we did what Jim Buchanan told us. With a sinking feeling of apprehension that things must be pretty bad if Glasgow was about to be evacuated, but a thrill of anticipation that the future would be different and exciting, we cycled swiftly back to the town. The Germans had invaded Poland that morning, so the one o'clock news on the wireless told us, and Mr Chamberlain had issued an ultimatum to the German government. And, with the greatest historic event any of us was ever going to live through beginning to unfold dramatically, we toiled all day in the Town Hall, filling hundreds of brown carrier bags with rolls, little packets of Kraft processed cheese, a small tin of Carnation milk and one Kit-Kat chocolate biscuit. These were starting rations for the children from Glasgow who began to arrive on Saturday afternoon. It was our task, then, to help show them to the houses on which they had been billeted and, towards evening, I found myself in charge of two small boys from Springburn who had been allocated to our house. They were certainly different from country children, sharper and harder and street-wise, once they had overcome the initial strangeness. But they were knowledgeable only in the ways of the city and were bound to be ignorant of country things. Understandably, small town life quickly became boring to them. Few stayed long and Glasgow received back the vast majority of her wandering sons and daughters long before Christmas.

Mr Chamberlain's ultimàtum ran out on Sunday morning and at 11 o'clock we listened to his sad, tired voice announcing that 'this country is now at war with Germany'. Some of the neighbours were sitting with my mother. Terry and I were tucked quietly under the dining table and decidedly sobered by what we were hearing. One of the women began weeping quietly. They must all have been in their early or middle 30s and would remember the Great War clearly. They could visualise their husbands taken for soldiers and the race memory of that other war was vivid. It was a sombre morning without the excitement and hysteria said to have marked August 1914. Lockerbie was a long way from any front line but the women knew their sons and husbands would have to go.

For boys, of course, excitement soon dispelled the gloom. The popular songs of the time were brash, over-confident or xenophobic. *Begin the Beguine* was the last pre-war tune I can remember trying to sing, but *Run, rabbit* . . . opened the war for me – a rabbit was said to have been the first casualty when the Luftwaffe flew

43

a sortie, supposedly against the Forth Bridge, that very day. The bomber, under pressure from defending fighters, jettisoned some of its bombs over a farm in East Lothian and the rabbit failed to run fast enough. *We're going to hang out the washing on the Siegfried Line* and *Bless 'em all* helped to raise spirits although I am sure the wiser thought there was an element of chicken-counting before egg-hatching in the first. In the circumstances return to school was an anticlimax made more irksome by the regulation which required us to carry our recently-issued gas masks in their horrid little cardboard boxes wherever we went.

It was the gas mask which was my undoing one day in that autumn of the phoney war. Our bus trip to and from Dumfries was enlivened by a good deal of horseplay on the upper deck. Seasoned adult travellers avoided the upper deck on the eight am service from Lockerbie and the returning bus which left the Whitesands in Dumfries a little after four in the afternoon. We did not break things; we were not rude to people, other than our own kind; we were not vicious, nor were we vandals. But we were noisy, given to practical jokes and sometimes one of the company would be singled out as the butt of our robust sense of humour. The chemist in Lochmaben, a village almost midway between Lockerbie and Dumfries, was a man called Bisset. The Bissets had two sons exactly contemporary with Terry and me and the elder, George, was in my year at the Academy. A feud between the younger brother and Terry spilled over onto George and me. The two Bissets were harmless enough boys but a bit precious and easy targets for ruffians. As George was leaving the homeward bus on this particular afternoon I followed him downstairs, threatening to kiss him goodnight and stepping down on to the pavement behind him for the purpose. Suddenly, without warning, I was attacked by a furious woman whom I recognized at once as Mrs Bisset. I turned to flee with such alacrity that the gas mask box swung round my shoulders and struck the lady. The conductor rang the bell, the bus moved off and I was frozen to the pavement by the enormity of my sin, having apparently attacked a defence-less woman. I would have run after the bus but I was paralysed with horror and, in any case, she had a strong grip on my sleeve. Before an enthralled audience she marched me off to the chemist's shop where I was confronted by Father Bisset whose natural stutter made him more and more incoherent as his rage and agitation grew. I had the wit to apologise but they were not

44

listening and it was made clear that this was a matter for reporting to Rector Lodge. It duly was, the following morning, resulting in my second and penultimate audience with Alfred Lodge, MSc. I had to write an abject apology, promise to be of good behaviour for the rest of my life, cease molesting George Bisset and compose an essay on chivalry. Mercifully, no-one at home found out and that was the end of the matter.

The *Athenia* had been sunk in the Western Approaches the day war broke out. In October Gunther Prien torpedoed and sank the *Royal Oak* at her moorings in Scapa Flow and the following month the Battle of the River Plate ended in the scuttling of the *Graf Spee* off Montevideo. One might have been forgiven for thinking that the only people at war were the navy. It was not so, of course, and, for us, my father's departure to the army as a volunteer in the late autumn underlined the fact that the war was going to affect us all directly. He had been a junior officer in the local Territorial battalion of the Royal Scots Fusiliers in Ayr some years before and, although his association had lapsed, he was at least better trained than most recruits. Whether he would have joined up quite as quickly had he not just lost his job is debatable for he was 38 years old and had a wife and family to consider; but, with the outbreak of war, there was very little civil engineering which required dressed quarry stone, there was nothing to sell and consequently nothing for him to do. Back went the company's Ford Popular, and the comfortable little house in Ashgrove Terrace, in which we had lived for little more than a year, reverted to the firm. We were on the move again and ended up in a flat converted from a shop in the south part of the town. From there my father left and whatever a private soldier was paid in 1939 was what my mother had to bring up four children. The rent of the flat was too much, the short lease lapsed and, early in the new year, my mother managed to find us two rooms in a farmhouse just outside the town. Muirhead Farm was owned by a rubicund countryman called John Kelly whose bustling, busy, competent wife managed a poultry flock of 1000 birds – quite a large undertaking for those days before intensive battery rearing. The Kellys had an excellent reputation as poultry breeders but he also managed his 120 acres as any other mixed farm. The house was a typical four-square Border farmhouse of lime-washed stone. The back door, facing the north-west, opened onto a square, unpaved yard the other three sides of which were occupied by stables and a byre on the south-west side, a large barn with a hayloft above and cart sheds alongside facing the back of the house and a row of outhouses and pigstys on the north-east side separated from the cart sheds by an alleyway leading to the midden behind. It was a substantial small farm, well managed by two able people and we were fortunate to find a haven there. The 18 months I spent under the roof of Muirhead Farm gave me an experience of the farming community and country life which I had first tasted only a year or two before in Sussex and which left an indelible impression upon me.

Almost as soon as we had arrived in Lockerbie, and established our credentials, Terry and I had become country children. It was inevitable because all our new companions had been brought up in country ways and we had to conform or be left out. After we moved into Ashgrove Terrace we somehow acquired a Lakeland terrier bitch called Gipsy which was the most wonderful natural hunter. She could take a darting rabbit cleanly by the back leg and hold on to the screaming, terrified creature until one of us reached her and gave the rabbit its coup de grace, releasing her to search for and pursue the next prey. Thus we caught for ourselves a very good dinner from time to time – or at least a good dinner for everyone except Terry who had never tasted rabbit because he didn't like it! Two boys with a small hunting dog were not the sort of trespassers the local farmers would tolerate if they could catch us. Rabbits were a pest; but dogs which hunted rabbits might easily develop a taste for lambs in season and were at risk from shotguns if they got within range. Long before we became his tenants we had recognized Mr Kelly of Muirhead as one of the most dangerous yeomen and, while two of his fields lying between a conifer wood and some marshy ground were ideal for rabbiting, we knew we would be in serious trouble if he caught us. He never did, but we learnt a great deal about the country by roving over it on what were unquestionably poaching expeditions, all of which had to stop when we went to live at Muirhead. Gipsy, accustomed to sleeping in a warm kitchen and being pampered by four children, was banished to the stable with the farm's two sheepdogs. Within a fortnight she had become a poor, miserable, ill-nourished creature having found it almost impossible to fight her way in to the feeding bowl. She had to go, and some kind-hearted woman on the other side of the town took her away and cosseted her for the rest of her life.

The Kellys were solid, dependable, unsentimental folk, and

practical. Small pet dogs which were not required for work were not worth care and maintenance. Animals were fed only if they worked, produced milk or eggs or could be fattened for market. The dozen grey Persian cats which lived about the yard and outhouses were marginal. They kept down vermin and so could be said to work, but they were allowed inside the house only as kittens, and beautiful kittens they all seemed to be. Mrs Kelly herself was a cheerful apple-cheeked lady with iron-grey hair parted in the centre and drawn back in a bun. As round as she was high, she was ferociously energetic in running her side of the business. If she was a poor cook and an indifferent housewife she was a generous warm-hearted friend. John Kelly looked like a benevolent Stalin without the cruel Georgian eyes. He was seldom seen out of gumboots in which he plodded steadily about his chores, knees slightly bent and feet splayed. He shaved only on Sundays and market days if he happened to be attending the market, and afterwards looked distinctly pink and cherubic if one discounted the Ol' Bill moustache. They were a hardy and independent pair and it says something for their good nature that they were prepared to let part of their house to a woman with four children in tow.

Apart from naval activity, leaflet raids over Germany and sorties against shipping in the North Sea, military activity had not yet become serious. From school some of the masters disappeared into the army and the RAF. One science master went off very early to become involved in something top secret which was whispered about as radio location. Robert Lyon, a conscripted private soldier by this time, won some notoriety when he chanced to be part of the guard looking after Rudolf Hess following his capture. The elder brother of one boy was lost in the *Royal Oak.* Some of the sixth formers from the previous year were known to have volunteered for the RAF but, in the main, the war by then had not turned nasty. The winter, on the other hand, became very nasty indeed and the early weeks of 1940 were among the coldest on record. Trudging up and down between Muirhead and the bus terminus in front of the town hall, through deep snow drifts, probably made one hardy but I should have felt better in a heavier coat and trousers which covered my knees. It seems incredible that, in those days, schoolboys – at least in Scotland – wore short trousers until they were well-advanced adolescents. It was the fashion at Dumfries Academy to eschew the proper grey school stockings and wear, instead, self-coloured hose, pale blue and lemon yellow being particularly highly regarded. These were worn very short, just about calf length and well below the knee, leaving a short portion of blue-white thigh, bare knobbly knees and about six inches of upper calf exposed to the winter winds. My own travail in walking a mile-and-a-half each way to and from the bus was as nothing, however, to the difficulties of looking after livestock on the farm. Almost as soon as we moved in I had volunteered for week-end work about the farm with Mr Kelly. I enjoyed it enormously but there was no other regular help and it was hard work, particularly because of the size of the poultry flock. Most of the laying hens were in a series of houses and runs in a 10-acre field just below the house. The route to it was badly drifted with deep snow and, having struggled to get there with a barrow-load of feeding pails, one had then to fight one's way into each stockaded run, break the heavy ice on the water pan, open up the houses and encourage the hens to come forward and feed so that the traps could be cleared of eggs and the house floor cleaned into the barrow. The first time I was sent I reached for the key of the hen-house door with fingers wet from breaking the ice on the drinking water. My forefinger froze instantly on the key and skin and flesh were ripped off as I tore it free. It was an early lesson in ice burn and the frailties of human flesh in sub-zero conditions which I never forgot.

In due time the thaw came and soon it was lambing time. Although the facts of life were well enough known to us all by hearsay my education was advanced by having to help with lambing ewes brought into the shelter of the barn when near their term. I found it neither frightening nor offensive – rather the reverse, in fact, for watching the birth of another creature seemed to me magical – one moment nothing but the heaves and groans of a ewe, the next another, small, bloody, wobbly, black-nosed perfect animal beginning to pulse with life after its first bleat. Some time later one of the small herd of four milking cows calved in the byre after a protracted labour. This was a larger-scale operation than a lambing ewe, but the spindly-legged, knock-kneed, brown and white Ayrshire bull calf which was eventually born seemed the most beautiful little beast I had ever seen - at least when it had been wiped clean with straw and its mother had licked it from truck to keel.

Farming is seldom about great and glorious moments of ecstasy or high emotion, however. Much, perhaps most, is concerned with improving and repairing fences, cutting back overgrown hedges, clearing drainage ditches, rehanging creaky gates, overhauling farm machinery often abandoned where it was last used, whitewashing pigstys, mucking out byres and stables, spreading manure and keeping the establishment in good order ready for the nodal points in the changing seasons. I seem to remember carrying several pounds of galvanised wire staples in an old paint tin round every fence on Muirhead. And I thought, at the time, that my ghost would be seen mucking out byres. Had it been seen at that fundamental task it would have been clothed in blue hand-me-down dungarees furnished by Mr Kelly and a pair of gum-boots at least two sizes too big from the same source made to fit by several pairs of thick socks. Thus I spent every week-end throughout that winter and spring, becoming a full-time farm labourer for the two weeks of the Easter holiday. My 'pay' was a shilling a week-end rising to 10s a week during the holiday. It seemed good to me and it was the first wage I ever earned, but I have only the haziest idea of how I spent it except to be quite sure that I did not hand it over in its entirety to my mother. Perhaps she persuaded me to save for the new coat I should certainly need before the next winter.

Muirhead boasted very little farm machinery. Before the war John Kelly had earned his money, for the most part, by fattening stock, his own and that of other farmers who leased those of his fields in which he was not running his own beasts. Quite early in the war, however, farmers were being encouraged to break more fallow ground for growing grain. I knew nothing of the economics of farming – and still don't – but what had been a depressed industry in the 20s and 30s was suddenly galvanised into new life by the injection of money in the form of a grant of, I think, £4 an acre for fallow land brought under the plough. Some 30 or 40 acres of Muirhead were ploughed for the first time for many years, a contractor bringing in his Fordson tractor and triple-bladed plough and turning over the good brown earth beneath the grey-green, sheep-nibbled grass. Ploughing is one of the elemental human tasks: there is some magic or witchcraft in the transformation of a field from its ordinary, placid, neutral appearance to something quite different, vibrant with possibility, merely by the passage of share and coulter. Even far inland the plough is followed by flocks of wind-tossed screaming gulls, like confetti at a wedding, white wings against the brown new-turned earth emphasising its richness.   When the frost had bitten into the furrow for a week or two, and before the rain could turn it into mud, the rake and the harrow were hauled over it to prepare for seeding. John Kelly sowed in the old-fashioned way. His small acreage did not justify the use of machinery when it could be done by hand. He did it with another man's help and me to keep their seed trays filled.   Each man carried before him, suspended by canvas shoulder straps, a kidney-shaped wooden frame under which hung a shallow canvas bag making of it a concave tray into which was emptied the corn seed. The sower then advanced across the harrowed field in a slow, measured stride, reaching into his tray with left and right hand alternately and casting the seed over an arc ahead and on each side of him. I do not know how long it took to sow a 10-acre field but, like so many rural activities, what seemed a slow and archaic method dealt effectively with the task before one realised it.   Afterwards the ground was raked over again and, within a very few weeks it seemed, the curving horizon of each ploughed field began to develop a faint, green shadow. As one looked closer the tiny shoots of corn poked their way through the earth obeying whatever law of life it is that makes a seed of corn reach for the sky. To me it was yet another wonder of nature and I find it odd to recall that such a childishly innocent sense of wonder could co-exist in the same frame, the same mind, as served the impudent, irresponsible, half-washed, ill-disciplined schoolboy the French mistress called – to his secret gratification – 'L'incorrigible'.   Such paradoxical opposites of thought and behaviour exist in most of us, I suppose, and to stigmatise an individual's finer feelings by calling them mere sentiment – or, even worse, sentimentality – is to miss the point entirely.   It is a poor spirit indeed which is not nourished by a close observation of the natural world around us.

The corn was hardly out of the ground when the German army in Europe suddenly erupted into Denmark and Norway, the real war began and, despite the high regard in which the third year at Dumfries Aacademy held the British and French armies, our side started to lose it. Holland and Belgium fell to the Wehrmacht and the Stukas of the Luftwaffe, Chamberlain resigned and Churchill became prime minister, France was invaded and blown wide open and the Maginot Line turned. Even boys looked at the future with foreboding, but everyone's resolve was stiffened by Winston

Churchill's oratory.   Many years later I was to have my own doubts about Churchill as a peacetime politician, and he was probably unbearable as a human being with whom to be in constant touch, unless you belonged to him.   But at that time he represented whatever was good about our country and without him we should have been lost.   Every person in the land hung on the news bulletins, first thing in the morning and at one o'clock when the day's news had already been created, at six o'clock and again at nine o'clock in the evening for the definitive sweep-up of the day.   The war, in which so little had happened for seven or eight months, had become incandescent and the campaign in France developed with frightening speed.   Von Runstedt, Kluge and Guderian were, all at once, household names – and saying them over, even now, nearly 50 years later, conjures up a memory of apparent German omnipotence; ruthless, relentless German efficiency – but not Hitlerian savagery which was something different, although that was not generally recognized at the time. The French army and the British Expeditionary Force seemed unable to do anything about the sweeping, victorious Panzer divisions and, by the end of May, it was all over.   Between the May 26 and June 4 the remainder of our own Expeditionary Force was evacuated, mainly through Dunkirk.   The elderly amateur strategists, whom we all knew, were putting away their *Daily Telegraph* maps of the Western Front and the coloured drawing pins with which they had been valiantly fighting the campaign.   Like everyone else, they viewed the future with vast foreboding.   My own deep concern – at the age of 15, with the sap beginning to rise – was that the Germans were reputed to be addicted to castration of all young males in the countries they occupied.   Such a fate, in the event of successful invasion, would not only seem distasteful but would be positively final.   Perhaps Churchill's defiance touched more than one chord of British resolve in those unimaginably fateful days, but I am sure that even the youngest of us would have killed anyone in order to avoid a fate worse than death, if we could have controlled our terror while attempting it.

From this time onwards the spirit of national identity and unity in adversity took all in its grip, at least in those parts of the country which did not suffer heavy bombing, undoubtedly demoralising even if not so admitted until long after the war. For most of us that summer was a time of foreboding and apprehension, but ultimately of glory and great relief. Dunkirk and the weather which made the evacuation possible were seen as a miracle, and so they were. And, again miraculously, the Germans spent the rest of the summer preparing for invasion and seeking to neutralise the RAF. When school broke up at the end of June we were living with the breathless hush in the close. My labours in the field, at the heels of John Kelly, put a stop to too much introspection about the future of the race, or at least my share in making a contribution. There was hay to be cut, dried and 'led' from field to loft and hayrick. Sheep had to be sheared by contract labour, dipped by John Kelly and a day labourer, and treated for maggots round the stern by the master assisted by me. This must be the cruellest medication it is possible to devise consisting, as it did, of upending the ewe with maggots, scraping away the offending flesh and dowsing it liberally with paraffin the ferocious nip from which sent the poor animal off, wriggling its backside and its stump of a tail and kicking its back heels high in the air. I imagine the sheep were looking for the nearest open water in which to dowse their distress but the treatment seemed to work and none died.

And so the long hot summer of 1940 wore on while we waited for invasion. Serious air attacks on southern England did not start until August. The Battle of Britain lasted from then until mid-September when the Germans postponed their invasion and lost the chance forever. Every day we listened avidly to the score as broadcast in the news bulletins believing the numbers implicitly since there was no reason to doubt them. If the BBC said 138 enemy aircraft had been shot down in a day that was good enough for the beleagured garrison, even if, years afterwards, it turned out to be an exaggeration. It was like listening for the score in some enormous but deadly Test Match and in that month the Spitfire legend was immortalised. No matter that far more Hurricanes took part in the battle it was the graceful, beautiful, elliptical-winged Spitfire which caught the public imagination and the courageous, God-like young men who flew and fought and secured the future. Terry and I, like half the boys in the land, built models of Spitfires and Hurricanes because they had become the religious icons of our generation. In our house Terry did most of the building because I was too busy farming and, in any case, he had developed his own passion for aeroplanes and flying which ultimately took him to Cranwell in the closing months of the war. After the apprehension of May and June it was a great and glorious summer, a time to have lived through and the kind of experience given only to a few generations.

Some time in the autumn, after the school term had started, my father came home on leave heavily accoutred and by now an NCO in the Royal Army Service Corps. He must have concluded that his opportunities to talk about the future, to his older children at least, might be few and far between and, early in his leave, he asked me if I had made up my mind what I wanted to do with my life. It needed no consideration. I had been doing well enough, if not brilliantly, at school having some talent for drawing and painting which might have taken me to art school, and for English which might have led to Glasgow University had I been whipped soundly enough to get the work done, as later happened to most of my peers. But I knew that their path was not for me. I could not become a Dartmouth cadet in 1938 but I still yearned passionately for ships and the sea. The *Duchess of Hamilton* had been but a hint of a much greater world beyond the Firth of Clyde. In any case the war now dominated all our lives. If it lasted another three years - and by then it was clear that it was going to last a long time - we would all be called up to the army with little chance of electing for any of the other services. Like everyone else I would have no choice. At 15 I did have a choice and so I told my father, there and then, that I wanted to go to sea as an apprentice or a cadet. It had happened that, a week or two earlier, I borrowed a book from the Ewart library in Dumfries which described, comprehensively, the state of the British shipping industry just before the war. It was well illustrated and one photograph I had found arresting. It was of a ship called the *Automedon*, a solid, rather splendid unit of the Blue Funnel fleet with whose name and trade to the far east and Australia I was familiar. Blue Funnel ships of that era were quite unmistakable to all seamen, and anyone of my generation would recognize instantly the uncompromising vertical lines of unraked masts, the tall blue funnel with black top, the numerous, brown-painted, cowled samson posts carrying standing derricks and the graceful sheer of the black hull. My enthusiasm for the picture of the *Automedon* made me suggest that Blue Funnel would be my preferred choice of companies in which to serve. Before he returned to his unit my father wrote to a Colonel Lawrie with whom he had served in the Territorials and who was an executive somewhere in the Alfred Holt group of which the Blue Funnel Line was the jewel in the crown. With great excitement I waited developments, delayed because the correspondence had to go to my father first and then be sent home. Having once committed myself I was hardly able to contain my impatience but, some time in November, I had in front of me at last the application form - to become, if found suitable, a midshipman in Alfred Holt & Company of Liverpool, the China Navigation Company, the Ocean Steamship Company, the Blue Funnel Line. It was duly completed and despatched and, shortly before Christmas, I received a letter instructing me to report to Liverpool in early January for interview and medical examination, a railway warrant being enclosed. This was pretty adult stuff and I was becoming involved in exciting new experiences. My impatience became unbearable and my mother had to remind me that I was still a long way from heart's desire. They might not accept me in the Blue Funnel Line.

In preparation for the interview I was outfitted, during the Christmas holidays, with my first pair of long trousers in which I felt decidedly self-conscious to begin with. Quite rightly, my mother took the view that, despite my short stature, I had better go seeking a man's job dressed like a man and not a preparatory schoolboy. As the date of the interview approached I became more accustomed to grey flannel around knees and ankles and, suitably clad, travelled south to Liverpool the day before I was due to present myself. It was a typical wartime journey on a main line train between major centres like Glasgow and Liverpool. Most of the passengers were service men and women in uniform, khaki gas mask satchels over shoulders, brown, white or blue duffle bags dumped at their feet, every compartment crowded and the corridors filled with standing passengers or those who chose to sit on their kitbags. Rail journeys in trains hauled by steam locomotives over tracks with open expansion joints which caused the wheels to make the familiar clickety-click noise were exciting in a way fondly remembered by my generation. The locomotives themselves thundered out their own exciting rhythm, blasting smoke behind them in a magnificent banner, straight and swift in the wind of their passage. To the natural excitment of any railway journey was added, for me on this occasion, a realisation that this might be a moment of destiny, although I would hardly have thought about it in quite such purple terms. The beardless youth in school blazer and his first long trousers was hardly of the glorious company of defenders of the realm by whom he was surrounded. But he was setting out on a journey which would be taking him into manhood. I doubt if I thought about it like that at all. I am sure I spent much of the time trying to remember the instructions I had been given for getting from Exchange Station to Ellesmere Port where I was to stay with Watson Callander. He had been articled to a firm of architects in Dumfries the year before the war broke out but had given it up because of lack of activity in the building industry. He had volunteered for the Fleet Air Arm but had to wait and, in the meantime, was working at the Shell refinery at Stanlow and living nearby with an uncle and aunt. The instructions must have been adequate for I managed to do what I was told and reached the Pierhead without losing myself. I gazed upon the Mersey for the first time and, in early 1941, it seemed to me as if Liverpool must be the greatest seaport in the world. A massive, grey troopship lay alongside the landing stage downstream from the Pierhead. The whole visible length of the cold, brown river was filled with ships at anchor, an outward convoy assembling or an inward one awaiting tide time for docking. I knew nothing of these mysteries. All I knew was that here were ships and this was the world to which I must belong. If I had thought Glasgow and the Clyde important they now seemed as nothing compared to this. As far as the eye could see, upstream and downstream, masts and derricks and funnels stood out against the warehouse roofs of the docks, solid against the darkening January sky. Gulls wheeled and screamed over the water and, to this day, I associate Liverpool with the sound of gulls heard anywhere in the city within a mile of the river. Ferries churned across between the Liverpool bank and Birkenhead and Wallasey on the opposite shore and that was the way I had to go. Watson Callander met me in Hamilton Square and, in the gathering gloom of the winter afternoon, we boarded an orange-coloured bus for Ellesmere Port.

At the appointed time the following day I presented myself at Alfred Holt's head office in India Buildings, Water Street, having been circling the site for at least an hour in order to give an impression of punctuality. The clammy palms of apprehension were much worse than any first day at school as a commissionnaire led me through endless corridors between dark oak partitions whose upper part was glazed with reeded glass behind which faint, grey shadows moved and the staccato rattle of typewriters could be heard. My only consolation was that, in alcoves along the way, stood models of company ships – grander ships than the *Automedon* and bearing names like *Ulysses*, *Patroclus*, *Hector* and *Ascanius*. I suppose I must have known, even then, that the ships of this great company bore the names of heroes from the *Iliad* and the *Odyssey*. Those names lent some kind of Homeric quality to the affairs of the company itself and to the men who served it, or so they firmly believed. This boy of little Latin and less Greek was then shown into a long, windowless waiting room with two chairs, a small table and that day's edition of the *Journal of Commerce* which he was afraid to touch. There he was left to quake for a while wondering, in his panic, why he was there at all but sustained, ultimately, by the memory of the models in the corridor outside. At last the door opened and a tall. silver-haired man wearing horn-rimmed glasses, with twinkling eyes and a small, pursed mouth, came out and identified the sole occupant of the room. 'King?' he said, and without waiting for confirmation, because it was hardly necessary, 'Have you had a good journey? Come in and sit down.' He ushered me into the adjoining, larger office. The far side of this room was taken up almost entirely by the window in front of which stood a wide, high desk facing into the room. A smaller, lower desk stood against it facing the window. Behind the larger desk, silhouetted against the light, another tall man stood. He addressed me in a deep, velvet baritone of studied masculinity, told me his name and that of his colleague which I promptly forgot and bade me sit down in a low chair behind the small desk and facing the larger behind which both of were now settling themselves with the light behind them, the classic interrogation situation as I was to discover much later. Brian Heathcote, of the dark brown voice, was the manager responsible for staff and Douglas Peirce – universally known by generations of Blue Funnel boys as Danny – was in charge of sea-going midshipmen. There might have been an element of over-kill in this inquisitorial situation and certainly the interrogation, for a youth not yet 16, was formidable. Heathcote and Peirce did not seem to be playing games and if they were making any concession to the youth and inexperience of the subject it was not apparent to him. When asked the name of the last book I had read – rather sharply – I was so unnerved that all I could say was that it was John Buchan's autobiography. Memory was not holding any door for me that day and, as time went on, I was convinced that I had failed miserably. This became doubly clear when the grey-haired one with glasses and a prissy mouth embarked upon

56

a long dissertation on the hardships and manifold disadvantages of a life at sea. I was not convinced in the slightest and thought I was being put off prior to being knocked down. But, wonder of wonders, after half-an-hour or so, Deep Voice announced that Alfred Holt and Company would be prepared to open my indentures, but certainly not until I had passed my 16th birthday and finished the present school year – and subject, always, to my passing a medical examination to which I would be exposed forthwith! Elation mixed with disappointment, I was almost there, but it would be another six months until the end of the summer term. If I passed the medical how could I bear the waiting? There was no time to think too deeply about it. Within 10 minutes I was in the medical centre, the attendant nursing sister had ushered me into a tiny lavatory with instructions to provide a sample of urine at once and I was in front of a doctor, naked as a baby, embarrassed at exposing myself for the first time to the critical gaze of others, self-conscious about what I thought must be my masculine inadequacies (at 15, for God's sake!), jumping up and down with one foot on a chair and coughing to order while blushing with the shame of invaded privacy. In the end the embarrassment did not matter in the slightest. The doctor told me I would do, the sister gave me a sealed envelope containing the verdict and I was back in another, smaller office being addressed by Peirce.

'Well, King – h'mm, h'mm,' he said, 'You seem to be fit. You still want to go on? H'mm?' His glasses flashed. He looked fierce and quizzical at the same time. His small mouth twitched, whether out of amusement or habit I knew not, but I could barely suppress a giggle. Self-consciousness, embarrassment, nerves – it didn't matter. All that was required of me was, 'Yessir.' and I was on my way with the warning that it would be some months before I should be called and I would receive instructions about uniform, kit, books and procedure in due course. I left India Buildings in a state of euphoria. The train from Liverpool Exchange took perhaps four hours to reach Lockerbie. It was just as crowded with soldiers, sailors and airmen as the southbound train had been the previous day, but I had grown a cubit or two. I had been accepted and was going home as a young man committed. What I didn't know was that the waiting might be protracted because of the reducing size of the Blue Funnel fleet. Alfred Holt and its associated Glen Line went to war with 94 ships. By January 1941 they had already lost 11, four of which had been sunk that month. Before the war was ended they were to lose another 33 of their own ships in addition to eight which they managed on behalf of others. But most of that was in the future. As the train carried me home to Lockerbie there were still at least 80 ships left and, in due course, one of them would be mine, one name would spring out of a page or from someone's lips and with that I should identify all the days of my life.

Winter turned to Spring. The Easter holidays were devoted to farming again and, somewhere about that time, we must have had a corn threshing. We had had them before, of course. The threshing machine was towed into the rick-yard behind the barn by a great, traction engine with thundering reciprocating pistons, sibilant steam hisses, monstrous fly-wheel and, once coupled up to drive the thresher, a huge, wide leather belt oscillating up and down as it raced around fly-wheel and drive drum. Threshing was a co-operative effort. Neighbouring farmers came and helped or sent a hand, and John Kelly reciprocated by attending other farmers' threshings with me in tow at week-ends and in the school holidays. It demanded energy and stamina, for the steam engine and the threshing machine could go on forever and had to be served. As each rick was decapitated and cut towards the ground the sheaves were cut loose of binder twine and thrust into the feed hopper. Dust and chaff flew everywhere and one had to run to carry away filled sacks of corn and get back in time before the next one over-filled and spilled on the ground. Particles of straw and dust stuck to the sweat, got inside one's shirt, stabbed at tender flesh, seeped down into gumboots and became unbearable. Rats scuttled from the rick base and were chased by the dogs. The machinery throbbed on relentlessly and one became thoroughly exhausted. A 15-hour day was not unusual and they were hard if rewarding hours. This was the ultimate end of the ploughing and sowing and bursting green shoots of the previous spring and, in its way, it set the seal on the pattern of the year. The hurdle of my 16th birthday came and went and Alfred Holt & Co began sending heavy brown manilla envelopes full of lists and instructions. There had been a hiatus in their own affairs in March when Liverpool was heavily bombed and the headquarters office in India Buildings severely damaged. Now the office was located near Sefton Park in the suburbs with a smaller, satellite office in Birkenhead Park on the other side of the river. There Danny

Peirce continued administering his midshipmen's department and from thence I was sent, in early June, a large package containing a vast assortment of brass uniform buttons and a company cap badge. No Knight Grand Cross of the Order of St Michael and St George ever received his accoutrements with greater pride, and I could barely wait to see them attached to the uniform which my mother was having to scrimp and save to pay for.

Dumfries Academy occupied my attention only to the extent that the staff were able to keep my nose to the grindstone. They were well accustomed to keeping adolescent noses to grindstones and I knew I still had to turn out a reasonable end-of-term report to guarantee my appointment – at least that was how it was put and that was how I believed it to be. I had been made art editor of the school magazine a little while before which meant the advantage of several free periods a week in which to attend editorial conferences in the library. On our way to or from one of those, I was following the editor, the assistant editor and the business editor, and no doubt looking like Dopey, the seventh dwarf, on his way home from the mine, when we were accosted by the Rector. He knew the editor, Ray, a sixth-year blue blood. He half knew the other two. He looked at me from a long way up and said, 'And who are you, boy?' He seemed surprised when I told him my name and function. Perhaps art editors were supposed to be more mature, or taller, or cleaner. But he let it pass. It was the third and last time that I was ever addressed directly by Alfred Lodge and I am sure we did not miss each other on parting.

My mother was then nearing her 40th birthday. Slight and fair-haired she still looked younger than her years except for the too frequent worry flickers across her brow. And worried she must have been because she and my father were on the verge of separation. This I did not know until many months later. I was too selfish and self-centred to appreciate the situation in which she found herself, bringing up four children on very little money, living a hand-to-mouth existence in someone else's house and having to find the means to launch the first of her family into the world. I suppose the cost of outfitting Midshipman King in those days was less than £100, but that was a fortune and, in her circumstances, a greater burden than she should have been required to bear. Part of that cost she could defer until I could make some sort of contribution myself, but that would not be a great deal and she had the daunting task of finding the means in the first place. Of the difficulties she made light. Of my imminent departure she made the best she could. It never occurred to me that I should not go. I had talked ships obsessively since I was 10 years of age and, whatever the circumstances of war, the time had come for me to depart. Boys, she knew, were apprenticed to the sea at 16. She had grown up knowing that – and the elder of her boys was now that age.

On a blazing morning in late June she and I walked down through Lockerbie to the station to await the 10.30 from Glasgow to Liverpool, the train I had caught in January to go for interview. My tin trunk had gone on to the station before us on someone's lorry. There it sat on the platform containing six sets of underwear, four shirts dress white, 12 collars stiff white, four pairs tropical shorts white, four tropical suits white, six cap covers white, a spare tie black, three dungaree suits blue, three working shirts blue, a hussif, six assorted text books covering navigation, seamanship, meteorology and ship construction, a pair of strong working boots and all my dreams. I thought myself the cat's whiskers, resplendent in navy blue reefer and trousers, the brass buttons from the brown paper package gleaming in the sun and Alfred Holt's cap badge adorning the front of my black-peaked cap. I might have been a shade self-conscious but I was stiff with pride and, as the train steamed into the platform, my mother embraced me very tightly and said, 'Well, George, this is what you wanted. This is your chance. Do your best, son.' If she was crying she kept most of it out of her voice, and the last I saw of her for almost a year she was standing on the platform waving after the departing train, the classic million-times repeated cliche of war-time partings. I felt a twinge of sadness but it had evaporated before the train had travelled 10 miles in the direction of Carlisle.

Chapter 3

THE INSTRUCTIONS WERE EXPLICIT: the tin trunk had to be checked into the left luggage office at Exchange Station and I had to take a tramcar from the Pierhead to Aigburth Vale. The Merseyside geography was to become almost as familiar to me as that of Lockerbie, but that first journey upstream, past Penny Lane two decades at least before the Beatles made a hit song out of it, seemed interminable. We passed Sefton Park where a group of WAAFs were struggling with a barrage balloon until finally the conductor called out, 'Riversdale Road next stop'. Several lusty young men, also in uniform and sporting the Alfred Holt cap badge, tumbled downstairs to join me on the pavement. They seemed enormous, self-confident and adult but, in an off-hand sort of way, recognizing me for what I was, they shepherded me in the right direction and I was sucked into the tribe. Riversdale Road was about a quarter-of-a-mile long and ended in open ground on the Mersey riverbank. Near the bottom the company owned a large semi-detached house which was known as the Midshipmen's Hostel. Alfred Holt's indentured apprentices - they were addressed as midshipmen on their mail and universally as 'middies' on board, except by the Chinese stewards who called them 'midshipboys' - were here accommodated when reporting to Liverpool. Usually there was a period of several days between reporting and appointment to a ship and this was occupied in classrooms at the Birkenhead office re-learning the navigation forgotten while on leave, or in the company's rigging loft at Vittoria Dock being instructed, in an atmosphere pungent with the odours of manilla rope and Stockholm tar, in rather advanced rope and wire splicing by elderly seamen pensioners invalided or retired from the fleet. Two widowed sisters of uncertain years administered the house efficiently, looked after us well but stood no nonsense. There was a good deal of it behind their backs, of course, but Mrs Asman and her sister were greatly respected. Furthermore, Brian Heathcote of the dark brown voice lived next door and where his shadow fell few liberties were risked. The house was large of its kind and the spartan bedrooms were furnished as dormitories. Mrs Asman's evening meal having been consumed in short order the inmates had the rest of the evening to themselves. 'Lights out' was at 22.30 and any midshipman who had a date with a WAAF from the Sefton Park balloon barrage site had to make his own arrangements to return late through a bathroom window and his peace with the senior hand whose duty it was to report to Mr Heathcote at 22.25 that all were accounted for.

That night I was still a long way from getting up to such tricks. After supper we congregated in a large downstairs sitting-room lined with bookshelves but hardly a library. I sat well back out of sight, listening with fascination but feeling young and inadequate. These great fellows of 18 and 19 seemed to have been everywhere and done everything. Sailors, when they meet, always talk about ships and this band was no exception – ships in which they and their friends had served, ships in which they hoped to serve and those in which they hoped not to serve, ships which had or had not been sunk, what they were going to say to Danny Peirce in the morning or what he had said to them today and, most important of all, conjecture about which ship each would be appointed to next. The ships' names meant little to me but everything to them. Worldly-wise and mature beyond their years, they were different from the sixth year Dumfries Academy seniors who were their contemporaries and who had been great bloods to me but a week earlier. By that time we had been at war almost two years: most of my new companions had begun their sea careers in the piping times of peace when the funnels were still tall and blue, the superstructures white and the topsides black with salmon-coloured boot-topping. Now the funnels were grey as was everything else, and these young men had seen two years of war. In any circumstances their calling would have matured them quickly; in those of war the effect was even more marked.

Fortunately, to begin with I was ignored; the cheeky, self-confident schoolboy had been cut down to size and was grateful to be consigned to the background. Some time after 10 we made our way to the dormitory. I was brushing my teeth at one of the washbasins when a tall fair bronzed young man beside me, wearing only pyjama trousers and displaying a great deal of fine blond hair on his chest, looked round and down as if seeing me for the first time.

'First trip?' he growled.

I confessed to the fact – it must have been obvious.

'H'm,' he said, 'I'm sorry for you.' There was a pause. 'If I were you I'd go back home tomorrow and forget it.'

My heart sank. 'First trip' – that was it. I had now been identified, to myself, as a 'first tripper', a new bug. They knew what I was – and wasn't – as did I. In an odd way it was comforting to realise that I was the bottom of the heap, for no-one could expect too much. I slept like a baby, but awoke in the morning to nervous tension and the pumping of adrenalin. Yesterday I had been required to do nothing; today I would be rumbled.

Breakfast was hearty but taken at great speed. Then, in groups of three and four, the midshipmen left for the local suburban train into Liverpool. In my now-established role of first tripper I had to be shown the ropes and the others were really quite friendly. The atmosphere was different from the school bus in far-away Dumfriesshire but the journey took about the same time and it was almost nine o'clock before we trooped into the Birkenhead office. Separated from the rest I was sent into a small room to be joined shortly by two others, one obviously another first tripper whose uniform had not yet settled to his frame and whose cap looked too big and too new as did mine. The other was different. If we three were first trippers the third youth was either well advised or not genuine. His uniform fitted. He was a hardy-looking customer and his cap had a battered look about it. He did turn out to be another first tripper but he had been a cadet in the training ship *Conway* which accounted for his more professional presentation.

Our seats had hardly been warmed when the door opened and in walked Danny Peirce his pursed mouth still pulled down at the corners. He bade us follow and presently we were seated uncomfortably on three upright chairs facing his desk which, predictably, backed onto the window. I cannot remember a word of Peirce's sermon that day, but I can vividly recall the embarrassment of suppressing giggles every time he looked at us quizzically seeking a sensible response. The lecture would have been to the point for Peirce was the right stuff, his life devoted to often undeserving midshipmen. He had served at sea as a Blue Funnel officer until his eyesight failed when he had been brought into the office where, in due course, he administered the training programme for the company's future deck officers. Legend had it that, as second officer of one of the ships, he had been supervising the discharge of some live pigs from the after well-deck, the animals being hoisted ashore one at a time in net slings. As Danny looked up at one lift, it was said, the pig urinated catching him in the eye, blinding him temporarily and changing the whole direction of his subsequent career. The story no doubt was apocryphal but any group or tribe depends upon its legends as part of the mortar which binds it together. Whether a pig ever pissed in Danny's eye will remain conjectural; what is beyond doubt is that he looked after us like a rather remote but caring uncle. Nevertheless, throughout my time as one of his brigands, I could never accustom myself to his pursed mouth and quizzical look which seemed to call for a reaction I could not provide. I have a feeling that he repeated, that morning, his homily about how hard life at sea would be. But this time we had no choice: we were committed, and it was becoming quickly obvious – difficult to bear so early in the adventure – that school desks, books and examinations would still occupy a major part of our time despite the fact that we had now reached man's estate and ought to be given real work such as looking at an empty horizon through a pair of binoculars. Back to the adjoining classroom we were sent to be introduced to Nicholl's *Seamanship* and Nicholl's *Concise Guide volume 1*, the basic manual of navigation. A hint that the schoolroom might have to be endured for at least a week carried with it a promise, too, that appointments were soon to be announced. And so it happened next day. Six of us from Riversdale Road were collared as we arrived in the morning and ushered into Danny's room. Assignments had been made to two ships which were due to sail within a few days. Four midshipmen were to join the *Idomeneus* and two the *Asphalion*. The first four names were called out but mine was not among them. *Asphalion* it was going to be then. Peirce turned to address one of the more senior hands. 'Hopkins,' he said, 'you'll be senior midshipman in the *Asphalion* and you will have King with you, a first tripper. It's up to you what you make of him, h'mm? Important test of your qualities of leadership, Hopkins, isn't it, h'mm? You look after him.' I identified Hopkins by a process of elimination for, although I knew all the faces from two nights at the hostel, no-one had been inclined to exchange names. Now he had become more important than any other individual in the building, indeed in the company. This was to be my companion for an indefinite time and, although I knew nothing about him except the sound of his voice and the eccentric shape of his cap, I was less than sure that I liked him.

Conrad John Hopkins was my prime mentor in the ways of the sea. He came from Sketty an aspiring suburb of Swansea, only child of a civil servant and his small, neat wife. He stood hardly five feet six in height – an inch taller than I – but at 18 plus he was broader, more robust. He had dark, curly hair, a dumb pimple on the end of his nose, brilliant little eyes and resembled, I thought years later, a more energetic and less liver-lipped Dylan Thomas. Being Welsh he talked a great deal and was full of anecdote, but his original accent must have been modified by his contact with others because I never really thought of him as Welsh. His reaction to my apparent ethnic origins was probably precisely opposite to mine about his. From that moment he addressed me as Jock and thus I was known by my peers throughout my Blue Funnel time. He answered to 'Hoppy' and seemed embarrassed by the name his parents used, Conrad. Taking his responsiblities seriously Hopkins instantly became a mother hen looking after a single chick – a rough, gruff, seamanlike, manly, pipe-smoking, cap-near-the-back-of-the-head (when authority could not see) sort of mother hen with a rather wayward, anything-but-fluffy chick. While his own studies were two years ahead of mine, he was supposed to – and did – catechise me on what I was learning from the nautical bibles with which we had been burdened. He began that very morning but, however well-intentioned we both might have been towards the books, he was far more concerned to get hold of news of where the *Asphalion* was lying and when we were to join. That event, however, was to be postponed for a day or two.

The ship's loading schedule was dictated, in part, by the outward convoy programme and there were a number of days in hand. Hopkins and I, with the four midshipmen joining the *Idomeneus*, were instructed to attend a DEMS course in anti-aircraft small arms at *HMS Eaglet*, a naval training establishment in Salthouse Dock. There we reported next day, tagged on to a motley crew of officers and ratings from other ships in the port, had the briefest instruction in the Hotchkiss machine gun, a lecture and a film on what they called eye shooting and were then released, singly, in an elementary simulator trainer which frightened the life out of us. To a man we used up all our simulated ammunition in the first prolonged burst of defensive fire only to be sunk by a second Stuka screaming down at us from the film projected on the wall. It was heady stuff, nevertheless – and safe!

• *Asphalion in 1924*

The following day, after some instruction in an infernal device called the PAC rocket we were taken by coach to Blundell Sands where each was permitted to fire a few rounds from Hotchkiss and Lewis machine guns. Thus instructed, we were ready to face the foe. On Monday Hopkins and I received our joining instructions: report on board the *Asphalion*, in Gladstone Dock, at eight o'clock the following evening. If that now seems an odd time to be joining a ship for the first time then I gave it no thought since the ways of ships and seamen were to me an unrevealed mystery. Had Hopkins said that the form was to paddle alongside in a barrel at dawn I would have accepted it.

Next day seemed endless by 10 in the morning; but time passes and, at seven in the evening after our last Asman supper, we caught a train from Pierhead station and set out for Gladstone Dock. The Overhead railway ran alongside the dock system where shipping activity in each basin could be seen clearly. Every dock was filled with grey-painted ships, great and small, working cargo, discharging what the last convoy had brought in, loading what the next would take out, an impressive spectacle. By then Liverpool had become the country's most important seaport and, in consequence, had been the target of heavy bombing earlier that year as the gutted shells of buildings and piles of rubble in and near the docks evidenced. Within half-an-hour we had reached Gladstone Dock station and made for the security barrier at the gate. Once through, we walked across the marshalling area in front of the warehouses and, as we rounded the first, the ships in the dock came into sight. Hopkins stopped for a moment. 'Well, there she is – that's your home for the next few months.' I looked in some puzzlement at the two elegant and enormous grey liners ahead of us and eventually said, 'Which one?' – a stupid remark since even I knew that neither was a Blue Funnel cargo ship. Indeed they were not, for one was the *Capetown Castle* and the other a smaller but still significant passenger ship of the same company, both commandeered as troopships. My gaze moved to the much smaller and humbler ship berthed astern of them further along the dock. That was her. This was the *Asphalion*, and my heart sank a little for, by comparison with the two liners, she looked small, unglamorous and dirty. Lockerbie seemed, suddenly, a long way away; but there was no time for idle reflection. Hopkins was off, leading the way round mooring bollards, between railway waggons, through silent cargo sheds and out again onto the dockside. We emerged somewhere in the shadow of the *Capetown Castle* and worked our way along under and over her mooring lines to where the *Asphalion* lay, a narrow gangway stretching up from the granite flagstones of the quayside to the deck abaft the bridge. The ship's funnel, masts and superstructure were painted grey but her hull was still peace-time black, the name on the bow supposedly erased but still faintly visible under the paint. The reason for her grimy appearance became all too obvious as we reached the gangway. A coal-burning turbine steamer she had bunkered that day before being warped into the Gladstone Dock, and coal was everywhere. A night watchman directed us over mountains of coal lying in, over and around number three hatch to where the chief officer's cabin was located on the lower bridge. Hopkins went off to report to the duty officer and draw keys so that we could get into the half-deck, as I had already learned to call the cabin occupied by midshipmen. While he was gone I surveyed the ship with mixed emotions none of which could be called love at first sight. For a fleeting moment I contemplated retreat and returning home as my blond colleague had advised, but pride and vanity denied me that escape. At that moment the *Asphalion* did not measure up to the dreams I had cherished for so long. In fact, she seemed little different from a vastly-enlarged Kelly coaster but without the smell of bacon and egg wafting from an open scuttle. The return of Hopkins with the keys put a stop to my miserable reverie, and the sight of the cabin cheered me up. It was a tiny box in the after part of the lower bridge house with one aft-facing port opening onto the upper deck at number three hatch. The cabin door was immediately inside the port fore-and-aft alleyway leading to the engineers' accommodation. In fact this half-deck, makeshift by the standards to which

I was to become accustomed in other ships, had been converted from a cabin for one junior engineer. In peacetime the ship carried no midshipmen, but they were now considered useful as bridge watch-keepers and convoy signalmen. Furthermore, with the loss of more than 20 ships from the fleet, there was a shortage of berths for those under training.

The cabin was square. Two bunks, one above the other, occupied the bulkhead opposite the door. Across the after end a settee, covered in brownish uncut moquette, ran under the bottom bunk. Against the forward bulkhead there was a chest of drawers with a pull-out flap for use as a desk and alongside that, where the cabin door opened, a complicated piece of mahogany furniture called a compactum. This had a toilet cabinet with mirror at head height and, below that, a tip-up hand basin which stowed flush with the front of the compactum. Beneath the basin was a cupboard containing a white enamel bucket placed to catch the slops when the basin was tipped back to the stowed position after use. The basin was filled with water, hot or cold to taste, obtained from the galley or the officers' bathroom in a miniature watering can painted and grained. These elementary arrangements obviated the need for complicated plumbing but there was a serious disadvantage. One had to remember to empty the bucket periodically and frequently or one's feet were flooded with grey, sudsy water. Completing the furnishings a large cane chair took up most of the available deck space. I have no idea why I should think this spartan cell so desirable, but I did. Hopkins, as the senior, promptly laid claim to the upper bunk. The watchman told us our trunks had just been delivered on board and, scrambling over the coal in the dusk, we carried them to the half-deck and unpacked. Before we went to bed Hopkins, having tutored me in a rather complicated technique of folding one sheet, two blankets and a blue and white counterpane to make them fit a single bunk, ushered me on deck again and up to the lower bridge to get a better idea of the ship. The foredeck, cluttered with beams and boards and tarpaulins, was covered in coal-dust. Nothing was secured for sea although I was in no position to know how this was to be accomplished. I went to bed in a complicated frame of mind but the dominant and saving thought was that at least I had arrived.

Five-thirty the following morning brought a rude awakening. Used as I was to a seven o'clock start the dawn had come swiftly and remorselessly. There was a knock on the door, and then instant activity from the top bunk. 'OK, Jock,' came Hopkins' voice, 'Rise and shine for the Blue Funnel Line'. Reluctantly I rose and took second place at the compactum while he disappeared to forage for tea and two enormous slices of toast thick with butter and marmalade. On that we started work at six o'clock, Hopkins dressed in workmanlike dungarees and a tan-coloured shirt, I in my stiff new overalls and the strong working boots prominent on the kit list, weighing several pounds each. By this time some of the crew had mustered on deck and were flaking out hoses under the eye of a large, tough-looking customer whom Hopkins identified as the bo'sun – 'Crusher' Wainwright. In a strong Liverpool accent he addressed us all, individually and collectively, as 'Tommy'. He was concerned to get the 'crowd' turned to, completing preparations for sea. Some were stretching additional tarpaulins over the hatches. The carpenter, a lean, leather-skinned Liverpudlian with brilliant blue eyes, followed them round checking the hatch bars in the cleats along the ends and sides of each hatch, knocking in long, triangular wedges heels towards the bow at the sides or towards the ship's side at the ends. Three or four men were hosing down the grime from the lower parts of masts and samson posts and then the deck from forrard to aft as the hatches were secured. Black water rushed through the scuppers into the dock which, in those days, long before people were aware of pollution, seemed its natural place. Hopkins and I had been instructed to clear and scrub out the wheelhouse and bridge wings. It was some way short of what a gilded young apprentice to the navigation trade thought he ought to be doing but there was no option. At least we were not getting too dirty which was important in view of the proximity of breakfast. By eight the ship was beginning to emerge from the dirt: the coal over which we had climbed the previous evening had been trimmed into number three hatch and the cross-bunker by the Chinese firemen and order was gradually being re-asserted. It was time to seek the nourishment of which I now felt in need despite the earlier tea and toast. Midshipmen ate in the officers' saloon where there were no concessions to the labour on which we had been engaged and the state into which we had got ourselves. You had to be properly dressed to enter the saloon and this had to be accomplished between 0800 and 0815 in our cramped half-deck. The trick to learn was the technique of washing to half-an-inch below the collar and above the cuffs, and remembering to brush one's hair. The other dirt stayed on, hidden under a nearly clean shirt and a tightly-buttoned reefer jacket. No-one paid the slightest attention to us in the saloon, a large square room at the forward end of the lower bridge house, heavy with dark mahogany, uncut moquette, highly-polished brass fittings and half-a-dozen ports facing the foredeck. Eight or 10 officers of various ages and shapes were disposed between two long tables running fore and aft with settees extending round the forrard and outer sides and revolving chairs secured to the deck in the centre. The Chinese cooks and stewards seemed exotic, the saloon steward a tall young Cantonese with dark brown eyes and a kind face who was to prove a great friend to the 'midshipboys' now occupying their places at the bottom of the junior table presided over by the third engineer. No-one on board appeared to have heard of rationing and we ate a copious breakfast in about 10 minutes washing it down with over-sweetened coffee laced with condensed milk. Speedy passage through the saloon at breakfast and lunch time allowed us to return to the half-deck, change back into working gear and smoke a cigarette before it was time to be back on deck. At that time I had not taken to smoking but my downfall was to be delayed only as long as it took to get to sea, open the duty-free bond and buy yellow-wrapped 50-tins of Gold Flake set up in cartons of 10 costing 10s. At that price I could not afford to be left out, but in the meantime I had to be content with watching my 18-year-old companion and guide fill, light and smoke a pipe very professionally.

After loading the last few parcels of valuable cargo in the strong room the ship was due to leave dock early next morning. In the meantime there was still much squaring up to be done before sailing time. Early that afternoon I came down the port bridge ladder with a bucket of filthy water which had to be dumped and replenished. My strong working boots made a brave sound on the brass treads of the ladder but I had moved hardly 10 ft when the chief officer, a tall forbidding-looking individual with short grey hair, a sardonic expression and wearing only his white shirt and reefer trousers with braces, emerged fuming from the officers' alleyway. 'What the devil are you wearing, boy?' he roared. 'Get those stupid bloody boots off and never let me see you with them again on the deck of this ship. D'you want to wake up the whole bloody port?' No-one had told me that, for those off duty in the afternoon on board ship, the time between 13.30 and 15.00 was

sacrosanct and must never be disturbed by noise.   Since Mr
McFee's cabin was alongside the port bridge ladder my working
boots had called him back to the surface only minutes into
slumber. Sacrilege. First lesson learnt. I removed the boots – not
without a twinge of guilt for the money they must have cost my
hard-pressed mother – hid them in a locker and never again wore
them.   Indeed, apart from rubber seaboots I wore no heavy
footwear aboard ship after that, having learned early that silent
movement about a deck is both desirable and courteous.   I
surmised that McFee was going to be an even harder tutor than
Alfred Lodge and, since I was living under his nose, there was no
chance that he would miss my sins of omission and commisssion.

The signal for the crew to go to stations for leaving harbour was
one prolonged blast on an officer's whistle: two blasts summoned
the watch stand-by man and at the sound of three blasts every
midshipman within earshot was in duty bound to make for the
bridge at the double and say, 'Yessir?' A few minutes before six
on a drizzly summer morning the single blast called us all to
stations. The chief officer had already given Hopkins his orders
for the two midshipmen. Hopkins was on the bridge in uniform
keeping the movement book and manning the telephones. I had
to report to the focs'lhead in working gear as part of the forrard
mooring party. In cargo ships this is normally controlled by the
chief officer and worked by the bos'un with the carpenter in
solitary dignified splendour operating the windlass and anchor
gear. Part of the midshipman's job was to relay telephone com-
munications between focs'lhead and bridge.

'Answer that, laddie,' called tall Mr McFee when the telephone
buzzer sounded for the first time. Scrambling over ropes and
steam pipes to get at it I shouted, 'Yessir.'

'Single up to the head rope and back spring,' said a distorted voice
sounding hollow and far away. The message was brief and easily
remembered for the short time it took me to reach the chief officer.

'All right, lad,' he said. 'Thank you. Do what the bos'un tells you
– but stay near the 'phone and pass the messages.'

'Here, Tommy – give us a hand here,' called the Crusher, having
disposed his men on either side of the windlass where they were
heaving in those mooring lines already cast off while two stood by
the wire back-spring below on the foredeck. The chief officer and
the bos'un were old hands, the crew experienced and the ritual
had been practised a thousand times. It was no different from the

way the *Duchess of Hamilton* had been handled – only it was a bigger and better operation and I was exhilarated to have a role however minor. The chief officer called out to tell the bridge that we were singled up forrard. I cranked the handle of the telephone, heard the whirring sound at the other end and then Hopkins' distorted voice saying, 'Bridge.'

'Chief officer says to tell you that we're all singled up forrard,' I reported, well pleased with the forward mooring party and myself. 'Thank you,' he snapped and clicked the instrument down. Later he instructed me in the proper, crisp, unadorned way to pass messages without attributing them to anyone unless so instructed. One tug was already secured aft as another bustled up the dock to be made fast forrard. A powerful voice emanating from beneath a uniform cap just visible near the wing of the bridge bellowed, 'Cast off, forrard'. Imperceptibly the ship began to move away from the dock wall, the bow being held in by the back spring until that, too, was cast off and recovered by a racing winch. Swung slowly by the two tugs the *Asphalion* was squared up for the dockgate now opening onto the swirling brown Mersey. Delicately she slid through and one sensed a faint tremble in the deck. Although the tugs were still secured alongside, the propeller agitated the water astern. As the tugs were cast off the ship turned towards her anchorage moving independently at last. Already the river was full of anchored ships with small craft bustling between them and the shore while a destroyer slid seawards. Along both banks the balloon barrage showed as tiny grey and silver specks above the buildings. Our west-bound convoy had assembled and soon would put to sea.

Early next morning the *Asphalion* weighed anchor and steamed slowly downstream towards the Bar Lightvessel. Over the bar she began to pitch gently to an easy north-westerly swell. A launch throbbed and splashed alongside, the dark-clad figure of the pilot climbed over the foredeck rails and disappeared down the pilot ladder. From the cockpit of the launch he waved a farewell and someone in the wing acknowledged. Deep in the engine room a bell clanged a ratchety pattern and another responded on the bridge. The ship began to gather way again, throbbing a little, as course was altered to follow in the wake of the line of ships ahead. A distant signal lamp blinked a message each word punctuated by a click as the hand-held Aldis lamp on the *Asphalion's* bridge transmitted one long dash of light, the letter 'T' meaning 'Received'. Back in the half-deck Hopkins told me that he and I were now on bridge watches, four hours on and four hours off, or 'watch-and-watch' as sailors would express it. Meanwhile he had to remain on the bridge until I relieved him later, although he would stay with me a while to show me the ropes. Watch-and-watch under the inscrutable eye of the captain. I had barely seen him except in his peregrinations to and from the office and the convoy conference in the previous two days. The chief and fourth officers kept one watch, the second and third, to which I had been attached, the other. It was as well that Hopkins' sense of responsibility made him stay on the bridge when I relieved him. Forming up a convoy, as I was to discover, involved much signalling between the commodore ship and the rest of us. Major instructions to all ships were signalled with International Code flags and the Admiralty signal code books called Mersigs, specific messages to and from individual ships usually being passed by Aldis lamp. All this involved frenzied action and smartly I was made aware that people took pride in responding quickly and accurately to such signals. I had never seen an Inglefield clip in my life until I boarded the *Asphalion*. Within a day or two I would be hauling out bunting from the locker, clipping the flags together in proper order, attaching the hoist to the appropriate signal halyard and hoisting it aloft with confidence. The International Code flags were easy to memorise; it took much longer to learn to read morse code transmitted by signal lamp, despite the signal-man's badge I had once worn on the sleeve of my Scout shirt.

In the evening, as we steamed in two columns through the North Channel south of the Mull of Kintyre, masts bridges and finally hulls of another group of ships hove up over the northern horizon, the Clyde section coming south to the rendezvous position. In the long summer twilight ships manoeuvered for an hour or two to position themselves in response to the commodore's joining instructions. Eventually, our 30 or 40 ships were arranged in eight columns abreast, each three cables apart, with four or five ships, two cables apart, in each column. The columns were numbered from port to starboard and the ships from the front of the column to the rear. The *Asphalion* was second ship in the fourth column, thus number 42. The commodore flew his flag in a neat looking ship called the *Kaipara*, leading ship in column five, 51. And away on the starboard side, in position 81 at the head of the extreme starboard column, was the *Idomeneus* her Blue Funnel outline instantly recognizable at a range of a mile or so. Perhaps a quarter of the ships were tankers in ballast and higher out of the water than they would have been homeward bound and loaded. Around the perimeter were stationed four or five small warships the senior officer of the escort in a destroyer a mile ahead of the *Kaipara*. The others, mostly Flower-class corvettes, a class of ship I came to love and admire, were stationed on the wings and astern while a former Western Isles steamer was positioned further astern still as a rescue ship. Night fell bringing almost total darkness; the ships displayed only faint blue stern lights – which could be switched on in an emergency – by which those astern could keep station on the ship ahead.

In the darkness I heard the officers refer to the Mull of Kintyre. Their business was to know where they were, mine but to pour tea in the dimmed-out chartroom and carry sandwiches to the bridge. Even if I had dared to look at the chart it would have been a mystery, but I knew about the Mull of Kintyre: I had been to Campbeltown in the *Duchess of Hamilton* and caught saithe off the end of the pier. Somewhere out there in the dark, beyond the starboard wing of the convoy, it lay and the realisation swept over me, powerfully, that we really were leaving home for far-away places and probably for a long time. There was a strange loneliness in those still unfamiliar surroundings, the deck scending gently under one's feet, the foremast sweeping small arcs against the midnight afterglow in the far north-west. I barely comprehended the danger but, for the first time in my life, experienced the wrenching sadness of parting from these islands outward bound. The last gaze towards the horizon beyond which I could visualise the people and places which were precious was to become the familiar reflex on departure over many years. How different the equally oft-repeated gaze ahead towards an unseen landfall when homeward bound. But one cannot experience the happiness of homecoming without living through the pain of parting: I was to wait long for the ecstasy but that night I learned the irrevocability of departure. Ross, the second officer, observed to Webb, the third, that the Mull of Kintyre was now well abaft the beam. He must have been inured to outward bound melancholy for, in the next breath, he suggested it was high time I made myself a little more useful and brought some tea and sandwiches.

By the following morning the convoy was well into the Western Approaches on a heading to take it just south of Iceland. After four hours of total oblivion in the cramped lower bunk I was back on the bridge with Ross, Webb and the helmsman to keep the morning watch. A watery grey dawn broke around 0500, the light spreading from the north-east while the sky ahead still looked heavy and dark with the last of the night. The commodore signalled as soon as flags could be seen. It might have been done just to sharpen up everyone, but the effect was to spread the ships further apart now there was more sea room. To my untutored eye the escorts had rather long stretches of perimeter to safeguard but the sight of them was encouraging. We were heading diagonally across a long Atlantic swell with enough wind to break an occasional wavetop. By no means heavy weather it was enough to cause the ships to pitch rather gracefully into it, rolling gently to the swell's lift. Pleased at feeling no ill effects as I looked aft towards the poop where two duffle-coated, balaclava-helmeted gun crew were on watch I realised that the stern of the ship was moving up and down a great deal more than was evident to someone standing amidships. Perhaps I was lucky. My stomach might have been more sorely tried had I, too, been keeping a watch aft. At 0800 Hopkins clambered onto the bridge and asked what was going on, information I would quickly learn to impart at the change of the watch without being asked. I told him what I knew, which wasn't much, responded to the chief officer's 'Good morning, boy' and hurried off to the gargantuan breakfast to which I had now become accustomed and had been anticipating for at least two hours. A more experienced sailor would have had the wit to get into his bunk in his watch below while keeping double watches. Over-excited I stayed up reading, going out on deck every now and then to stand by number three hatch and look across at the other ships. On one outing a voice from two decks above called down. The captain beckoned me. In some trepidation I found my way to the door of his dayroom which opened onto the starboard side of the lower bridge where he called me in. I tripped over the high storm step, recovered and stood on the thick bass mat just inside the door. I was surprised at the smallness of his dayroom, but the dark wood gleamed, the fittings were highly polished and the carpet bore the marks of a vigorously-applied brush. My impression was of solid, if austere, good order. On the desk stood a silver-framed photograph of a middle-aged woman with no other ornament or decoration to be seen. Captain James Beer turned out to be a great gentleman.   A

Londoner, he had served most of his life in the Glen Line which had been absorbed into Alfred Holt and Company in the early 30s although the ships, whose names all had the prefix *Glen*, retained their individuality, their red and black funnels and their trade which was exclusively with the Far East. Sea-going officers were interchangeable between the ships of the associated companies and Captain Beer was in one of his Blue Funnel phases. Of medium height but slim and upright, he looked taller than he was. He had straight iron-grey hair, a sallow complexion, a quiet voice and a kind eye if a rather remote manner. In uniform on board or civilian clothes ashore he was always impeccably dressed. A reserved man, Captain Beer was not given to displays of emotion or temper. I count myself fortunate that the first shipmaster I served under should have been such a man. That morning I am sure he wanted only to put a young boy more at ease. He knew perfectly well that the next 10 or 12 days were going to be physically taxing but he told me that I would find my feet soon and that it would be easier after the convoy had broken up, wherever and whenever that should happen. Some of our cargo was marked for Melbourne, Sydney, Brisbane and Adelaide but our route to Australia was not a matter of public knowledge and how far we would sail in convoy remained to be seen. Captain Beer did not keep me long. I suspect he found it as embarrassing having nothing to say to a 16 year-old as the 16 year-old found it to have no answers. But I decided I liked him and would even try to like Mr McFee who was a tough but mostly silent customer with the fierce eye of a bird of prey, receding grey hair, a ruddy complexion and no nerves that he ever displayed. He must have been only a little younger than Captain Beer and a year later he had his own command. I never quite lost my awe of him but I don't know why for, like many other strong but reserved men, he was fundamentally gentle although misdemeanour and stupidity would draw from him a few words of biting criticism infinitely more effective than a loudly raised voice. In fact his loudest shout, in my experience, was when he consigned my working boots to perdition and such a manifestation of wrath was never repeated in many months of quartering the globe.

Ross, the second officer, was even quieter. Tall, cadaverous, balding with pale, translucent skin he had the style and appearance of an ascetic, bookish monk. In vivid contrast was the third officer, Ronnie Webb, a short square hook-nosed Yorkshireman from Hull, proud of his north-east coast tramping company origins in the 30s, sometimes sarcastic about Blue Funnel pretensions but quick to defend what he regarded as the company's better qualities. A sternly practical seaman, both Hopkins and I learnt a great deal from him during the time we served together. The most junior of the deck officers, Cedric Hurt, not more than 23 but seeming to me a man of immense sophistication, was a delightful character who had been apprenticed to the Anglo-Saxon Petroleum Company, Shell's tanker fleet, and had arrived in Blue Funnel only after passing his first examinations. The age gap being so much less in his and in Webb's case, they were more approachable and less daunting than the more senior officers but, for the first few days, I saw little of Hurt since I was not on his watch. Indeed, we saw little of anyone to begin with other than our own watch companions. With the exception of Mr Kellock, the taciturn, ginger-haired chief, the engineers were for long virtually unknown to me, but the septuagenarian medical officer, Dr Duncan McPherson, quickly became a familiar figure as he stumped up and down whichever was the lee side of the upper deck abaft the bridge each morning and afternoon. Why a ship with a crew of 71 and no passengers required a surgeon at all was to puzzle me later when I knew more about the running of ships, but at the time I took it for granted although Dr McPherson's was obviously not a strenuous occupation since it consisted of two 10-minute daily surgeries with seldom a patient at either.

At a range of almost 50 years it is difficult to put names to every one of a crew of 71, although faces are more easily recalled. Thirty were Chinese – fitters, firemen, cooks and stewards; 20 of the crew were sailors, six engineers, one purser, two radio officers, the doctor, four gunners, four deck officers, the captain, and Hopkins and me. Some are unforgettable – Peaston the purser, Harry Haworth the radio officer, the chief steward, Leo Galvin the carpenter, 'Crusher' Wainwright, Pollock the third engineer, Tobin the Australian gunlayer, Paddy Malone – or was it Finucane? – the Irish lamptrimmer, Charlie Buckley the oldest and smallest AB with the face of an ancient puzzled gnome and eyes like black currants. Charlie, always convinced that the ship was about to be sunk, preferred being in port – preferably Liverpool or Birkenhead – to anywhere else. But Hopkins is the best-remembered of all for it was from him, by precept, example and force of personality that I learnt more seamanship and ship lore than from anyone else. We were not bosom companions. In many ways we were not compatible, but he took his responsibilities seriously, was proud of his growing mastery of his calling and wanted to pass on the knowledge. I did not always agree with him but I respected him unreservedly.

The ship herself was becoming familiar. It would be some months before she was as etched upon my mind as Muirhead Farm but, in due course, she became so much a part of me – or I of her – that it is easy to recall her in detail and to name her parts. I did not then love her because I did not know her well enough but first ships are, perhaps like first love, specially memorable. The *Asphalion* was a five-hatch, dry-cargo ship of 6000 gross tons, 450 ft long, 52 ft in beam, drawing 26 ft laden and built by Scott's of Greenock in 1924, one year before I was born. The five holds were divided into lower hold, orlop deck and 'tween deck, number three having deep tanks in the lower hold and number four being refrigerated. Driven by a double-reduction geared turbine fed from two coal-fired Scotch boilers she was capable of 14 knots on a good day with the correct boiler check-valve settings. This was a knot or two faster than the average ocean-going cargo ship of that era but was necessary for her to maintain her normal peace-time schedule. Each hatch in the welldecks was served by two 10-ton and two five-ton derricks, the latter permanently 'standing' and stepped on cowl-topped samson posts. Each hatch also had a larger derrick stepped at the heels of the masts, of 20-tons safe working load at numbers one, four and five and the so-called 'jumbo derrick' of 40-tons serving number two hatch. Deck and engineer officers were accommodated on two decks of the bridge house, petty officers on either side of the engine-room trunkway and sailors, firemen and catering crew in the poop-space. At that time the ship was armed with a four-inch anti-submarine gun mounted on the poop-deck and four Hotchkiss machine guns, two in the bridge wings and two in small gun emplacements built on the boat deck, for air defence. In addition, on the upper bridge, there were two PAC (parachute and cable) devices but these were considered so potentially hazardous to life and limb on board that it was doubtful if they would ever be fired except accidentally. The gunlayer was responsible also for two Ross rifles kept on the bridge but to what end was not clear. With the exception of the four-inch gun which could be trained only over an arc aft of the athwartship line this armament was more dangerous to the ship's company manning it than to the Luftwaffe, but it did create a comfortable illusion of capacity to respond to attack.

Of attackers, however, there was none. For 10 or 11 days the convoy plodded westwards through a depression which for a time gave us gale force winds and heavy, breaking, Atlantic rollers. Despite becoming more and more sleepy with what seemed almost continuous watch-keeping my apparent immunity to seasickness caused me some elation. A fortnight earlier I had been a schoolboy, yet here we were pounding into an Atlantic gale and I could still manage three square meals a day. The first-trip gunner who kept his watch on the poop shared no such elation and privately I was quite glad that I had only to go to the ends of the ship on rounds after each watch. Flag signalling had become second nature now. Our eyes were always peeled for the first flutter of bunting from the commodore's bridge or the blink of an escort's signal. The officers read the code flags as they whipped aloft into the wind one by one and our hoist, acknowledging or repeating the signal, was half prepared before the commodore's signalmen had tightened their halyards and made fast. The movement and behaviour of other ships in the seaway caught my imagination and I developed a huge admiration for the crews of the corvettes which made the most violent gyrations of all. Some of these little ships were dazzle-painted, others dark grey, but all had anti-fouling paint below the water-line which had started out a maroon shade but had faded and discoloured the longer the ship was out of dock. The anti-fouling at the fore-foot and the single propeller and rudder seemed to be perpetually alternating as the corvette pitched and rolled violently, seas crashing over the bows and streaming aft through the waist to tumble in white cascades around the depth-charge racks on the after deck. How anyone remained upright was a mystery. The tough, rugged, slow, under-armed and unglamorous Flower-class corvette was the first engine of war of which I was directly aware. Later one became accustomed to Hunt and Atherstone-class destroyers, Castle-class frigates and sloops like the *Londonderry* and *Black Swan* which so frequently seemed to be part of our escorting force. But the humble corvette had a special place in my affections. It might have been otherwise had I ever served in one when my unblemished record of never having been sea-sick could have gone by the board.

Somewhere south of the Grand Banks the flag signals, seemed to engulf us. The convoy, now with a different escort, was dispersing, some to Halifax, some for New York and Baltimore and the rest proceeding independently as indicated in the captain's secret sailing orders. The *Asphalion* was routed independently to Jamaica and thence to the Panama Canal. Groups of ships broke away to reform again in smaller convoys as they disappeared over the western horizon. The independents drew clear of the ruck and, by nightfall, had all but disappeared from sight. Suddenly the ocean was empty and our darkened ship, now released from the constraints of convoy, throbbed with increased power, pushing out a more urgent bow wave. Hopkins came down from the bridge and announced that we were to settle into normal watchkeeping. I was not due on the bridge until midnight. Bliss! After dinner I fell into a deep sleep from which I was aroused at 0730 the following morning when Hopkins himself was called. No-one had called me for the middle watch. The second officer either didn't know I should have been with him or chose to turn a Nelsonian eye on my absence. Everyone thought it hilarious. I felt humiliated - but refreshed.

Soon the *Asphalion* made her landfall. It was a brilliant summer morning as she brought up off the port of Kingston, the Jamaican landscape gold and green and the distant mountains blue, the water of the harbour clean and clear so that the bottom, 40 ft below, was visible but bent and distorted as the sunlight flashed down from the scintillating surface. I had seen nothing so enchanting as that tropical island in the morning sun as we idled on deck and threw an occasional coin for the tiny cocoa-coloured Jamaican boys to dive for from their flimsy canoes. Captain and purser went ashore in the agent's launch. 'Routeing orders,' said Hopkins mysteriously. I was more familiar with the jargon now than I had been on departure from Liverpool but, in any case, it hardly mattered for the captain was soon back with his orders. We were under way by noon, past Port Royal and heading south for Cristobal at the northern entrance to the Panama Canal. At Cristobal we coaled again, great truck-loads hoisted into the air and dropped from on high into the cross-bunkers and number three 'tween decks between the bridge house and the engine room casing. The coal was trimmed by large heavily-muscled blacks controlled by an autocrat in a sweat- and coal-stained felt hat who sat at the top of the hatch. 'Hey you down deah, Mistah Robinson, suh! Ain't yo' got no interest in yoh perfession? 'Fyoh doan' git

80

dat coal pushed out to d'side ah'll come down deah an' chistise yoh mos' sorely!' The coal was trimmed, the ship hosed down and, while we waited for clearance to transit the canal, Hopkins and I were allowed a run ashore for a couple of hours. Apart from Argentina which, of course, I could not remember, this was my first adventure on foreign soil – and it was foreign. American rather than Panamanian the Canal Zone military presence was spectacularly evident. On our way back to the ship the heavens opened in a tropical downpour. Trying to shelter under a tree we were shortly aware of a voice calling us from of an adjacent house. We ran for shelter and were welcomed into an American household with all the warmth that that can mean. From that moment on, I was aware of America and Americans in a way which has lasted all my life. They can be the most exasperating, infuriating, bumptious and self-satisfied people in the world – except, perhaps, for the British, the French, the Germans and everyone else. At the same time they exude a simple, homely, welcoming warmth which I have seldom found elsewhere. Hopkins and I, two boys in their teens, were treated as if we were Greek heroes. This was five months before Pearl Harbour and we were made to feel, by an American staff sergeant, his wife and three children, that we, personally, had been defending the entire free world almost single-handed. It was embarrassing but flattering and when the rain stopped we were sent on our way with magazines, candy and a 200-pack of Lucky Strike. And so through the Canal the following day with electric 'mules' secured by towing wires to bows and quarters to heave us through the locks, and heavily-armed US Marines stationed on the bridge, in the radio room and at the engine-room control platform. We cleared from Panama late at night, slowing down only to disembark the pilot and the military. Then we headed south-westwards into the Pacific bound for Melbourne four weeks away.

The impressions created by different geographical locations must lie fallow in the mind. Once out of sight of land both Atlantic and Pacific remind the observer that they are huge immensities of ocean, but the shape of their edges lurks in the brain, how far here is from there and in which direction the wind will blow or the current will stream. Embattled Britain seemed an infinite distance and an age away. The great albatross which rode the wind astern for day after day was beyond normal experience; here, was the endless, blue Pacific Ocean seen for the first time barely five weeks after the parting from green and faraway Dumfriesshire. We were now off watches completely and, under Hopkins' tutelage, the ways of the ship were becoming familiar to me. There was no convoy, no U-boats, no need to spend time understudying the watch-keeping officer who seemed to me, in my ignorance, to have little enough to do himself most of the time. Hopkins and Crusher Wainnwright, Leo Galvin, 'Lamps' and the older crew members like Charlie Buckley started to make a sailor out of me; but Hopkins was the chiefest of these. He it was, the first time we had to do some awkward job aloft who told me, 'One hand for the ship and one for yourself – and keep the better hand for yourself'. Ironically, he forgot this fundamental sailor's truth himself 10 years later when he was chief officer of a Shell tanker. Standing on the bridge rail to tighten an awning one night in the Indian Ocean he slipped and fell to his death on the foredeck 30 feet below.

As we steamed through Melbourne Heads and started the 20-mile passage to Port Melbourne there was a great sigh of relief on board. It is not difficult to recall the wonder with which one looked across the water at night towards the brilliantly lit city we were approaching. There had been one brief interlude in Panama but Melbourne, seven weeks out from Liverpool, was a city one could understand in terms of European cities, whose lights had not shone like this for two long years. Two neon signs on dockside warehouse roofs burned themselves into my memory – Swallow & Ariel's biscuits and Penfold's wine. Next day some of us managed to sample the delights of Australia, but it was neither biscuits nor wine that took my fancy. Instead, I brought back to the ship two one-pound blocks of Cadbury's milk chocolate which Hopkins and I demolished in short order. After a week in Melbourne discharging cargo, there was a short run up the coast to Sydney. As we steamed up the harbour, four great, grey troopships lay at anchor – the *Queen Elizabeth, Queen Mary, Aquitania* and *Mauretania*, all preparing to take more of the Australian Expeditionary Force to the Middle East, a spectacle, etched against the so-familiar outline of Sydney Harbour Bridge - the 'Old Coat Hanger' - never likely to be seen again. After ten days in that splendid city we moved on to Newcastle and then to Brisbane. We had joined the *Asphalion* after her loading had been completed and I had never actually seen the inside of a stowed cargo hold. Hopkins and I were placed on cargo watch alternating with each other in whichever hatch the most valuable and vulnerable cargo happened to be exposed. The men of the stevedoring gangs, leather-faced, some lean, some with beer bellies hanging over their belts, all seemed to be called 'Bluey' or 'Snowy'. They were adept at securing for themselves what they considered to be their share of the cargo. Bottles of whisky disppeared from crates to be hidden inside rolls of linoleum and Rolex watches evaporated mysteriously from stoutly secured cases. I suppose our presence at least caused them to be circumspect, but against such professionals it was unlikely that we would be very effective. From our point of view the real benefit – not appreciated at the time – lay in seeing how a ship's cargo was stowed, and we got plenty of practice in watching and recording that. Being moderately neat of hand I early carved for myself a niche as the reasonably trustworthy keeper of the working cargo plan. I could measure and draw and tint and letter but, of course, I had not the faintest idea of how to calculate the effect of a weight removed from here or another placed there – much the most interesting aspect of cargo handling. I did not have the wit to ask and no-one had the wit to tell me, other than the edict, 'We have to put heavy weights in the lower hold – but not too much! Some weight may be needed higher up or she'll roll too fiercely.' It took some time with the stability book to establish why that should be.

The ship became only where we lived and worked. Six in the evening saw the great release and a rush for the bright lights, if the chief officer sanctioned it. We seldom returned before the small hours of the morning and sometimes as dawn was breaking. We were not questioned so long as we were on deck for the uncovering of hatches at 0600, and I do not know where the stamina – or the finance – came from. The indentured pay of a midshipman was meagre – in my case nine pounds a year! This was supplemented by a war bonus of £10 a month for everyone over the age of 18 but of only £5 a month for the likes of me. Hopkins, in his third year and over the age of 18, received £15 a year and the full £10 a month war bonus. Soon after we arrived in Melbourne Captain Beer gave Hopkins two pounds for us to share, a fortune in our circumstances and a sum which would have to be multiplied by at least 10 to produce the present-day equivalent. Inevitably our resources dried up rather quickly, but we had recourse, then, to the Flying Angel Seamen's Mission, an Anglican charity operating worldwide. These missions were particularly good in

Australia and dances, at which girls from local churches acted as hostesses, were frequent. It was an innocently effective way of enabling us to mix with Australians for we were often invited to homes at the week-ends and, so long as we behaved ourselves properly, we were hospitably entertained. Hopkins was a blade and in Sydney met a girl whose address he had brought with him from Swansea. She had a friend – inevitably – and, in the three or four times we passed through Sydney during the Australian summer of 1941-2, the four of us had a wonderful time. Noel Coward has said it all about the potency of cheap music and it is by the tunes popular in Australia in 1941 that I recall a golden time so vividly. Most insidious of all was *A Sleepy Lagoon*, heard times without number as the signature tune of the Desert Island Discs radio programme, but first heard by me on the ferry crossing from the Sydney landing stage to Cremorne Point on a starlit, semi-tropical night – as it should always have been heard. We had an old HMV gramophone on board and some even older records – *Blueberry Hill, My Blue Heaven, Tea for Two, Begin the Beguine, What'll I Do?* Heard now, any one of them takes me back, hauntingly, to what was almost peace-time Australia in the months before Pearl Harbour.

As the ship was discharged we began to re-load – military equipment and stores for the Middle East. The *Idomeneus*, whose outward itinerary had been similar to ours, was running behind us because of calls at two US ports outward bound but received orders to load for home. In a way I was envious. After three months it would have been wonderful to have arrived home at Christmas and be in a position to brag about far away places. On the other hand rumour had it that our cargo was bound for Egypt and that to me was much more exciting. From Sydney we sailed to Adelaide and Fremantle. Then we were off across the Indian Ocean towards Ceylon that beautiful island whose swift sunsets over Colombo harbour both enthralled and made me deliciously melancholy at the same time. Are beauty and art essentially tragic? I don't know but Ceylon, like so many beautiful places, filled me with mixed but intense emotions. We bought pairs of carved ebony elephants cheaply but of a quality not to be seen now. We stocked up with small wooden cases of Broken Orange Pekoe to take home to starving Britain, or at least those natives to whom we had a personal attachment. And then we were off again, independent ship, towards the Barren Rocks of Aden, the

Straits of Bab el Mandeb and into the Red Sea. Some of our military cargo was for Massawa and Port Sudan to re-equip the army which had just liberated Abyssinia from the Italians. In the port of Massawa there must have been 40 Italian merchant ships scuttled in its shallow waters, lying on the bottom in grotesque postures their superstructures still poking above the surface. Manoeuvering to the berth with an inadequate tug was a delicate operation and the diminutive, elderly Italian naval officer who was acting as pilot was acutely nervous. The operation began to go disastrously wrong and suddenly Beer lost his temper, ordered the Italian out of the wheelhouse and took over himself. It was the only time I ever saw a shipmaster peremptorily dismiss a pilot in the middle of an operation.

Much of our heavier cargo went ashore in Suez Bay and at Port Said. The Mediterranean was a closed sea except for heavily protected convoys to Alexandria and Malta. Luckily the *Asphalion* was not swept into that stage of the Mediterranean war for we were ordered back to Australia by the same route as we had come - Aden for coaling, with tiny Arabs climbing up one flimsy plank bearing baskets of coal on their heads and scuttling down another plank to reload; to Colombo for onward routeing and back towards Fremantle. At 0755 on the morning of December 7 the Japanese attacked Pearl Harbour and, with the Americans now totally involved, the war, which had seemed far away in Europe, Russia, the Atlantic and the Middle East, took on a new dimension. The *Asphalion* was within a day or two of Fremantle: Hawaii was thousands of miles away but a look at the atlas was enough to indicate that nowhere was safe from now on. Loading for England took us round the coast again to Fremantle, Port Pirie (a small ore port in the Bight where the trains ran down the middle of the main street. As there was only one berth for deep-sea vessels visiting a ship was considered locally to be a suitable Sunday morning outing), Adelaide, general cargo in Melbourne and Sydney, frozen meat in Brisbane and back again to Sydney to top up. The ship was in Brisbane at Christmas and we had a splendid time with the friends we had made previously. Here a girl called Hope Chesterfield (whose sisters' names were Faith and Charity) tried to teach me to dance and took me home to Sunday lunch. And, just before we sailed, Hopkins and I paid a visit to a hog-backed American freighter lying nearby with the Stars and Stripes emblazoned on her topsides as if she were still neutral. The crew were the usual friendly Americans, less boisterous and far more pensive than once they might have been but as generous as their nation always is so that we returned to the ship with innumerable back numbers of the *Saturday Evening Post* and *Life* magazine. It is from this and the tiny incident in the Panama Canal that I date my life-long love affair with the United States and my affection for its people. It is odd how the silliest details remain fixed forever. In one copy of *Life* there were photographs of perhaps two dozen of that year's crop of American society 'debutantes'. One name – Patty Lou Saunders – sticks to this day whether because I thought her the prettiest or was just intrigued by the name. Since she could have been no more than a couple of years older than her anonymous admirer in far-away Queensland she is probably alive, and prospering – a blue-rinsed grandmother in Richmond, Virginia?

In Sydney my friend, Judy Lindley, scared by newspaper stories about the intrusion of a Japanese submarine into the approaches to Sydney Harbour, was convinced that arson, murder and rape were about to break out all around – and who could blame her? I am afraid I was as unsympathetic and severe as it was possible for an almost beardless youth to be. Never having heard a bomb explode in my life I reminded her that London and other British cities had suffered a lot more than a rumour of a Japanese submarine. But the Yellow Peril – Japanese or Chinese, it didn't matter which – was a potent bogey in Australia, whose soldiers were busy in the Middle East fighting Germans. I think we parted on good enough terms and I hope that, like Patty Lou Saunders, she survives and prospers. She and I walked across Sydney Harbour Bridge together as the new year rang in – 1942, and who knew then what would happen to us all.

What happened to the *Asphalion* was that she joined a convoy from eastern Australia to Wellington, New Zealand. If it was not the first convoy across the Tasman Sea it could not have been far from it. It seemed bizarre, in a semi-tropical summer, to be going through the Atlantic routine, a grimmer ocean by far at that time. Perhaps it was not quite so brisk and professional but the Royal Navy and the Canadians had been at the business of convoy in the Atlantic for more than two years and were the acknowledged experts. Our stay in Wellington was brief but the ship in the adjacent berth was the full-rigged ship *Pamir*, her German crew interned in New Zealand and the ship laid up until someone decided what was to be done with her and mustered a crew capable of doing it. Her watchman allowed Hopkins and me to walk the decks at will. By now I had a far more informed respect for the men who understood and sailed such complicated ships than I could bring to bear when the *Abraham Rydberg* lay in Ayr harbour before the war.

The Pacific was just as wide as it had been outward bound and took as long to cross, but it was tranquil and the Japanese were still far away. Homeward bound we were putting the ship back in shape after the ravages of a long passage to and from the Middle East and intensive trading around the Australian coast. Being a 'day man', in these circumstances, was idyllic. The two midshipmen were called by the stand-by man at 0545 every morning. We took it in turn to get mugs of tea and thick wedges of toast from the galley, eaten and drunk sitting on number three hatch. I remember lying back on top of the hatch, looking up at the tall grey funnel and wondering what it must have been like to have been at sea before the war when the funnel had been blue, a yearning even then for the piping days of peace which would surely come again, if we survived to see it. We painted ship from stem to stern and truck to keel - true it was all in grey but it looked better for a fresh coat. We made repairs. We spliced new cargo slings and wire snotters and odds and ends that would be required next voyage. We overhauled lifeboat equipment and replenished water breakers. In war-time the boats were kept swung out on the davits and I loved working in an outslung boat, looking inwards to the ship, diagonally up to the bridge or vertically down to the racing turquoise and white water swirling along the ship's side. We stopped for a 15 minute 'smokoh' at 10 o'clock in the morning and then beavered on until 1215 when it was time to go through our standard drill of washing up to the cuffs and down to the collar before donning a near-white suit to enter the saloon. At three we stopped again for another 15 minutes, for tea and 'tabnabs' - whatever kind of cake the cook had exercised his art upon. Tired, sunburned, inevitably hungry, we finished at five and took our baths in the washplace using a white bucket sitting in a hole cut in a wooden plank which straddled the bath. The smell of carbolic reminds me of it to this day. About six o'clock the officers gathered for a gin before dinner, the 'sundowner' which I always associate with this delightful time of day on board a quiet ship forging her solitary way across a limitless ocean. After the Canal transit we threaded our way through the islands in the Gulf of Mexico and steamed hard up the coast of Florida. No black-out had yet been established and, even 20 miles off, the loom of Miami lights could be seen in the night sky. U-boats were beginning to take advantage of this cavalier attitude to war, but on board the *Asphalion* we saw nothing and heard only vague radio reports of ships attacked further north. Beautiful, balmy weather greeted our approach to the latitude of Cape Hatteras early one evening as we gathered for dinner still in tropical whites. But by midnight the bottom had fallen out of the glass. We had cleared the Gulf Stream and a freezing force eight was blowing. Next morning we weathered the worst sea conditions I had yet experienced. Despite my doubts about her capacity to survive near-hurricane conditions, the ship's behaviour was beautiful, as she lay hove to with just sufficient power to keep her manoeuverable, riding enormous seas, blown spume like lace over the grey-green water. Now and then she was struck by a rogue wave subtly out of rhythm with the rest. The port wing of the bridge was badly damaged by one such wall of water but, in the late afternoon, the weather abated almost as quickly as it had risen as the centre of the depression moved off into the Atlantic. Heavy weather, but at least it had kept the submarines down.

Halifax, Nova Scotia, like Freetown in Sierra Leone, was one of the great convoy gathering places of the Second World War. As we steamed towards its harbour on a bitter February evening, out of the darkness a long skiff-like boat suddenly appeared with two men in singlets pulling, another in a red and black checked mackinaw steering and the pilot sitting disconsolately in the bow. The two in singlets must have been doing it for a bet as the temperature was well below zero. The port was full of ships and seamen. Nova Scotia's licensing laws were odd: to get the rationed bottle of beer, one required a signed chit which had to be stamped by the supplier, possibly the well-known local cafe-inn called the Green Lantern. It was hardly worth the trouble because Halifax, feet deep in February snow, was not the world's most alluring place. Charlie Buckley, again, was convinced that the *Asphalion* would be sunk on the homeward run which appalled me. I had a wooden box full of carved elephants, tea from Ceylon, koala bears from Sydney and meat products from Brisbane with a side of lamb buried somewhere in the ship's refrigerator. This represented an enormous capital outlay and I was determined it should reach its destination. In any case the yearning, after eight months, to be back home again was too strong to be denied by the presence of belligerent U-boats between Halifax and the North Channel. I might be frightened but I was not ready to give in.

Hopkins and I had long since completed our course papers for Danny Peirce, each set designed to fill the idle hours of a four-month voyage. We had been out twice that time but luckily no additional papers had arrived. Mail, precious mail, was an infrequent and longed-for luxury which did not extend to additional examination papers! I had but one task to complete – to write an essay, near the end of the voyage, on my impressions of a career at sea. This I wrote during the homeward passage from Halifax when we reverted to double watches with a commodore enthusiastic about frequent signals.

'Rendezvous for noon the day after tomorrow will be XYZ.'
'Keep closed up - submarines are reported in the vicinity.'
'Number 43 - make less smoke.'
'Convoy will exercise Scatter drill at 10.00 tomorrow.'
'Zig-zag pattern number 17 will commence at 14.00.'
'All ships indicate noon position at GMT minus 4 hours today.'

I must have been weary and vexed, despite the warm glow of being so close to home, for my essay had little good to say of the sailor's life, that of the watch-keeping deck officer being dismissed as wasted in walking up and down looking for something which was not there and might never materialise. There was certainly a discrepancy between my love of ships and my temporary disenchantment. The essay was slipped into an envelope with my journal and the rest of the papers and promptly forgotten as the Atlantic general chart on the chart table was replaced by one of a larger scale showing the north-west of Ireland. For the first time I was experiencing the condition sailors call 'the channels' – the elation of homecoming which is one of the compensations for the pain of parting. There was deep satisfaction, too, in the familiar names of navigational marks, headlands, islands, beacons, the sea passages of the British coast. Those names, on the rim of the Western Approaches, were familiar to a wartime generation of mariners – Aran Island, the Bloody Foreland, Malin Head, Inistrahull, Rathlin Island, the Mull of Kintyre. There is a picture in my mind, a vignette of the war at sea, as this unassailed convoy steamed through a grey, March dawn north-west of Rathlin Island. Following a flurry of signals the Clyde-bound ships were

• *Asphalion under escort*

formed into two columns on the port wing of the convoy with the Liverpool and Bristol Channel ships in two columns to starboard, the *Asphalion* leading the inner one. Out of the murk one of the escorts closed us her signal lamp flashing a message which Ronnie Webb read as I recorded. The rust-stained, salt-encrusted warship, throwing heavy spray over her thin, sharp bow closed abeam of the bridge, pitching more heavily than the *Asphalion*, the water between the ships boiling with conflicting bow waves. *HMS Londonderry* had been merely a low, grey shape on the starboard flank for more than a week. One day she had suddenly hoisted a long black pennant and steamed off at great speed towards the southern horizon following some contact her sonar or asdic had picked up. But it was spurious and she returned to her watch-dog role, remote, impersonal but there. Now she was alongside, a markedly different kind of ship from ours, so much smaller, so cluttered and yet so lethal. And on her open bridge and about her decks were the men who had hoisted the black pennant, who had run to action stations to defend us, whose role was so different from ours and yet who performed that duty in the same conditions of weather and weariness. They were men just like ourselves, wrapped up in duffle coats, seen close-to for the first time. Did they, too, get the channels? Perhaps not; *HMS Londonderry* had probably been at sea for three weeks; the *Asphalion* was coming home almost nine months out from Liverpool. What the *Londonderry* people probably experienced was seasickness.

We thought we were Liverpool-bound but were directed instead to the Bristol Channel and, on a fresh March afternoon, we anchored in Swansea Bay. For Hopkins it must have been a superb experience to come back to his own home town. For me, the brown Welsh hills and the town encircling the bay, spelled tranquillity. We had been away for what seemed an eternity with the centre of the universe travelling with us. What had happened to the *Asphalion* and those who sailed in her had seemed all-important. Suddenly came the realisation that, while we had been away, nothing fundamental had changed. Swansea was in the same place as was Liverpool. The centre of the universe had been variously located squarely above the heads of those contemplating it – as it had been when the *Duchess of Hamilton* slid alongside at Ardrossan an hour out of Ayr, long before the war. It was a humbling but reassuring thought for surely there would always be some stable, unchanging Swansea to come back to.

The ship berthed next day. Hopkins was released at once. His father, a small bespectacled and cheerful man helped him home with his gear. I was invited to tea and the chief officer, probably with a middle-aged version of the channels simmering under his tough exterior, let me off the leash for the evening. It was strange to be in a house I had been hearing about for nine months and wonderful to be spoiled by a voluble Welsh lady, so grateful and relieved to have her only son home again that it overflowed upon me. It seemed a perfect end to a long saga and the following day I was sent on leave myself.

I did look back at the ship as I left her in King's Dock that morning, unaware of what she would mean to me for the rest of my life. In February 1944 the *Asphalion* was torpedoed in the Bay of Bengal and abandoned. When she failed to sink the crew returned to salve her. Two torpedoes had struck her in line with the boiler room super-heated steam engulfing the engine room and the spaces above, one of which was Leo Galvin's cabin. Dreadfully scalded he died in agony in the lifeboat, a sun-burned, blue-eyed, humorous, kindly and courageous Liverpudlian. With him and his kind, under a gentleman captain, professional officers and nurse-maided by an ebullient, voluble, hard-working, knowledgeable, aggravating little Welshman only two years my senior – 'One hand for the ship and one for yourself ' – I had grown up.

Chapter 4

THE SIEGE OF LENINGRAD STILL RAGED.   Singapore had fallen and the *Prince of Wales* and *Repulse* sunk.   German bombing of British cities continued and Bomber Command were mounting heavier and heavier raids on Germany.   At sea the U-boat wolf packs had enjoyed their 'happy time' in 1941 and were still formidably successful in what had come to be known as the Battle of the Atlantic.   In nine months the *Asphalion* had steamed many sea miles over much of the globe but had seen no action and heard only the occasional distant reverberation of depth-charge patterns.   The citizens of Lockerbie did not know that, of course, and my credit was as good in the community as other more deserving young men from the town, who were serving in the army and RAF.   'Young lad, King, up by Mairheed - comin' oot fur a captain,' was the jocular remark of one old farmer to another, overheard by John Kelly in Lockerbie market.

My mother, still slim, fair and younger-looking than most of the other mothers, was clearly under strain.   She had separated from my father during my absence and was now working as a shop assistant in Dumfries, the only work an untrained housewife of 41 could obtain easily.   Travelling 12 miles each way daily was becoming increasingly burdensome and looking after a 15 year-old schoolboy and two girls of 12 and nine in someone else's house far from easy.   But the Kellys were good to her, and Terry and the girls were conspicuously well-behaved and disciplined.   Terry, a sergeant in the school Air Training Corps, was determined to join the RAF as soon as he could.   Later that year Thelma was to live with Tot and Isa and go to school in Prestwick while Eileen, a sunny-natured child with a will of her own but who knew where the line was drawn, would become my mother's closest companion.   My leave lasted 21 days, from March 19 until April 9.   After a week at Muirhead I took off for Ayr to visit aunts and friends and to establish some kind of a rapport with a girl I had known at Dumfries who was now at Ayr Academy.   Arriving on her mother's doorstep in the late forenoon of my first day I was asked if I were Tom King's son.   On confessing that this was the case I was sharply told by Mrs Lawrie that, in that case, she would keep an eye on me!   I was not to know then that she and my father had

- *Top: Terry, left, and George King*
Bottom: Mum flanked by Eileen, left, and Thelma. Both photo-
graphs survived the sinking of the Polydorus

been contemporaries in Ayr during the first world war and that he
had been quick off the mark with the girls of his generation. As
it happened her daughter and I had an off-and-on relationship of
an innocent kind for two or three years during which time Mrs
Lawrie and her old mother could not have been kinder. Frequently Granny would slip me a 10s note for the best balcony seats
in the Broadway cinema where the back row, as always, was much

94

sought after by the fancy.   Alas, Elsie was clever and became intellectual on entering Glasgow University in 1944. She thought, wisely, that at our age it was a better idea to play the field and eventually it all came to an amicable end. She married an engineer called Hamilton after the war, started to use her second name, Jane, and, as Jane Hamilton, is alive and well to this day. But she was my first heart-throb - if you don't count Judy Garland in *The Wizard of Oz* and jolly Judy Lindley in far-away Australia.

Back in Lockerbie in early April I awaited the dread telegram. I was reluctant to return to sea. Apprenticeship seemed a long hard grind and although so much of shipboard life appealed strongly homesickness, I knew, would ever persist. The low range of hills behind Lochmaben, to the north-west of Lockerbie – my 'blue remembered hills' – were real and dear, seen from the 10-acre field below Cemetery Wood. Pride prevented my saying anything to my mother, adding another worry to her burden.   However, I must have said something to a school friend, Porky Morrison, who was as thin as a lath despite his nickname. He reported it to his father, a schoolmaster I think, and a rather superior sort of a fellow. Father Morrison had a solution: the local dairy needed a boy to help the milk roundsman. I was aghast at being patronised as it seemed to me, scarlet-faced with shame at ever having exposed my thoughts to his son.   Blue Funnel middie to errand boy! Instantly, I had no more doubt. There was no turning back and, when the telegram arrived, followed by a letter of instruction and a rail warrant for Liverpool, I went cheerfully, promising my mother to eat plenty of fresh fruit and cure the acne which now humiliated me.

To Riversdale Road again, and Mrs Asman. This time I was no shy newcomer on the Aigburth Vale tramcar. My uniform cap had as good a Western Ocean roll as anyone else's, a fact instantly recognized by my companions with whom I felt on equal terms. The tram conductors were now more circumspect approaching Riversdale Road. Some time before they had developed the habit of calling out, 'Next stop Riversdale Road - for Holt's Baby Farm'. A week or two previously, when this call had gone up, the last two brawny midshipmen to come downstairs picked up the conductor by his arms and elbows, belled the driver to carry on and marched their prisoner some distance up the road before releasing him. By this time the tram was far away. There was a great row. Someone – probably Brian Heathcote – had to apologise to Liverpool Tramways department and disciplinary action was taken! But the conductors were more careful.

Danny Peirce appeared taken aback as I reported to the office. I was sent for at once. 'Didn't expect you back, King – h'mm?', his eyes drilling me from behind the thick glasses, his lips pursing into a miniscule 'o'. I could have exploded into self-conscious giggles again. His effect on me was exactly the same as it had been the previous year and was so to remain until the parting of our respective ways. 'Yessir,' I spluttered. It hardly seemed adequate, but he hadn't explained himself and I could only surmise that my voyage essay had been taken as resignation as turned out to be the case; but Peirce did not harangue me for expressing my views. He treated me as an intelligent observer, which I was far from being, and was prepared to debate my contentions although I had undermined my case by returning to the fold as soon as the whistle blew. He also reminded me that he had emphasised the hazards and hardships when I joined, which was no more than the truth. At the end he sent me off in a glow by telling me that Captain Beer had given me a good report. As an example of man management it was impeccable, and I have always been sorry that I had no opportunity to talk as an adult to Danny Peirce or to get over the effect he had on me as soon as he started to speak.

The war was even more serious and professional now than it had been the previous year. There was no question of catching up on the ex-meridian altitude problem by studying in the office. Half-a-dozen of us, led by Conrad Hopkins who had just turned up, were despatched once more for a week's gunnery course at *HMS Eaglet*. We had a great deal of four-inch gun drill.
'Still. Missfire. Carry on.'
'Striker not gone forward.'
'Shift striker.'
'Ready.'
'Up two hundred, left four.'
'Down one hundred.'
'Open fire!'
It was brave and warlike stuff, in a depot with experienced professionals pushing and shoving us into the right places and getting us to react like trained naval ratings. Anti-aircraft training had advanced spectacularly since the previous year. We now fought off Stuka and Messerschmitt 110 dive-bomber attacks in a thing called a Dome Trainer, a much more sophisticated version

of the film projected on the wall which had sunk us on our last visit. Now cine-films of actual attacks were projected on a curved wall, the sound-track delivering at what seemed like about 120 decibels. The trainee was strapped in a mock-up of an Oerlikon gun which sounded realistic when the trigger was pulled. It stopped after 99 rounds had been fired - the capacity of a genuine magazine. Still we failed to conserve our ammunition, fired off our magazine at the first attacker and had nothing left to repulse the next two aircraft which screamed down at us out of the clouds.

After the course I found myself appointed, with Hopkins again and two first-trippers, to a ship called the *Phemius*. We joined her in what was left of one of the Canada Docks and within hours were anchored in the river once more, awaiting convoy. On anchor watch somewhere off New Brighton pier I saw our new captain for the first time – or, more correctly, heard him. 'Boy!' came a loud cry from the chart-room as I slowly paraded the wing of the bridge out of the officer-of-the-watch's sight. Leaping forward I was confronted by a short, bull-necked man with a face like a beetroot, fair hair and small blue and bulging eyes. He looked me up and down deliberately in a very unfriendly manner, chewing one side of his lip the while. 'What's your name, boy?' he rasped, and I detected a Scots accent. "King, sir." I answered.
'Are you the boy from Scotland?' he said, menacingly.
'Yes sir.'
He looked even more truculent.
'Did your mother give you a bible when you left home?'
'N-no sir.'
'Oh, she didn't, didn't she. Well, we'll have to teach you the lessons from the Good Book, won't we? Here – take this chit to the Chief Engineer – and keep your eyes open when you're on watch!'

I was taken aback. I could remember nothing in the Good Book covering the bearing of chits from captains to chief engineers or keeeping a good lookout on the bridge. Come back Captain Beer, gentleman.

Captain Johnston was nicknamed 'Pinky' or 'Piggy' because of the colour of his face and neck I guessed. He came from Edinburgh and had not been long in command. At sea he always wore black silk pyjamas (because they didn't have to be laundered so often, some wag claimed) but he forbade midshipmen to undress when they went to bed in case they had to get up to abandon ship! I thought him odd. We sailed from the Mersey in a large convoy with many troopships. The *Phemius* was bigger and faster than the *Asphalion* and had a reputation. In the early 30s she had been caught in a hurricane in the West Indies, rode through the eye of the storm, was laid on her beam ends, seriously damaged and lost her funnel. The episode was later used as the basis of a novel entitled *In hazard,* and we always swore that the replacement funnel casing, fitted in Galveston, Texas and still in place in 1942, was several sizes smaller than that of any of her sister ships. It was supported by thirty-two funnel guys instead of the normal Blue Funnel 16 or the eight which would have been sufficient in a lesser ship! The half-deck, after the *Asphalion*, was palatial. It occupied half of the starboard side of the house around the engine-room casing and consisted of a square dayroom with a fixed table, settees round three sides, a tallboy and a long book-case. Immediately abaft of it was a bunk room with upper and lower bunks on either side of a narrow fore-and-aft gangway leading into a shower room and toilet. On joining the ship Hopkins, who knew the drill, went at once to the book-case, took out the bible and gave it a smart shake to make sure that nothing was hidden inside. Legend had it that Mr Laurence Holt, the chairman – the true 'owner' come to that – during his customary pre-sailing inspection had once slipped a five-pound note into the half-deck bible. When the ship returned four months later from her pre-war Far East voyage he went straight to the half-deck, took the bible from the book-case and retrieved his five pounds, proving to his own Unitarian satisfaction that his four young men were heathens. That was the story and it was sufficient to ensure that the bible was checked each voyage for banknotes, invariably its only outing during the trip. As no bank notes were ever found in his other ships Mr Holt's prudence was established for ever.

Four midshipmen in a proper half-deck made a difference. Conrad Hopkins was very much the senior for this would be his last voyage as an apprentice before he went ashore to study for his Second Mate's Certificate examination. As second senior, after only one nine-month voyage at that, the heady fumes of power rose in my nostrils but I had to be careful for number three was a hulking ex-Liverpool Collegiate boy called 'Shaggy' Thomas. The most junior was a tall fair shadow from Pinner, whose name escapes me. Double watches lasted only a few days on this occasion and then three of us remained on single bridge watches while the fourth became a day-man. We steamed west a long way before the convoy split into two parts, one group continuing towards Halifax and a bigger section turning south-easterly in the direction, ultimately, of Freetown where we arrived unscathed 20 days out from Liverpool. Refuelled and reformed, we sailed a day or two later for Capetown in what had now become a fast troop convoy made up of ships like the *Empress of Canada*, the *Reina del Pacifico*, the *Orduna* and the *Orbita* and two Dutch passenger ships with short stumpy funnels the tops of which were cut parallel with the deck and which gloried in the names, *Maninx van St Oddagaun* and *Johan van Oldenbarnevelt*. I took great pride in learning and remembering those two names but I might have found a more productive use for my time.

On passage towards the Cape we saw a great deal more of Captain Pinky. At evening twilight he sometimes liked to take star sights with the chief and fourth officers. As he swept from one side of the blacked-out bridge to the other he called out, 'Ping! Ping!', either to warn off on-coming traffic or, like the bat, to establish his own position with reference to the next obstruction. The first time I heard this on watch I naturally leapt to action stations at the sound of my own name and called out eagerly, 'Yes, sir.' 'You silly boy,' he fumed as he came into the dimly-lit chartroom, 'I said Ping, not bloody King.' One evening he spent nearly an hour dealing with reductions of the moon. As I passed through the chartroom on some errand near the end of this saga he threw his pencil down violently and said, 'Boy, learn this once - navigation is NOT an exact science.'

From Freetown to Capetown the battleship *Resolution* formed part of the accompanying force but spent all her time tucked into the centre of the convoy near the *Riena del Pacifico* with which she almost collided one memorable Sunday afternoon due to some misunderstanding over the zig-zag. Table Bay was full of troopships and our bunkering call alongside lasted only a few hours during which we got no further than Adderley Street and saw nothing of the legendary South African hospitality. Off again we rounded the Cape bound for Suez and Port Said where the atmosphere, in the summer of 1942, was as fraught as it had been the previous year. The desert war had not quite been lost but it looked as if it would never be won. From the Middle East war zone we were routed back to South Africa again and, north of the Mozambique Channel, picked up a lifeboat with survivors from a Norwegian ship which had been torpedoed the previous day, presumably by a Japanese submarine, several of which were known to be operating in the area. The survivors included a small Cairn terrier which seemed to be coping well with the war. It didn't know how lucky it was that the submarine had not surfaced to conduct a Japanese interrogation which tended to include a machine-gun attack on the survivors. Early next day the alarm bells jangled, the ship's speed increased as we zig-zagged wildly and closed up to action stations. The gunlayer had sighted a torpedo track which missed astern and, for several hours, we remained at action stations in case the attack developed. Not unreasonably, the Norwegians were anxious not to be torpedoed twice in 48 hours, and equally reasonably the rest of us were keen to avoid a first experience. But no attack developed and we disappeared through the Mozambique Channel at maximum speed to reach Capetown and land our survivors.

The ship was to load for the United Kingdom in several ports on the West African coast, the first being Matadi some distance up the River Congo which I thought of then, and still do, as 'Heart of Darkness' country. The Congo announces its formidable presence, far into the Atlantic, by discoloration of the water on a broad front. What it lacks, however, are good navigation marks. The *Phemius* was steaming slowly in the direction of the river mouth - a general sort of term in the case of the Congo – one Sunday, when the captain espied two fishermen in a tiny canoe. Altering course to bring the canoe close under the port side he took himself to the wing of the bridge and called out, 'Is this the Congo?' The only response to this bizarre, if logical, question was for one of the men to hold aloft a large fish and call out, 'Feesh, feesh'.

We were to load palm oil in number four deep tank which had carried artillery and motor transport on the outward passage. Preparation of this tank took almost a fortnight during which time we lay alongside a rickety berth. Matadi held little to attract us ashore, but we four impecunious midshipmen procured the services of an enterprising 10-year old boy who would shop for us every day or two and bring back from the local market fruit which was delicious and eggs which were tiny but fresh. We had no need to supplement the ship's more-than-adequate rations but we enjoyed the trading and our 'agent' no doubt made a handsome profit. At Lagos, Accra and Takoradi we completed loading but, sadly, many of us succumbed to malaria despite the daily administration of liquid quinine followed by a generous measure of rum to remove the bitterness and – so said the doctor – reduce the quinine-induced heart rate. One gunner, a quiet bank clerk in his mid-30s with a wife and two young children in some leafy Surrey town, died in hospital ashore, a casualty of the war as surely as if he had been killed in action. The rest of us sweated it out on board but it left me a legacy of recurrent attacks for the next 25 years or so. It was a great relief to sail from Freetown in convoy back home to the Mersey and straight into Bromborough Dock where the palm oil was to be discharged. Fortunately that was none of my business. At the end of our six-month voyage all four midshipmen, after de-briefing in the office by Danny Peirce, were sent on leave. Conrad Hopkins was to stay at home for two or three months studying for his Second Mate's Certificate, the rest of us for 10 or 12 days freedom. If I was not sorry to see the last of Captain Johnston who had ridden us so hard, I had developed a greater respect for him as a shipmaster. He was an eccentric and at 17 one does not know how to deal with eccentrics, especially those in authority.

The pattern of this leave was similar to my first in the early spring. By early October I was back in Riversdale Road and had been appointed with indecent haste to one of the Blue Funnel Dutch-flag ships, the *Polydorus*. There was no way in which I could have anticipated the adventures which were to befall that ship's company; but I was delighted with the appointment because it was something of a privilege for British midshipmen to be sent to one of the six Dutch ships which did not normally carry midshipmen, but whose food and conditions were considered to be superior to those prevailing in British-flag ships. To tell the truth they were not, merely stranger for being Dutch. In peacetime the ships traded between Hamburg, Rotterdam and the Dutch East Indies. In consequence they were permeated with the cultures of Holland and Java rather than England and Hong Kong or Shanghai. One drawback was said to be that the Dutch officers were sometimes a deal harder to please than the British. As I had met few of the latter who were easy to please to me it seemed no drawback at all.

The *Polydorus* was a similar ship to the *Asphalion* but built a year or two later. She, and the five other Dutch-registered ships of the Oceann Company, had been at sea when the Netherlands fell to the Germans in 1940. Since then they had been operated from Liverpool as part of the British fleet with their original Dutch officers and Chinese crews supplemented by British midshipmen, an occasional junior officer and DEMS gunners. A tiny half-deck had been created out of two supernumary cabins on the starboard side of the lower bridge house with just enough room for four bunks in double tiers and a washplace and lavatory. The four of us who joined the *Polydorus* in early October did not mind that. The privilege of serving in a Dutch ship was thought by some to be a present for a good boy although, privately, I could see a flaw in the argument. After Pinky Johnston, who had once sent me up to the crow's nest of the *Phemius* for leaning on the bridge rail and then forgot me for four hours until I had to come down to the lavatory, I wondered how I fitted into the 'good boy' category, but I asked no questions and enjoyed my good luck.

John Leslie, the 19-year old senior midshipman, was a man already, and a very handsome, blond, Aryan-god of a man at that with formidable self-confidence. He came from Carnoustie in Fife where his mother ran what sounded like rather an exclusive hotel in which John had picked up social graces and sophistication beyond his years. He was a different animal from Conrad Hopkins and I walked respectfully. His previous voyage had been in a fast Glen Line ship, the *Glenorchy* which had been sunk off Sfax while sailing in the Pedestal convoy to Malta the previous August. The ship's company had endured real hardship in North Africa and had reached home only with difficulty. The two others, junior to me by a few months, were Peter Postlethwaite Bracewell from Formby and Geoffrey Bridden from near Preston. They had served together in the *Deucalion*, an Ajax-class ship - a class I admired enormously by this time - which had also been sunk in the Pedestal battle although nearer Malta than the Glenorchy. Plucked from the water by the destroyer *Bramham* and transferred to the tanker *Ohio* to support an exhausted crew both Bracewell and Bridden had thus become involved in the epic of that ship's last few limping miles into Malta. They came home eventually in the submarine *Clyde*. In the face of such war experience shared by the other three I, who had put in 15 months without hearing a shot fired in anger, walked small and quietly. But we got on well and settled down quickly.

• *Polydorus*

The Dutch officers tended to be taciturn, demanding but well-enough disposed to us: certainly the social atmosphere on board was more relaxed than in my two British ships. Much of this must have been due to the personality of Captain Hans Brouwer; bluff, avuncular, good-humoured, urbane, cosmopolitan, cigar-smoking, he spoke perfect idiomatic English with only the faintest hint of Hollander rotundity. For me he epitomised all that one would expect of a Dutch shipmaster with centuries of maritime history in his bloodstream. Van Vurre, the chief officer, had a treacle-deep voice but lacked the sparkle of the captain. At least he did not try to drive his four midshipmen too hard. The second officer, Salomons, seemed quite young and was excellent with us youngsters. Van der Most, the third, might have been Van Vurre's younger brother. The fourth was a Welshman called Evans on temporary secondment, as were we. The Dutchmen, with their engineering colleagues, had served in the ship since 1940 and took only what short leave they could in England simply to get away from the ship for a day or two. Most had wives and children and all had relatives in occupied Holland. The strain on them must have been so much greater than that endured by their British counterparts but they were stoical. About this time Princess Juliana, as she then was, gave birth to her third daughter, Margriet, a cause for celebration and the dispensing of mementoes to us all.

But our business was at sea. Again we went through the ritual of undocking, anchoring in the Mersey, preparing for sea and then steaming slowly in a seemingly endless line of ships to form up in convoy west of Liverpool Bay. The *Polydorus* was bound for the Middle East with military equipment, clothing, trucks, motorcycles, barbed wire, ammunition of every calibre and sea mines stowed near the centre line of numbers two and three holds and surrounded by such padding as bales of battle dresses. There was even a substantial consignment of army forms and stationery but this I did not know until about three weeks later. On the after deck were lashed two massive army vehicles and several small launches. Each side of the fore deck was occupied by a large RAF air-sea rescue craft resting on skids secured by heavy wire lashings over bow and stern. The foremast rigging had had to be released to get them into position and then set up afresh. They were sleek and handsome boats, each powered by three Rolls Royce engines and they made the mouths of 17-year-old sea urchins run with saliva.

With four of us on board there was no doubling of watches

although the convoy work was just as arduous. Life, indeed, was comparatively easy. We had a messroom but the rigid protocol of the saloon still applied and we had to dress properly for meals, no hardship when every day brought some gorgeous Javanese or Dutch culinary surprise. A dish called Nassi Goring became a tremendous favourite and we even had a Rijstaffel which was a great deal more than was being enjoyed on board most ships in the convoy. Despite our ultimate destination we were routed a long way west before the dispersal signal was hoisted on the eighth or ninth day. With the arrival of the new western escort the main body of ships re-formed and steamed off into the sunset towards Halifax, Boston and New York to be attacked, a day or two later, and quite badly mauled. A dozen or so of us altered course south-easterly and we made off, independent ship, towards Freetown some 2000 miles away. As one of the faster ships the *Polydorus* had put most of the others hull down astern by nightfall and was set on a shallow zig-zag pattern with the eyes and ears of the lookouts wide open. It was mid-November, 1942. There had been rumours of imminent landings in North or North-west Africa; the approaches to the Straits of Gibraltar and the African coast as far south as Dakar were known to be under constant German surveillance. The route to Freetown passed through troubled waters.

Despite their initial taciturnity the Dutch had turned out to be a delight and I thought myself particularly fortunate to have been put on Salomons' watch. Certainly the twelve to four was the 'graveyard' watch and one got one's sleep in two three-and-a-half hour spells, after supper and before breakfast, with four hours of deep, dark night in between. But Salomons talked to me, if not quite as an equal at least freely, and assumed some grains of intelligence on my part. I learned much about Holland in just a week or two. A fastidious man he liked his supper sandwiches served on a plate with a napkin covering them so that my grubby little fingers would neither contaminate nor offend. A day or two after we broke away from the convoy watch-keeping ended for the midshipmen who could be employed more usefully than getting in the way on the bridge. One afternoon Bridden and I, who had been checking stores in the out-swung lifeboats, were sent to resecure equipment and covers in one of the launches on the after deck. We were working away and no doubt chattering, for Bridden was an accomplished raconteur with an ability to quote whole pages of Shakespeare – 'Alas, poor Yorick. I knew him, Horatio. He was a fellow of infinite jest' – springs instantly to mind as he was particularly strong on Hamlet. We both happened to be looking to seaward when there a was sudden eruption of water some distance away on the starboard quarter followed, a moment or two later, by the flat thud of an underwater explosion and a strong vibration through the ship's hull. Almost at once the alarm bells rang out for action stations. The explosion was surmised, later, to have been a torpedo 'premature' or 'over-run' and Captain Brouwer, now on the bridge, put the ship into a more complicated zig-zag as the rest of us closed up – Leslie on the bridge, Bracewell and Bridden in Oerlikon pits and I at the telephone behind the four-inch gun aft. Nothing happened. The tension slowly eased and, as the afternoon drew towards the sudden low-latitude twilight, we stood down and the ship returned almost to normal and certainly to supper.

Suddenly, just before 2100, there was a flash of gunfire out of the night from the port beam and a shell whined overhead followed by a burst of what sounded like Oerlikon fire. After the warning earlier in the day the response was instantaneous: the alarm bells were ringing before the reverberations had died down. A tremendous crash and flash from aft followed. Running to my station, I realised the four-inch had been fired. By chance Widd, the RN gunlayer, had been training the gun, as part of his end-of-the-day drill, at the moment when the first flash had come out of the night. Without thinking, Widd pressed the trigger firing the round left in the breech since our action stations in the afternoon. Off into the night it hurtled, missing whatever was there wildly but suggesting that the soft target at least had its eyes open. A few minutes later the U-boat fired again and the *Polydorus* responded with her two port Oerlikons which probably served only to give the submarine a more exact target reference. Two or three small-calibre shells pierced the funnel casing, the engine room skylight and one of the lifeboats. Within half-an-hour the attack was broken off but we stood to at action stations until almost midnight by which time we were sufficiently exhausted to fall into our bunks and instant oblivion.

Shortly after five o'clock next morning the ship's company was galvanised into action again by the alarm bells. As we grabbed lifejackets and steel helmets it was clear that the ship was heeling under full rudder as she turned to avoid something. Dawn was breaking and, in the early morning light, Van Vurre, the officer of the watch, had sighted a torpedo track coming in swiftly from the port side. His alteration to starboard caused it to miss astern. Within seconds everyone was closed up at action stations with thudding hearts, boiled eyes and dry mouths. A minute or two ticked by. Salomons, the ship's gunnery officer, called me from the telephone and told me to give two others a hand to bring up more four-inch ammunition, shells and charges in scarlet bags stowed in heavy cardboard containers, to supplement the dozen rounds in the ready-use locker behind the gun. As I staggered up a ladder from the ammunition locker there was a small, bright-red flash in the dark grey to the east. A second or two later, a shell exploded in our wake. Salomons and Widd reacted like Eaglet instructors.

'Target, submarine, red one five oh, range five thousand, open fire when ready.'

'Range five thousand, deflection nil.'

'Layer on - ready.'

'Fire!'

Wham! Off went the first four-inch shell to God knows where; but it was impressive for 'a peaceful merchant ship about her lawful occasions', even if filled to the gunwales with war materiel.

At that range the U-boat was becoming more visible in the gathering light, a low, dark, innocently nondescript shape with a hump in the middle, oddly unlike a ship but instantly sinister as the gun forward of the conning tower flashed or the quick firer abaft the bridge sent across a short burst. From a bigger, more stable platform, and at a comparatively short range, Widd's gunlaying was at least as accurate as that of the U-boat which gradually opened the distance until she was near our gun's extreme range. At that distance, 10-11,000 yards, the U-boat was much more difficult to see. She pressed her attack, firing regularly and following Brouwer's every move. By now all our ammunition was racked. In a lull in the firing I was sent to the bridge with a message because the gun-deck telephone had been put out of action. As I reached the bridge an incoming shell found the range and struck the rescue launch on the port side of the fore deck, entering through the transom and exiting through the starboard bow, the explosion carrying away some of the port rigging as well. Hurriedly, I was sent back aft which seemed to me safer anyway as we had a gun there and it was the forward end of the ship which was being hit! I discovered later that John Leslie was spotting from the foremast crow's nest at the time, too close to the effects of that shell strike for comfort.

When I reached the gun-deck Salomons asked if I knew how to set sights, the sight setter having been hurt and sent below. Thank God for *Eaglet*. Yes, I knew the sight setting drill, and for the next hour or so I had plenty of real-life practice. Once the first terror of realising that those bastards out there were Germans and serious had passed it was surprising how quickly the gun's crew settled into the drill of exchanging fire. I felt perfectly safe on the left-hand side of the gun, both hands outstretched on the two circular sight-setting scales with Widd on my right, hunched against his padded shoulder-rest, eye to telescope, hand to trigger. Even the crash of the gun became near-acceptable and I was fascinated by the swift, straight recoil of the barrel just above my knuckles as the blast and flash from the muzzle engulfed us in acrid fumes. Salomons, standing to one side with binoculars glued to his eyes, was a confident and steadying influence. Unexcitedly he concentrated on estimating range and deflection and the future position of the U-boat from its aspect through his glasses. Crude gunnery but seemingly effective defence. Once he thought we had scored a hit but it was probably just a close splash - enough, however, to keep the U-boat out at his gun's maximum range. Once or twice he managed to hit the ship but caused only superficial damage except to the port side lifeboats which suffered badly.

By now it was full daylight, but the submarine had disappeared behind a bank of dark grey smoke disgorged from one of the smoke floats which Evans, the fourth officer, had been dropping on instructions from the bridge. Then the low black shape hove back in sight as it came up-wind of the smoke floats to find the target again. Long range fire resumed and continued sporadically for another hour. Captain Brouwer manoeuvered the *Polydorus* as if she had been a warship, taking every advantage of cover behind the heavy smoke, spoiling the German commander's target by presenting the least possible aspect to him and using the ship's 15 knots to advantage by heading into the weather whenever possible. The head seas which did not trouble the *Polydorus* would make life more difficult for the U-boat's gun crew on her slippery foredeck. Around 0830 Brouwer managed to head for a substantial rain squall, gained it and the flagging U-boat was lost to sight. When the rain cleared 30 minutes later the enemy had vanished.   Gradually the ship was turned back east-south-easterly towards Freetown 800 miles away. In due time we were stood down from action stations but spent the rest of the day on double watches and checking the ship for damage.   The funnel casing and main engine-room ventilators were riddled with shrapnel holes. Two of the port side lifeboats were badly damaged as was the large rescue launch on the port side of the foredeck. One shell had penetrated the shell plating and entered number three 'tweendeck a foot or two above the waterline.   The hatch was opened and the chief officer led the damage control party into the hold. Battle dress remnants and cartons of War Office stationery were scattered some distance from their original stowage but the cases of ammunition were intact as were the mines even further down.   But the RAF launch looked rather sad. At first sight the damage seemed minimal - a hole about six inches in diameter and much splintering in the counter with more damage in the starboard bow. Inboard, one Rolls Royce engine was wrecked and the other two damaged. But the *Polydorus* was still afloat and making 15 knots.   In little more than two days we could be safe in Freetown now alerted by our frequent 'submarine sighting' radio transmissions which we hoped would result in the despatch of a Sunderland flying-boat to help us.   Relaxing, I envisaged our triumphal entry into Freetown harbour having fought off single-handedly a ferocious U-boat. I was distressed by the thought that only the undamaged starboard side would be visible from the town as we steamed into harbour, and the battle-scarred port side would be facing mangrove swamps.   I was proud of the ship. Later that afternoon it was my turn for two hours lookout in the barrel near the truck of the foremast. Doubtlessly, I should have been concentrating on the horizon throughout my watch but, for a while at least, I looked down on the deck of the stalwart ship as she thrust her way through the sea. My eyes took in the details of the deck machinery and equipment on the foc'slhead, the neat symmetry of the foredeck hatches now that the debris had been cleared away. Down on the bridge Salomons, alert and watchful, paced the starboard wing.   Behind him brown smoke from the fore-shortened grey funnel streamed away to leeward. On the boatdeck, Oerlikon pits with a keen-eyed gunner in each and outswung lifeboats like barbettes along the ship's side were silhouetted against the white race of boiling wake.   Just visible behind the mainmast stood the four-inch gun with which we had fought that morning. So vivid was the spectacle that beautiful afternoon that it remained etched in my memory ever afterwards. We went to bed exhausted, elated but still on edge. Perhaps we hadn't lost the U-boat. Despite our 15 knots he could still be there somewhere if the commander had correctly interpreted Brouwer's intentions. He could have manoeuvered ahead into a firing position again. Submerged he could not hope to keep up with the *Polydorus* but on the surface he could. Six or seven miles away he would be out of sight whereas our high masts and funnel smoke would still be visible to him. He might, just might, be waiting.

He was. A little before 0300 on November 27 1942, in latitude 9° 1'N 25° 32W, Kapitanleutnant Reiner Dierksen in command of U-176 found his target. Two torpedoes struck the port side in number four hold immediately abaft the engine-room. Instantly awake it was obvious that the first explosion was different from anything we had previously experienced. The second explosion, much louder, emphatically confirmed that. As the ship heeled heavily to port I was tipped out of my bunk on top of the other three already scrambling about the deck. The cabin was in total darkness. For a second or so there was silence and then, above our heads, the urgent sound of running feet, cries and the harsh clang of the alarm bells. Not 'Action Stations' this time, but 'Abandon Ship'. None of us panicked. We had been sleeping in shorts so all we needed were lifejackets, shoes and our 'jump' bags which we kept by our bunks at night. As we burst out into the alleyway leading aft to the upper deck a figure filled the dim light of the open weather door. Captain Brouwer had come personally to make sure we were all right. He counted us out, told us to hurry and returned to the bridge. Through the darkness we scrambled our separate ways to boat stations amidst loud shouts, thuds and rattles as the first arrivals released the boat gripes and prepared to launch.

Number one boat on the starboard side of the lower bridge deck was Salomons' boat - and mine. By the time I arrived he was already there, sent down from the bridge by Brouwer, and trying to control a gathering crowd of Chinese sailors and firemen. 'Get into the boat before we release the gripes,' he shouted to me. It was standard drill, practised over and over again in other ships and at least three times since we had joined the *Polydorus*. The officer stayed on deck in charge of the operation while the mid-shipman or a petty officer, with one or two hands to handle the gear, was lowered in the boat to take charge until the officer himself could get down and take over. I scrambled in and released the tiller lashed to the inboard gunwale. Two Chinese sailors stood by the bow and stern blocks ready to release the hooks as the boat took the water. On Salomons' order the gripes were slipped and the boat swung violently at the davit heads for a few seconds. By now the ship had thrown off the list she had taken when the torpedoes struck but, although the engines were stopped, she still forged ahead making a good deal of way, the black water swirling malevolently under the swinging lifeboat. The men on the falls began to lower away jerkily and we parted company from deck level, the ship appearing to rise above the boat. She was settling by the stern now and the boat rope stretching from the ship's foredeck to a fairlead abaft number three hatch, to which the lifeboat was made fast by painters fore and aft, was dragging in the water. The starboard was the weather side and diamond points of black water were driving against the hull through the grey-green lacework thrown up by the ship's forward movement. The sounds of wind and waves, creaking blocks, thuds and crashes from above, cries in the distance and steam released from the boilers made a wild cacophony in the night. It was difficult to see the bow and to have any kind of control. Suddenly the boat hit water, bounced and was afloat as the sailors, by instinct and training, threw off the blocks from the lifting hooks. At once the ship began to leave the boat behind. Then the rudder struck the wreckage of another boat already sinking under its davits. One of the pintles snapped off and the tiller was loose and useless in my hands. I could hear the roar of Salomons' voice above, yelling instruction, but could distinguish nothing in the tumult. My limited experience however suggested one obvious solution. If the rudder was useless I would have to use the steering oar. Smaller than the pulling oars, its blade was painted white and it was stowed, blade aft, on its own and not blade forward with the five others lashed to each side thwart. It stared me in the face. With the help of a sailor, I shoved it through the wire grommet secured in the stern sheets for that express purpose. Now I could steer the boat either into the ship's side or veer away. And then I realised, suddenly, that even with the steering oar I had no control of the boat which started to describe a wide semi-circle out from the ship's side. I knew then that the forward painter was no longer attached to the boat rope; only the after painter secured us to the ship. The waves drove the boat back in towards the ship again but this time with the bow facing aft. We were being towed by the after painter. At that moment I became aware of a pale, streaming face and a lifejacket in the water alongside. I grabbed a reaching hand and with my right arm round the steering oar and my left clutching whoever was in the water I lost control of the boat which was now driven hard towards the ship's side. The ship was steady but still moving ahead. The boat was being thrown up and down six or seven feet and rolling heavily in the waves and about to smash into the starboard side. Just before it struck a white-clad figure leapt from the boat deck above but sadly for the Chinese fireman he missed the boat where he might have got away with a broken leg. He plunged between ship and out-of-control lifeboat just at the moment of impact. His poor, thin body acted as a fender and then I was submerged by a wave of bodies sliding down man ropes and Jacob's ladder, Salomons among the first. He grabbed the oar and grunted, 'Good fellow'. Now I was free to deal with whoever was still clinging fiercely to my left wrist. At that moment the doctor reached over the gunwale and grabbed the lifejacket of the man in the water. I had precious little strength left to help him but, with my faithful Chinese sailor, we managed to drag the man into the boat. It was Owen Nulty an engineer en route to West Africa to join another ship. As number one boat took the water he had started down the rope ladder to come to my assistance. When the boat sheered off suddenly he had been torn from the ladder and had dropped into the sea. Later Salomons told me how one of the Chinese, who had gone down in the boat with me, had picked up the emergency axe and chopped through the forward painter severing our most dependable connection with the ship.

Over the turmoil Salomons' strong, assured voice began to exercise calm. I was grateful that he was now in charge and that there were others in the boat. As Nulty lay hawking out sea water in the bottom of the boat, the doctor and I hauled in the injured fireman. With his face sagging in the water he looked like a bundle of old clothes. As he came inboard it was like handling a sack of loose sand. There was no blood, no broken skin, no obvious injury but a green pallor of death was upon him. The doctor ran expert hands over his body and we made space to stretch him out on the side thwart, but he was already dead.

Salomons ordered the after painter cast off and called to the crew, now settling on the thwarts in some semblance of order, to clear the oars and lower them into the crutches. 'Give way,' he ordered and in ragged fashion we began to pull away from the ship. Another Chinese fireman was seated behind the aftermost oar on the port side. Standing in the cockpit facing him I pushed as he pulled, the doctor giving the same assistance to the man on the starboard stroke oar. I soon became aware that I was pushing more than my shipmate was pulling. The doctor motioned me to stop to see the effect. The oar rotated once and then began to trail alongside. The man's eyes were glazed. 'Drugged,' whispered the doctor so we pushed him out of the way and took over ourselves. With eyes now used to darkness it was possible to see the outline of the *Polydorus* 50 yards or so away. No longer making much way her stern had sunk low in the water, the four-inch gun barely clear. There was no discernible damage but it was obvious that she was doomed. Salomons urged us to pull harder to get well clear. She might go at any moment and we could be engulfed in the down draught or smashed by the wreckage thrown clear as she went under. We pulled against the weather for what seemed an eternity but were hardly more than a quarter-of-a-mile off when Salomons, realising that the ship had sunk no further, ordered us to stop rowing and rest. If she was not going to sink we might return, so we need not get too far away. A faint light on the eastern horizon gave a hint of the dawn to come when, all at once from deep inside the ship, there was a rumbling crash. The poop slipped slowly under the water as the bow rose clear. Within seconds the curved forefoot was in sight while the afterdeck, as far forward as the mainmast, had disappeared. As fittings and cargo broke loose there was a continuous, thunderous rumble punctuated once or twice by a louder explosion as a bulkhead ruptured. Slowly the bow pointed towards the sky. Scarlet-tinged smoke, flame and soot spewed from the funnel. As the ship reared beyond 45 degrees the funnel itself collapsed in a cascade of fiery red sparks and fell into the sea. There was a great tearing sound as more and more broke loose, the bow reared vertically, seemed to hesitate for a moment and then slowly, inexorably, and with great dignity, slid with gathering speed into the boiling cauldron and disappeared in a continuous submarine thunder of noise.

Stunned, none of us moved until Salomons yelled to start rowing. We had not pulled far away when the consequences of the sinking were upon us: pieces of wreckage, great and small, boiled to the surface pushed swiftly in all directions by the up-currents. Some 30 seconds after the ship disappeared, the wooden foretopmast shot into the air at an acute angle like a stick thrown obliquely into a stream recoiling out again. Slowly it turned end-over-end and splashed back into the sea 50 yards away. Salomons had been right. Gradually the rumbling noises became fainter. The wellings and upsurges subsided and we were left in the gathering dawn with nothing more than the wind, the splashing of waves, quieter now, and the grunt and grumble of oars in crutches. Watching the *Polydorus* sink had been the most dramatic if not the most profound experience of my life. It was the classic climacteric repeatedly portrayed in films of the period; but the intensity of our feeling, as we sat in the boats and saw, heard and smelt it happening to the ship which an hour before had been our home, hearth, warmth and comfort, defies description.

Faint calls could be heard some distance off, but it was not yet light enough to identify other boats half-a-mile or a mile distant. The occupants of number one boat had no idea how many others had managed to escape from the sinking ship, how many boats there were or the condition they might be in. Daybreak would expose the whole, grim story. Suddenly a larger, darker shape eased out through the darkness and headed towards us. The unfamiliar outline of a German U-boat, close-to, manifested itself. The slow throb of high-speed diesels, throttled down, came across the water. Slowly the submarine manouevered alongside our boat. An officer and half-a-dozen men stood on the forward casing with one or two aft. From the conning tower the U-boat's captain called out orders in clipped German which fell passing strange upon the ears when one had heard it only in films before. How odd it was, in the middle of the Atlantic with a tropical dawn about to break, to realise that these young men were the enemy. And not just the generalised enemy but the very ones we had been fighting the previous morning. To hear the German language, of which I knew no more than three words, was neither frightening nor infuriating, just infinitely strange. To confound matters further the Germans themselves looked like anyone else. Salomons, of course, spoke German as fluently as he spoke English and engaged in a lengthy exchange with the officer on the fore-deck. Later he translated the conversation for the benefit of those who did not understand the language. The Germans knew exactly what the *Polydorus* was and where she had been bound.

113

Although they had had to fight for their kill this officer, at least, was civilised. He checked the position and distance to land with Salomons who, having been on watch, was likely to be the best informed of the the ship's company. He asked if anyone had been wounded or if we were short of anything. He regretted that they could not supplement our fresh water supply as they themselves were short but offered cigarettes and magazines which Salomons refused. Throughout the interrogation, one German rating kept a cine-camera trained on our people in the boat. After 10 minutes dialogue the figure on the bridge grew agitated and called out some instruction to his own men. We were cast off summarily. The U-boat went astern to clear us then swung away, slowed as he passed another lifeboat, now visible half-a-mile away in the gathering light, and then accelerated to full speed. Within seconds he started to submerge and that was the last we saw of Kapitanleutnant Dierksen and U-176. Six months later, almost to the day, he and his crew perished when the boat was sunk in the Straits of Florida. But I only learned that 40 years later.

With full daylight contact was established with the three other boats which had managed to clear the ship. Rowing through the sad debris of the sinking we discovered that the two RAF launches, in some mysterious way, had torn clear of their lashings as the ship sank under them. Remembering how they had been secured, and the trouble to which the shore gang in Liverpool had been put in shipping them, it seemed miraculous that they had not gone to the bottom trapped under the rigging and manacled by their own lashings. One of course had been damaged by shell fire but the other, with a large cabin and three Rolls Royce engines, was in good shape apart from having no fuel. On this craft the four lifeboats homed and made fast. Captain Brouwer and the officers went on board to count heads and conduct a council of war. Miraculously, the one fireman killed while abandoning ship had been the only serious casualty. My three companions were all in good shape although John Leslie, the senior, displayed a spectacular amount of blood about his face and head and over his lifejacket which turned out to be the result of a superficial cut sustained when he banged his head on a loosely swinging davit block as he abandoned ship.

There were 81 of us and, after examination, three sound boats out of the four which had got clear of the ship. The *Polydorus* had gone down about 750 miles west of Freetown. Innumerable

'submarine sighting' calls had been transmitted but, at that distance, we must have been near the limit of any intervention or succour by Sunderland flying boat - and who knew what others might be in the same plight within the Freetown orbit? We midshipmen had nothing to do with the decision-making but, for the officers, there were three choices - stay where we were and hope to be picked up by someone responding to our calls, head for the African coast 750 miles away but against the Equatorial current, or turn west and steer down wind and current for South America 2000 miles away. They decided to aim for the African coast and, after re-distributing men, water and stores equitably among the three sound boats, we set sail in company. My chum, Peter Bracewell, the lugubriously-cheerful comedian from Formby, had now joined us in number one boat. Salomons set three watches and I was flattered to be put in charge of one with Owen Nulty, now fully recovered from his ordeal, and the dependable Chinese sailor to support me. It was a beautiful blue and gold Tropic of Cancer flying-fish day - tranquility after ordeal. But the salt spray kicked up by our two-and-a-half knot progress quickly dried and burned on the skin. From the first moment we were strictly rationed – a half beaker of water morning and evening and one biscuit with pemmican. Brouwer and the officers had estimated that we faced a 30-day sail which controlled the ration. The following morning there were some among our company of 27 in number one boat who seemed to have given up the idea of survival - a surprising number of the Chinese and one or two Europeans. It is a commentary on the human condition that those of us who were active in the boat – perhaps seven or eight – had calculated that the rations would last longer than planned because in a week's time there would be fewer left to share them. Personality and leadership were everything and Salomons lacked neither.

At night we kept station on the other two boats by requiring the helmsmen to display their battery-powered lifejacket lights. Each boat had almost 30 of those so the practice was long sustainable. Daytime was a trial of torturing sun because of the salt spray and lack of shade. Night-time was no more comfortable because of the cold and cramped conditions which did not allow all to stretch out and sleep at the same time. But it would have been infinitely worse had we been torpedoed in the North Atlantic. I had the watch until midnight of the second day, handed over to Salomons and tucked in alongside Bracewell to fall fast asleep within seconds. Suddenly, I was rudely awakened by Peter shaking me. 'Jock, Jock. Wake up. It's lights. Look - lights.' The others were stirring and noisy with excitement. And there, in the distance, was a concentration of small, bright lights - one ruby red and two white above - the steaming lights of a ship underway and bearing down upon us. The other two boats, at least half-a-mile ahead, had set off flares two of which were drifting down towards the sea surface as I awoke. Salomons fired one for us lighting up the boat and the eager faces in a bright red glow. But the boats had already been sighted and the steamer's navigation lights showed her altering course towards us. Half-an-hour later, grateful and elated, the crew of number one, the last of the three, scrambled up the pilot ladder swinging from our rescuer's foredeck rails. Acting as bowman I was the last to leave. Before reaching for the ladder, I looked around wondering what I might take as a souvenir and on impulse tore off the varnished board screwed to the gunwale bearing the ship's name. Then I spotted the compass by which we had been steering so I took that as well. Thus burdened, I struggled up the ladder on to the deck where a swarthy sailor with a thin black moustache thrust a glass of water into my hand. Bliss! I downed it in a gulp - but the water was some kind of coarse spirit and, unused to anything stronger than lager, I almost brought it back up again. Another cheerful sailor handed me a cigar. Each survivor seemed to have been given one too and glowing red ends were visible all around the deck. With great bravado I took a deep draw - and then quickly disappeared round the end of the house to drop it over the side before I shamed myself and everyone else.

We had been sighted and saved by a small Spanish cargo ship called the *Eolo* homeward bound to Spain with a cargo of Brazilian tobacco and, as a neutral, lit up like the Blackpool illuminations. The *Eolo* was a ship of about 2000 tons with 'death-trap' well decks fore and aft, so-called because they were so short that they filled quickly in a seaway and trapped anyone who happened to be caught in their vicinity, a woodbine funnel, a crew of 25 and all the fresh meat for the voyage alive and on the hoof or the wing in cages on the after deck. The Spaniards were as poor as church mice, simple, decent and warm-hearted. They had little enough for themselves, and had just picked up 81 assorted Dutch, British and Chinese for whom, in a ship like the *Eolo*, it would be difficult to find water far less food. Captain Urgelles, the tiny, elderly Spanish shipmaster, discussed the matter with Brouwer - having first picked up all three lifeboats with one of his cargo derricks – and decided to alter course towards Las Palmas in the Canary Islands. His men clothed us from their meagre possessions and fed us three times a day on some rich and inexhaustible supply of vegetable broth containing kilos of horse beans or Lima beans, depending upon the day, until, six days later, we made landfall at Las Palmas. We were hurried ashore by the authorities, a great deal less friendly than the simple souls on board the *Eolo*. She continued on her interrupted passage with the *Polydorus'* three lifeboats stowed carefully on her foredeck, a gift from Brouwer to Urgelles. At once we were taken under the wing of the British consulate, led to a local outfitters and given more appropriate clothing. Rumour succeeded rumour throughout the day, but the consul was anxious to get us off the islands as soon as possible and on to mainland Spain where our chances of repatriation were thought to be greater. Late that evening, barely 12 hours after our arrival, we were mustered and marched through brightly-lit streets to the dockside and on board a rather smart-looking passenger steamer, the *Ciudad d'Alicante*, which traded between mainland Spain and the islands. There were a number of Spanish army officers aboard but they, and every other Spaniard, ignored us during the three-day passage to Cadiz. On arrival there almost the first people on board were representatives from the German consulate sent to woo the Dutch officers back to the Netherlands with promises of immediate repatriation and reunion with their families. Not one was tempted. Their scorn was obvious – but it must have taken courage and character to turn down such a chance, for they had no more idea than anyone else how much longer the war would last or whether they would ever see their families again.

Our final destination was Seville further up the Guadalquivir River where we were accommodated in an hotel with guards on the corridors. One midshipman was heard to complain that he was not anxious to spend the best years of his life interned in Spain which caused great peals of laughter from the Dutch and the captain's smiling comment that it was ladies who spent, or mis-spent, the best years of their lives, and not midshipmen. In Seville we seemed likely to be detained indefinitely, a different rumour circulating every day: we would be handed over to the Germans in Vichy France, we would be kept in a prison camp in Spain, we would be sent to North Africa, we might be released next year, we might not be released next year. The British consul sent for the four midshipmen soon after our arrival.

'I just want to warn you,' he said, if you have any ideas of escaping and heading for Gibraltar – don't. You'll never make it, and you'll spoil your chances of being released until the war's over.'

We had been contemplating exactly that and, quite certainly, would have contemplated it again, despite his warning, had the most dire of forebodings seemed imminent. But time rolled on. The authorities marched us to a bull fight one day. On another we were taken to Seville Cathedral and the Alcazar Palace. I admired the view from the top of the Cathedral tower but it took a second visit more than 40 years on to appreciate what we were shown then. In the gardens of the Alcazar I stole six lemons from a tree thinking myself unwatched; but afterwards Captain Brouwer ad-monished me gently – and then suggested I might try to get them home if we ever got the chance. A day or two later, on December 22, there was a sudden upsurge of excitement when Captain Brouwer and Mr Beymerwerdt, the chief engineer, returned from their daily visit to the consulate.

'Pack tonight, boys,' Brouwer told us in the hotel foyer. 'We're going in the morning. Train – to Gibraltar.'

And so we did. At 0600 we were taken to the station and locked into the compartments of a segregated coach. Each had a card-board box of coarse sandwiches, fruit and a half bottle of wine, and we said goodbye to Seville. Later in the day, when we saw the country we would have had to traverse had we attempted escape, it became clear why the consul had warned us against it. About 2100 our coach was uncoupled and shunted into a siding in the little port of Algeciras opposite Gibraltar. We were hustled off the train and on board a Royal Navy dockyard tender lying alongside in total darkness. In less than an hour we were climbing up the gangway of a small troopship en route to England from West

Africa. She harboured the largest cockroaches I have ever seen and was in a poor state of repair. I was promptly mustered in a watch and shortly afterwards we put to sea and joined a home-ward-bound convoy on Christmas Eve, 1942. West of the Bay of Biscay a Focke Wolfe Condor sighted the convoy and attack seemed imminent but the winter weather closed in and our passage to Loch Ewe and thence through the Pentland Firth was unmolested. At Methil, on January 9, we disembarked. Within 24 hours I was back at Muirhead, my telephone call from the Callander's house on the way home from the station being the first my mother had heard since a message on November 30 telling her that the *Polydorus* had been sunk and nothing known of survivors.

A week later I received a telegram from Liverpool telling me to report, in uniform without fail, two days hence. If I had no new uniform the office would arrange it provided they knew in advance. But I had. My resourceful mother had decided we should visit Paisley's in Glasgow and I was already much better equipped than I had been before the sinking. This time a grateful government would be paying most of the bill so my mother need be unconcerned. Arriving in Liverpool as instructed - travelling pleasurably light for once - I was promptly instructed to report to Danny Peirce. He was solicitous about my health, the dreadful *Asphalion* essay was lost in the mists of the past and my credit appeared good.

'King,' said Peirce, 'Captain Brouwer is going to see Sir Max Horton tomorrow. He wants to take you with him.'

Sir Max Horton might have been the Lord High Executioner for all I knew, but it sounded impressive and, despite my ignorance, it did not take long to establish that he was the admiral in command of the Western Approaches and that he functioned from a palatial bunker under Derby House. I was flattered and excited and, although I didn't know why Captain Brouwer required my presence, the opportunity delighted me.

Next day I reported to the office as instructed and met a jovial Captain Brouwer again. Following him into the car put at his disposal we were driven to an insignicant-looking entrance to a building near the Pierhead. A Wren officer took charge of us through interminable cream-painted corridors, lit coldly from above, to a small ante-room. My homework overnight had established that Sir Max Horton had been a famous submariner at the end of the First World War, a bachelor, keen golfer and the emergent successful commander of our forces in the Battle of the Atlantic. Had I been a junior officer in a corvette I should not have had to discover all this - it would have been as Holy Writ. We were quickly ushered into his large office, one wall of which was glazed and looked down, as if from a mezzanine floor, into an enormous plotting room, the far wall of which was a black-coloured chart of the entire North Atlantic with symbols which spoke for themselves – convoys with their identification numbers, independent warships and merchant ships, groups of submarine hunters and the U-boats themselves. Wrens picked up messages from the control desks, climbed library steps and made adjustments to the chart symbols. So fascinated was I by this that I had to pull myself away forcibly and listen to what the admiral and Captain Brouwer were discussing. Sir Max, who had asked to see Brouwer following the report of the *Polydorus* action, wanted the unvarnished story and he got it, succinctly and accurately in flawless idiomatic English with a faint mellifluous flavour of the Netherlands. Thus told it sounded splendid and I was proud of this man I admired so much. The admiral asked one or two pertinent questions and, as a submariner, suggested what might have been the U-boat commander's intentions at different stages of the action. It was all very professional and I had the wit to realise that I was privileged to be listening. After 20 minutes or so Sir Max turned to me and said,

'Well, young man – interesting experience. Were you frightened?' I had no time to dodge the straight question; besides I didn't think dodging admirals was a good idea.

'Yessir.' By this stage I was becoming excellent at 'Yessir'. Getting beyond that response required a little time, but in this case it didn't matter. If I'd said anything else he would not have believed me.

'Good man. You should never be afraid to realise you're frightened. I used to be, every time I went into action. The thing is to keep it to yourself.'

With a few more polite words and a brief guided tour of the Atlantic plot we were shown out. It was the end of the *Polydorus* saga, the apogee of my war. I still do not know why Brouwer chose to take me with him; but I have been forever grateful that he did.

Chapter 5

HARDLY HOME FROM OUR AUDIENCE with Sir Max Horton – for me a bit like having been marched into Field Marshal Montgomery's campaign caravan to say 'Good morning' – I was instructed to report forthwith to the Outward Bound School at Aberdovey, Merioneth for a four-week course. This struck me as being something of an imposition.   I was supposed to be a survivor – a protected species – recuperating from the rigours of war looked after by adoring women.   Alas there had been little enough of the latter and the reputedly uncompromising nature of the Outward Bound course seemed a poor alternative.   Aberdovey, then in its infancy had already earned a reputation for rigour. Kurt Hahn, headmaster of Gordonstoun, and Lawrence Holt, Blue Funnel's chairman were friends with similar views on education and training.   Gordonstoun School had been evacuated from Elgin when the Moray Firth became a restricted military zone. Now located in North Wales its regime was no less spartan despite its move south.   The muster on early Outward Bound courses consisted of Gordonstoun boys, *Conway* cadets – Lawrence Holt supported that establishment too – a mixed bag of young men from factories and offices throughout the British Isles sent by their employers and half-a-dozen or so Blue Funnel midshipmen whose chairman was probably funding most of the start-up costs as a pledge to his own ideological and altruistic convictions.   We six Blue Funnel middies were all survivors on leave, a year or two older than the others and with a great deal more worldly experience.   Part of the Aberdovey Code of Honour was to pledge that we would not smoke.   All of us signed – and smoked on as discreetly as we could.   We were also not to be afraid of reporting back-sliders, loyalty to the code being thought nobler than misplaced loyalty to our fellow criminals.   Unfairly perhaps, we considered that the Gordonstoun boys, probably through long practice, were good at this part of the code, and treated them accordingly.   The warden, Hogan, was a wavy-haired, be-spectacled, Harris-tweed jacketed social worker from the Midlands and our relationship with him was cool.   The academic staff were standard-type schoolteachers with a bent for the outdoors.   The nautical staff, who supervised the boat work and cruises in the schooner *Prince Louis* and the ketch *Garibaldi*, were Blue Funnel officers on secondment. They included Captain Beer, sick, heavily jaundiced and a shadow of the man I had last seen on board the *Asphalion* barely a year previously. Another officer called Fuller joined the staff about this time. He had an awesome reputation because he had recently survived 36 days in an open boat following the sinking of the *Medon* west of where the *Polydorus* had gone down. Eventually he became the director of the Aberdovey Outward Bound School where he had a distinguished record.

Despite a guerilla war with the staff, because we resented being there in the first place, we had to admit that we were beginning to enjoy it after a week. Expeditions over the Cader Idris range, pacing ourselves with litte success against Marine Commandos under training who were stationed near Barmouth, athletics every day, sailing and pulling heavy naval cutters in the Dovey estuary, orienteering, even compulsory cold showers each morning at Brach y Celyn, the dormitory house, and a mile run in the rain, failed to daunt our spirits. Sadly but inevitably, some of us were caught smoking, not once but several times. In addition, the Blue Funnel group were thought responsible for the potato stuffed into the exhaust of Hogan's car causing him acute distress. One youth created a major diversion when, after filling a cigarette lighter with fuel, he inadvertently dropped the empty bottle into the fireplace where it exploded – fortunately quite a small explosion since it was quite a small bottle. It blew the cast-iron grate into the middle of the room where it smouldered on the floor boards while a group stood round extinguishing it with tumblers of water. There were no casualties; but after a stewards' inquiry the delinquents' list lengthened. Nemesis struck, however, and hubris received its just desserts when a small group, of which I was a member, were sent to Pwllheli to join the *Prince Louis* in February weather conditions too severe for the schooner to cross the bar inwards to Aberdovey to effect a crew change. At Pwllheli it was obvious that boarding in the bay would be just as hazardous. The ship had sighted the party on the beach and signalled by lamp that they would send in a boat with the crew who were leaving and embark us when the weather had eased. Someone in our group decided that this was unsporting. A rubber dinghy belonging to the Marines lay near one of their outposts and I was nominated to engage the guard in conversation while the others stole the dinghy and dragged it down to the beach. The intention was to use it to ferry us to the ship but, as a paid-up natural coward, I was having none of it. The others put out and within 100 yards bitterly rued their decision. After a struggle which lasted about half-an-hour they arrived on board where there was a most unholy row. The captain ordered his cutter launched and the culprits were rowed ashore with instructions to return the dinghy with apologies and take the next train back to Aberdovey. Reduced thus to size that is what we had to do. I was as implicated as the others despite having been restrained, by cowardice or caution, from undertaking the trip out to the schooner. The following morning at 0830 the three Blue Funnel midshipmen who had been involved were on the train for Liverpool. Two *Conway* cadets had also been sent back to their training ship at Bangor, and the Gordonstoun boys had a field day thinking the retribution visited upon us richly deserved. As, indeed, it was.

The *Conways*, who were junior cadet captains, were said to have received 12 of the best over the backside and were demoted. We three – 'Tiny' Paine, Arthur Borthwick and I – were put through the hoop in Liverpool, first by Danny Peirce and subsequently by a lengthening list of executives culminating in Brian Heathcote whose voice developed an even darker shade of brown. Cancellation of indentures was hinted at. We had committed what seemed almost a capital offence, and I was decidedly worried. 'Young King up by Mairheed – comin' oot fur a captain,' – and busted for insolence and riotous assembly! The thought was unbearable. That afternoon Heathcote told us, very severely, that Mr Holt was deeply distressed and required us to report to his house at 2000 that evening. In great trepidation we were ushered into his impressive Victorian mansion by an elderly retainer in a stand-up collar escorted by a rather fierce-looking dog. He showed us into a small room lit in a sea-green, ancient kind of light and lined with darkly-bound books which did not seem to have been disturbed for a long time. Ten minutes or so later a door opened and Lawrence Holt appeared, a stooped, grey man with a nonconformist chin and an intense, penetrating gaze.

'Well, young men,' he said, 'Come into my room.'

He motioned us through to a sitting room.

'Have you had something to eat?' he enquired. We had eaten heartily of over-cooked fish and lukewarm chips in the Ocean

Club but, even if this had not been the case, it was unlikely that we should have confessed. Lawrence Holt then treated us to the most stimulating monologue on the formation, development, ethos and style of Alfred Holt & Company that we were ever likely to hear. He claimed that he knew, personally, every one of the company's shipmasters and chief engineers – as he probably did. He was an old-fashioned shipowner, and he knew about ships. After an hour the dissertation drew to an end and his expression darkened. 'You fellows have been misbehaving yourselves,' he said.

We flushed. I was already thinking of the excuses I would offer my mother when my indentures were cancelled.

'What have you been up to?' he asked, 'It sounds disgraceful.'

We had no defence and mumbled only apologetic words.

'I know perfectly well what you have been up to – and, if you can't do it properly the first time you will have to go back and do it properly the second time, won't you.'

Oh, joy – indentures not cancelled! Oh, hell – back to Hogan. It was crystal clear that there was no alternative. Back to Aberdovey and make amends, or else . . .

'Do you want to say anything?' he asked.

There was a long silence.

'Sir,' I eventually piped up, embarassed by our gauche silence, 'could we go home first and have our laundry done?'

It was spur-of-the-moment stuff. I was not noted for being particularly concerned about laundry, but I hated an empty silence and thought the chairman deserved a response.

'All right,' he said, surprising us, 'go home for two days and be back in Aberdovey by Friday.'

In retrospect, of course, he was absolutely right. We were repentant sinners and not entirely incorrigible but needed to be brought to our senses. There was no more suitable sentence than to send us straight back, tails between legs, to start again. Thus it transpired, at least in Borthwick's case and mine. Tiny Paine took ill at home and escaped to hospital.

Our second course was different. We signed the pledge and stuck to it. We met all the County Badge athletics standards and Borthwick, a natural athlete, achieved all with the best figures. I did them in barely adequate figures, but did them. We had to run two miles in something like 13 minutes and 30 seconds, at one stage. I was no great runner but I knew that if I kept the acknowledged runner in our group within my sights I could not go far wrong. With some difficulty I contrived to do that when, 600 yards or so from the finish, plodding wearily a long way behind, I became aware of a steady pad-pad-pad of overtaking plimsolls behind my shoulder. I glanced round and was chagrined to catch sight of the seven stone weakling from a Northampton boot factory who spoke through his adenoids and had, until that moment, been beneath the notice of the bloods. He padded alongside looking like death and then padded ahead. And then further ahead. I was in the process of learning another lesson, that the external appearance sometimes belies the quality underneath. I must have known the boy's name at the time but haven't remembered it for decades. He had the heart of a lion and he taught me a lesson I never forgot. Even Aberdovey seemed pleasanter when we were trying and not bucking the system. I had a wonderful three days acting as bo'sun of the ketch *Garibaldi*. Conned by her master I steered the ship under sail over the Aberdovey bar and back to haven at the end of one cruise and my heart swelled with insufferable pride and joy at having a ship under sail in my own two hands.

By the end of the course Borthwick had achieved a Gold Standard County Badge and I had managed a silver. We were required to complete some other task after the end of the course before we could have the certificates and for some reason I never did it. Now it seems a pity for we had re-established ourselves by effort spurred by fear. Within a week we were appointed, with two others, to the same ship, an ancient and not particularly honourable Blue Funnel ship called the *Rhesus*, an extension of our punishment we feared but we bore it with fortitude. I recall little about that particular ship. Her master's name was Simpson, a pale-faced man with mandarin eyes who lived in the select end of Gourock, than which there is nothing more select at the Tail o' the Bank unless it be at Rhu or Shandon on the northern shore. The *Rhesus* acted as commodore ship from Liverpool to Freetown. Twenty days out, as we were manouevering into two columns in line ahead approaching Freetown, Captain Simpson turned to Commodore Manners, a true-blue product of Britannia Naval College.

'Do you know, Commodore,' he said, 'This ship is 32 years old.'
There was silence for a moment or two.
'And she looks every minute of it, sir,' said Commodore Manners without turning round.

A week or two later the *Rhesus* lay at anchor off Takoradi shipping some baggage into an open surf boat which was scending up and down mightily in the heavy Gulf of Guinea swell. The luggage, belonging to some English government people, included their small Highland terrier which was tied in a canvas bag, its head poking out. Because it was a delicate operation and I was supposed to be in charge I climbed outside the guard-rail to tend the heaving line and make sure the little dog did not get bumped. Half-way down, the knot tied by one of the Chinese sailors, slipped. Bag and dog fell into the sea astern of the surf boat. Without thinking I dived after it and for the longest few seconds of my life on the way down I realised that the stern of the boat, lifting in the swell, was coming up to meet me and swinging out at the same time. A picture of the limp body of the Chinese fireman killed when he jumped from the *Polydorus'* boat deck flashed before my eyes but luck was with me. I cleared the gunwale by no more than an inch, grasped the terror-stricken dog and held it up for the two natives to take into the boat. They would have none of it. Their eyes were round with fear and in the end the line had to be made fast again and the dog hauled back to the loving arms of its owner. My stock, quite low at this time, went up remarkably, at least for a short while.

Of the details of that voyage I remember little. I heartily disliked the West African coast and was glad to be steaming out of Freetown harbour, homeward bound. And, as it happened, I was never to see that part of the world again for my path followed quite other directions.

Ten or 11 days later, north-west of Cape Finisterre, the convoy was sighted by a Focke Wolfe Condor operating out of Brittany. As it circled, keeping out of range of our frigates' guns, another aircraft appeared from the north. The new arrival turned out to be a Coastal Command Liberator which must have been patrolling in the vicinity and had been directed towards us. At once the German turned towards the east diving to sea level pursued by the Liberator. There was a sound of distant machine gun bursts and then the Condor's wing appeared to strike the water. It cartwheeled upwards and exploded, a column of black smoke burgeoning into the evening sky. With one propeller feathered the Liberator turned across the convoy and headed for home, obviously damaged. It was rumoured, later, to have crashed into the sea a few miles short of the Cornish coast, its crew recovered by the air-sea rescue service. We had been spectators at a rather bizarre display of aerial combat between two four-engined aeroplanes but, as we stood down in the twilight, we feared that the Condor's sighting signal would attract more attention to us, probably in the form of U-boats. During the night two cruisers, the *Sheffield* and *Scylla*, joined the convoy and took up station in the centre where they would be less obvious to an observer. About nine the following morning the senior officer of the escort warned of the approach of enemy aircraft - 'bandits'. Five or six black shapes broke cloud cover and started a bombing run from astern.   At once the cruisers detached themselves from the merchant ships.   *HMS Edinburgh* steamed out ahead;   *Scylla* stationed herself at the rear.   As the Focke Wolfe bombers approached, both ships opened fire with heavy anti-aircraft guns the rapid cracks of the shellfire sounding aggressive and exhilarating in the morning air. The Germans must have been taken by surprise at the ferocity of such a box-barrage defence and at the presence of two powerful warships whose overnight arrival on the scene they could not have anticipated. They wheeled away climbing high to make another run only to be met by a similar furious pattern of black smoke puffs all about them. Determined, they pressed home the attack as long as they had bombs to drop although, from their height, it was random and inaccurate. No ships were hit, the closest bomb exploding between the *Rhesus* and the CAM-ship leading the next column. At the time I was strapped into the Oerlikon in the port wing of the bridge, my action station. The attacking aircaft were far outside the range of a 20-millimetre cannon but suddenly the captain shouted excitedly, 'Open fire! Open fire!' His head was tipped back, binoculars glued to his eyes and his tin hat pushed over his forehead to keep it on. I was about to say, 'But, sir...' and then thought better of it. What the hell, why not? I looked up the sight at a distant dot in the sky, pressed the trigger and had the greatest satisfaction of shooting, personally, in the general direction of the Luftwaffe. The line of tracer hosed into the sky and dropped in an arc far short of any aircraft. I fired again out of sheer excitement but Captain Simpson must have recognized its futility and shouted to cease fire.   As I looked around the CAM-ship – so-called because it carried a Hurricane aircraft on a trackway extending from the foremast over the bow along which it could be catapulted into the air – prepared to fly off its fighter. The engine of the old Hurricane revved up to full pitch, there was a loud explosion and a flash of flame along the ship's foredeck and it hurtled off its trackway, dipped perilously close to the sea and climbed away in pursuit of the 'bandits'. By this time the Germans were turning for home and the Hurricane followed, sadly losing them in cloud before causing any damage. Forty minutes after take-off the pilot returned, flew slowly up the column at about 1500 feet and then ejected through the open canopy by diving the aeroplane into the sea. His parachute opened at once and he drifted down into the water a few hundred yards from his mother ship which launched a boat and picked him up safely. The CAM-ship-launched Hurricane was a one-shot weapon of air defence since there was nowhere for the aeroplane to land once he was air-borne. Our admiration for the courage of the pilot knew no bounds and we hoped he was paid extra for his trouble. The Germans had disengaged but another attack of some kind, probably by U-boat, seemed inevitable now that the presence of a strongly escorted convoy had been so well publicised. Inexplicably, it never transpired. The two warships disappeared in the night as silently as they had come and went back to whatever station they were patrolling to await the next opportunity.

The convoy plodded on, west of Ireland and north towards the Hebrides, coming to anchor in Loch Ewe on a beautiful highland summer evening. The orders for the *Rhesus* meant joining a coastal convoy bound through the Pentland Firth and down the east coast to London. The mail told me that my mother would be in Portsmouth visiting her widowed and recently remarried father by the time the ship reached the Thames. Thus, it was the Portsmouth train out of Waterloo that I caught when released from the ship and not the Glasgow train from Euston. It was strange to be in a seaport so different from Liverpool. Portsmouth has its own atmosphere, the essence of the Royal Navy. Liverpool spelled commerce, trade, merchant shipping. The contrast was enormous, the binding common factor our seafaring heritage. My grandfather, Percy Bartholomew, still impressed me but I was enchanted to find that we could converse over a shared experience, as I suspect was he. He knew all about the life I now lived and the things I could talk about, and I knew that he understood. This rapport however did not extend to his second wife, Winifred, who was a pleasant enough woman not much older than my mother but did not fit into the family pattern as I carried it in my

128

mind. When my grandfather died towards the end of the war Winifred disappeared into the bosom of her own family and was never heard of again, taking with her the gold half-hunter I was sure was my inheritance. Ah well, I never cared much for pocket watches anyway.

At the end of my leave I was sent to join another ancient ship, the *Gleniffer*. I was by now senior midshipman in a half-deck of four. My companions were a solid young man from Newcastle called Scott, Tom Ireland a first tripper from Markinch in Fife and another first tripper whose name and identity are lost forever as are most of the ship's company, with the exception of the master. Captain Evan Williams was a tough old rooster from North Wales with a square-rigged master's certificate, much experience of Cape Horn and hands like burst packets of sausages. He lurched along, knuckles towards the ground like a prize fighter, had a fierce and bloodshot eye, a marked Welsh accent, no sense of humour and a habit of chewing one side of his lower lip ferociously. He did not like midshipmen and they were wary of him. He did not much like anyone who had not been to sea in sail, a point of view not uncommom among his generation. The *Gleniffer* was an old Glen Line ship built long before that company had been absorbed by Alfred Holts and very different in shape and layout from the Blue Funnel ships with which I was familiar. She had seven enormous hatches, five coal-fired Scotch boilers and about 40 of the roughest, toughest Liverpool firemen one could meet. The big, clear hatches were ideal for handling army transport including tanks, so the ship was despatched to the Mediterranean where, in the summer of 1943, the Sicily campaign was at its height. By the time we reached Malta the Italians had surrendered, Italy had been invaded and the landings at Salerno were in full swing. For the next three months or so we trekked backwards and forwards between Bizerta and Bougie on the North African coast and Malta, Augusta, Taranto and Brindisi, always in heavily escorted convoys, occasionally under air attack but never seriously, and just a little behind the main part of the land battle. Sometimes there were flashes of beauty in a dreary autumn – one particularly splendid sunset as the *Gleniffer* lay in Bizerta lake waiting to go alongside, a walk in the hills behind Bougie which reminded me of Wales, the pale dawn as we approached Catania where, only a week or two before, Tiger tanks had been firing over open sights at everything to seaward. We had our moments of drama and excitement too.   The ship's small barrage balloon, tethered close to the mainmast, was struck by lightning one night in the middle of a spectacular electrical storm in the Gulf of Taranto. As shattered nerves were recovering the Dutch ship in the next column to the *Gleniffer* struck a mine and was left behind badly damaged and sinking. One part of that convoy, led by the *Gleniffer*, was routed to Taranto; the remainder broke away and continued to Bari on the Adriatic coast. Those 18 ships, secured stern-to along the mole at Bari a night or two later became the victims of a 'domino' explosion during a German air raid.   One bomb struck an ammunition ship which exploded igniting several others until, ultimately, most of the ships in that part of the harbour were damaged. We had visited one of the ships in Bougie only the week before. An apprentice on board, who appeared to us to be fairly demented, explained that his post-war ambition was to be a trader – pirate? – in the South Pacific for which he had equipped himself with an Italian sub-machine gun which he showed us in great secrecy. Fortunately for him he had no ammunition. His ship was one of the Bari casualties and we never heard of him again.

There were also lighter moments. Entering Augusta harbour on one occasion the *Gleniffer* was leading ship with the King's Harbour Master, taking passage with us from North Africa, acting as pilot. I had been ordered into the chains to take soundings with the hand lead, standard Blue Funnel practice which would have been recognized by Nelson. As the ship was approaching the harbour entrance at five or six knots it was impossible to get the lead onto the bottom immediately under the bridge before it was swept aft in the wake. Not to be outdone I sent one of the junior midshipmen forward onto the foc'sl'head with the lead. 'When I call, "Let it go", you drop it and that should give it time to get to the bottom before it comes aft to me,' I explained in a confident and seamanlike manner.   We were approaching the gap in the boom defence, moving more slowly now. The chief officer and the carpenter were on the foc'sl'head with the anchor lowered out of the hawse and the cable held only on the windlass brake. I roared, 'Let it go!', and Tom Ireland dropped the lead from a hundred feet forward of where I was waiting, giving me the opportunity to obtain a very satisfactory sounding. 'By the mark, 10,' I sang out, like Mark Twain's leadsman.   But my triumph lasted hardly a second and was subsumed in the crash and roar of the anchor cable running out as the chief officer ordered the carpenter to 'Let go!' From three or four knots we pulled up all standing with virtually the whole of the starboard cable in the water leading tightly aft and taking a vast strain. The rest of the convoy had to veer sharply away and it took 30 minutes of frenzied manoeuvering to heave up, get clear and enter harbour more sedately. The good Captain Williams was beside himself with rage, first at me which was natural, and then at the chief officer who was quite emphatic that he had heard the order to let go called from the bridge and had seen someone make the appropriate signal with his hands.

'Keep your pluddy po'sun's voice to yourself, poy - and stay away from the pridge until I send for you.' was all I got; but the chief officer must have had a worse time. The King's Harbour Master took it all in better part and made a joke of it. The following evening he brought a party on board to dinner and, as they entered the saloon, he espied me cowering at our small table in a distant alcove. He burst out laughing and turned to his companions. 'There he is,' he said, 'the snotty who dropped the anchor.'

Evan Williams was difficult to please. On another occasion the fourth officer took ill and was clearly going to be out of commission for a while. The captain promoted me, as senior midshipman, to be acting fourth officer until further notice. About six o'clock the following morning, some 12 hours into my new-found glory, I was on the starboard wing of the bridge hauling up a flag hoist in a great hurry in response to the commodore's first 'wakey-wakey' signal of the day. The midshipman and I gave a final heave on the halyard and there was a sudden crack above our heads. Another halyard further along the triatic stay had parted and the string of heavy bronze signal lights it had been carrying crashed onto the bridge a foot or so from where the captain was standing. Once again he flew into a towering rage and, as the nearest to him, I got the full benefit. He shouted at me that signalling equipment was the fourth mate's responsibility and if I couldn't look after my gear better than that he would find someone who could.

'Send Scott up here to me,' he roared. I wakened Scott and sent him up to the bridge. He was back in five minutes, sadly subdued. 'What happened?' I asked.

'He made me fourth mate,' he said. 'I said I didn't think I could do it – so he fired me. He wants you back up there at once.'

I was reinstated, at least until the end of the morning watch by which time the captain had had his breakfast, was in a better frame of mind and had decided to forget all about it. But I was glad when the fourth officer recovered and I could sink back into a position of near-irresponsibility. Hard and unpredictable was my impression of Cape Horners from North Wales but Evan Williams, without doubt, must have been a marvellous hand on deck as a young fellow when it was blowing force 10 south of Tierra del Fuego and the ship was lying on her beam ends.

The *Gleniffer* consumed vast quantities of steam coal for her modest performance so her Mediterranean career lasted but a few months. On Christmas Eve she was lying at anchor off the port of Taranto, the ship's company embarking upon a modest Christmas party, when our new orders were announced - to Gibraltar and thence to New York first for dry-docking and then to load for an unspecified destination which was instantly assumed to be the United Kingdom. A trip to New York was a sufficient justification for raising the temperature of the party by several degrees. Far to the north the armies floundered in a sea of mud and the Anzio landings were only days away. Mr Churchill was in Tunis recovering from pneumonia after the Teheran conference, but the *Gleniffer* was celebrating Christmas. During the evening Tom Ireland was missed and a frenzied search of the ship initiated in case he had gone over the side. Found at last in a bathroom somewhat the worse of drink – for this was his first experience of alcohol – little sense could be got from him except for a repeated whimper.

'Oh, what would my mother say – and me a Rechabite.'

The west-bound passage of the convoy was without incident and all at once, on a January afternoon, the *Gleniffer* was steaming up the Ambrose Channel in another long line of ships. My first view of fabled New York, seen a hundred times on cinema screens, was disappointing. The Statue of Liberty came wholly up to expectations – we anchored half-a-mile from Bedloe's Island and the scale of the great copper-green figure was self-evident. But the skyline itself, familiar as were the buildings, did not extend the entire length of Manhattan Island as I expected. There was a cluster of skyscrapers around Battery Point then a much less impressive section until the eye reached the Empire State Building some distance uptown. At least that was recognizable and significant, for had not King Kong balanced himself on top of it only half-a-dozen years before and swiped attacking biplanes from the sky before plunging to his death a hundred floors below? My disappointment was never subsequently repeated. On my next visit, a few months later, the skyline seemed magical because I knew what to expect and for almost 50 years it has continued to be special whether seen from 35000 feet on a crisp, clear January day en route from London to Washington, or crossing the Queenborough Bridge inward bound on an early autumn evening just as the lights are beginning to make their own jewelled magic of the city's awe-inspiring buildings. Rough, tough – but so attractive: rude, crude – but the most exciting city in the world.

The Brooklyn Navy Yard was a reasonable base from which to enjoy a first taste of New York. Our duties were normally ended by about five o'clock in the afternoon. By six we were on our way uptown. By seven we had picked up whatever theatre tickets or other hand-outs we might obtain from the USO. New York's wartime generosity was overwhelming and applied equally to American and allied servicemen and to merchant seamen. We were treated as Uncle Sam's children and the city made sure we would remember our brief respite from the war. I did not then appreciate that I was witnessing a legend at Radio City Music Hall when Scott and I were given tickets for a Glenn Miller concert with the 8th US Air Force Band - even if we did have to applaud on cue. Since then I have never been able to take any studio audience seriously. A night or two later we saw *Brigadoon*, but my fondest memory was of *Porgy and Bess* which could only have just opened. I cannot hear *Summertime* without being transported ineluctably to wartime New York when the ultimate outcome of the war was no longer in doubt but so much of the battle had still to be fought. In Sydney, two years before, I had gone to see the film of Margaret Mitchell's *Gone with the Wind*. Since then I had read more American history than I had studied navigation and was almost overwhelmed now by the realisation that I had reached the promised land at last. A year or two elapsed before the glamour was tempered by a more realistic view; but I have never lost my admiration and affection for America despite my awareness that it is not quite the earthly paradise it then seemed.

Out of the water, the *Gleniffer's* shape was by no means as elegant as the *Asphalion's* had appeared when high and dry in Cockatoo Island Dock in 1941. But she carried more and, following her short spell in the Navy Yard, she loaded a mixed cargo ranging from bulk and bagged grain to Martin Maryland bombers co-

cooned on deck and jeeps by the score. We delivered them safely to Liverpool and four happy midshipmen left the ship without a backward glance. By now my sea-time was adding up and one more short voyage would enable me to sit my first professional examination for a Second Mate's Cerificate. Wartime concessions permitted this at the age of 19 instead of the normal 20, with a corresponding reduction in the required sea-time. I would have to study for a month or two at the Royal Technical College in Glasgow, 'The Tech' to generations of engineers and mariners, now long-since absorbed into the University of Strathclyde. My mother, who had taken some thought about this, approached her friends the Irvines who lived in Hyndland, a western suburb of Glasgow. There we went one day early in my leave to establish whether I might find a haven for the duration of my study. I remembered the Irvines from Marchfield Road days in the 1930s. George Irvine was the head cashier of the Singer Manufacturing Company in Clydebank and had virtually been sanctified by my two aunts in Prestwick. His wife Kate, a native of Perth, had quite an air of highland aristocracy about her, a private but impressive person. They had a daughter, Cath, a year or two older than I and, at that time, a secretary in Singers. Into this household I might be welcomed later in the year, provided that I got back. The second front in Europe had been talked about for more than two years and now, in March 1944, invasion was a word on everyone's lips. I had no idea when I might return to 94 Queensborough Gardens but the prospect was pleasant however long deferred.

Soon afterwards I joined the Blue Funnel flagship, *Priam*, surely the handsomest and most prestigious vessel in the fleet, a piece of pure luck for me. She was modern, fast, heavily armed and had radar, a mysterious device capable of identifying the range and bearing of any other craft or solid target within 15 or 20 miles. Of merchant ships only large troopers and fast cargo liners like the *Priam* were fitted with this equipment and the ship's company derived a certain gratification from association, however tenuous, with such an up-to-date miracle. Operated by naval personnel the radar was under close armed guard all the time so that, for us, it was nothing more than an opaquely-glazed five-foot diameter cylinder, six or seven feet high, sitting on top of the bridge and a voice on the telephone saying, 'Echo - green, three eight, range six point four miles – closing.' Although the *Priam* was the flag ship the commodore master who normally commanded her was on leave for this one short transatlantic voyage. His relief, Captain Brown, was amiable and a welcome relief from the old shellback, Williams. In a small convoy of about 12 ships, with fast destroyer escort, we were in New York 10 or 11 days out from Liverpool. This time the skyline lived up to its reputation as did the USO and the British Apprentices' Club. But in little more than a fortnight we were steaming back down the Ambrose Channel at full speed towards the rendezvous point, overtaking the *Rangitiki* in the process which caused a frisson of pleasure that the *Priam* had the legs of some of the big names. Our sole disappointment was that the actress, Veronica Lake – or was it Lucille Ball? – rumoured to be joining us for the passage to England, had been allocated a seat in a Liberator bomber instead and we had to be content with a mixed bag of American and Russian army officers none of whom bore the faintest resemblance to either lady.

By the time we reached the Mersey I had served barely two months in the *Priam* but I have always remembered her with pride and affection for she seemed to be a promise of what ships would be like when the war was over. A twin-screw motor ship of 10,000 tons with passenger accommodation, her appearance, while still retaining Blue Funnel perpendicularity, was more modern than any ship in which I had served previously. She breathed efficiency. With hindsight I am less sure she was as wonderful as she seemed at the time, but I was impressed and the *Priam* confirmed for me that I was a Blue Funnel man through and through. Called to the office on arrival in Liverpool I had a rather sobering experience. Before being sent off to study and sit my examination I was first hauled in front of a tribunal investigating the cause of damage to part of the *Gleniffer's* grain cargo three months before. I knew little and was wary for fear of saying something which might implicate others. The case hinged upon the manoeuvres of a tug assisting the ship while we were swinging compasses in New York harbour and which was thought might have smashed a deadlight in number five 'tween deck thus allowing sea water to wash into the hold in small but damaging quantities. The penetrating interrogation made it clear that the office would turn out every cupboard to get to the bottom of the incident. The company's reputation as a safe and careful carrier depended upon such things not happening to a shipper's goods. Such were the standards we had been brought up to and would be expected to maintain if we became Blue Funnel officers.

A few days later I was installed in Queensborough Gardens, catching the number 24 tramcar from Hyndland to the city centre each morning. Quickly I became immersed in the life and work of what was, in effect, a crammer. The Blue Funnel voyage papers had done their work and I had little problem with the contents of Nicholls' *Concise Guide* but, like most apprentices from all companies, I lacked experience of navigational practice and procedures. I could take compass bearings and estimate the error of the magnetic compass but had held a sextant only once or twice in three years. I could work out dead reckoning problems in a notebook or on the small and flimsy practice diagrams which came with the book work, but I had seldom been allowed to lay off a bearing on a real chart. Like my contemporaries I had been turned into a passable sort of a seaman, was not afraid of going aloft and working 70 or 80 feet above the deck, could splice rope and wire, was a competent hand behind a mooring rope or a wire back-spring, could chip, scrape and paint as well as anyone, knew about lifeboats inside out, could sail a dinghy and handle a motor launch and could run, jump and fight with anyone else my own weight; but what I, and the others, had learned had been largely by osmosis. If we had picked up anything at all about how to be officers, how to accept responsibility, how to deal with men and with awkward human situations, how to keep a proper bridge watch and be responsible for a ship and 60 or 70 lives, we had learned it by precept and example and not through formal and direct instruction. For the most part the officers under whom I had served were superb professionals, but they were not instructors, and it would have been naive to have expected that of them. The colleges and crammers we attended put a gloss on the theoretical knowledge we had gleaned from long nights on board ship with the text books open. Additionally, they hammered into us the *Rules and Regulations for Preventing Collisions at Sea* – the 'articles', all 30 pages of which we learned by rote to the last dot and comma – and taught us how to manoeuvre ships within that set of fundamental rules; enough to persuade our examiners that we were fit to be let loose in subordinate roles without too much risk of endangering ourselves or anyone else. I cannot claim to have thought it through then but I have never really been convinced that apprenticeship is the only, or the best, way to train young sea-going officers.

Long before my professional inadequacies had been exposed to the examiners, however, and about a week after I had started at the Technical College, the long-awaited invasion of Europe exploded. D-day, June 6, 1944, to my generation of Europeans and Americans, is one of the most significant dates of the 20th century. When the *Priam* had paid off in Liverpool the previous month every man had been asked by the supervising shipping master, 'Volunteer for the invasion?' Before he had time to open his mouth each individual's Discharge Book had been stamped with a 'V'. 'Good lad!' exclaimed the shipping master, and the lad was committed. Quite right, too. If we'd been in the army or the navy we should have had no choice. We had no choice as it was, but it was made to sound so. Home less than a month when the great day dawned, I expected to be recalled after ships had been sunk by the score and men had to be replaced. But it was not like that and, for many of us seated comfortably at desks, there was a guilty feeling of being 'men abed in England . . .' coupled with the disreputable thought that it was, of course, easier to get killed in the vicinity of Normandy than in the Royal Technical College, George Square. For me the summer of 1944 passed in comparative tranquillity. During the summer I was called to London to attend a function as a guest of the Netherlands Government in exile. It was a joy to meet Captain Brouwer again accompanied by Beymerwerdt, Salomons and Widd the gunlayer. We were to be presented to Queen Wilhelmina and, just before she entered the room, Brouwer whispered, 'Now, King, you must note what the Queen is wearing - your mother will want to know.' I was proud to be presented to Her Majesty, but I forgot the captain's advice. The only disconcerting feature about my two-day adventure in London was the occasional distant explosion of a flying bomb homing in from the Pas de Calais. I was lucky, that summer, to have nothing more serious to worry about than an examination. By the middle of August it was all over, my stickiest patch being an inability to tell the examiner who was conducting my oral how to wind a chronometer. It seemed silly that I had never actually looked into which end of the instrument the key was inserted – indeed humiliating. The examiner sent me off to find out and, the following day, with half-a-dozen others, I was released upon an unsuspecting world with a brand new Second Mate's Certificate and a single band of gold lace on my sleeve - half a band to be exact for, in wartime, the lace was sewn only on the outside of the sleeve.

I had greatly enjoyed my stay with the Irvine's. Cath, devoted

- Catherine Justice Irvine in 1945

to a pleasant fellow from John Brown's drawing office, treated me
indulgently as a rather wayward younger brother, a role I was
happy to adopt.   It was also an opportunity to renew some
Dumfries friendships with several of my contemporaries now at
university. But the lotus-eating had to come to an end and soon
I received my first letter of appointment addressed to 'Mr' and not
'Midshipman'. It instructed me to report for what turned out to
be a dreary spell of relieving duty on board ships in the dock. By
that stage in the war Alfred Holt had lost half its fleet. There had
been some replacement by standard-built ships – Empires, Oceans,
Forts and Liberties – inferior to Blue Funnel ships. But the vastly
reduced fleet had resulted in a surplus of officers. Fourth mates
with new tickets added to the embarrassment. Throughout the
autumn a group of us relieved those who had just come in from
sea. We supervised the discharge of cargo, dry-docking and re-
loading so that permanent staff could take over again after leave.
Sensible though the system was it would obviously delay the
accumulation of watch-keeping seatime young men like me needed
before sitting the next examination. Besides, Liverpool in early

winter was particularly dreary if most of one's time had to be spent managing someone else's ship in the docks. By Christmas I had had enough and thought seriously of going off to the local Shipping Federation offices where the 'Pool' system would have ensured an early return to sea if only on board the rougher type of ship to which I did not wish to become accustomed. But in the end I did not have the courage to resign from the company and become a free-lance, euphemism for a casual. Salvation came from an unlikely quarter when a friend's father engineered an interview with the Henderson Line's chief marine superintendent, Captain Cattanach, irreverently known as 'Old Joe'. Cattanach was a gruff, tough, square little man but he appointed me third mate of the *Daldorch*, a 5000 ton cargo ship which Henderson's had acquired from another company together with her sister ship, the *Dalhanna*. I parted from Blue Funnel at the end of the year while the Battle of the Bulge was at its height in the Ardennes and joined the *Daldorch* in Glasgow in January which suited me splendidly. Third mate's watch-keeping time counted for more than fourth mate's and the *Daldorch* was a fine, solid if unpretentious little ship. When I joined her she was already loading for the Middle East and would bè sailing shortly. In the meantime my leisure hours were pleasantly filled for the John Brown's draughtsman was in eclipse and I began to spend a good deal of time with Cath Irvine. Eventually loading was completed – pipelines and machinery consigned to Abadan in the Persian Gulf, a place I knew only by its reputation for being in the centre of the burning, fiery furnace and stinking of oil. Little did I know what lay ahead of me. The *Daldorch* finally sailed at the beginning of March under the command of Captain Norman Waiter, a taciturn Englishman but recognizably of the same breed as the Blue Funnel masters under whom I had served as, indeed, were the other officers. The crew, signed on from the Glasgow 'pool', were a motley lot compared to the Blue Funnel men who had been virtually company employees signing on for voyage after voyage. This became clear as we dropped the pilot off Toward Point and steamed down the Firth to join the convoy now forming up ahead of us. It was my first bridge watch on my own. The captain was on the bridge, of course, but, as the steward rang the hand-bell for breakfast, he looked around at a fairly clear sea.

'All right, mister. Keep her going as she is. I'm going down to have some breakfast. If you get up near the other ships before I'm back look for Number 72.'

Our pennant numbers were seven three, bravely fluttering in the breeze. As he disappeared I was suddenly petrified. What should I do next? What would happen if we caught up with the other ships? Oh God, what am I doing here? And then I pulled myself together. The *Daldorch's* maximum speed was about 10 knots. The other ships were making at least eight knots and were four or five miles ahead of us, so it would be half-way to lunch time before we were anywhere near them by when Captain Waiter would surely be back. Instantly, I was more confident and with a pair of 7 x 50 binoculars slung round my neck, I felt like Lord Louis Mountbatten. All at once I was aware that the ships ahead were sliding swiftly to port and were now well out on the bow instead of being straight ahead. One swift glance at the wake provided the explanation. The helmsman was in difficulties. I ran into the wheelhouse and called to him to come back onto his course.

'Mister mate,' he called, 'Ah canny see the compass. Ah've left mah specs doon below.'

A blast on the whistle summoned the stand-by man but when he was told to relieve the wheel so that the specs could be found he looked chagrined.

'But mister, ah canny steer,' he spluttered. 'Ah wuz a galley boy last trip.'

Fortunately, the third man of the watch could steer and did not need glasses. With that, to my great relief, the captain returned and my bacon was saved.

The outward-bound convoy to Gibraltar was the last in which I was to be involved and, one night, west of the Bay of Biscay, we were witness to the most spectacular U-boat hunt I ever saw. A starboard wing escort picking up what he thought was a contact dropped a pattern of depth charges which sent us all to action stations. Star shell followed and some of the other escorts moved swiftly through the columns of merchant ships in support. The action went on for at least half-an-hour, gradually being left astern as the convoy advanced. Slowly it subsided and then the show was over, the contact lost. Six or seven weeks before the end of the European war I had heard my last shot fired in anger. A few days later, steaming through a placid Mediterranean, the forenoon watch lookout reported an object bobbing in the water fine on the port bow. I altered course slightly away and called the captain to the bridge. We decided, simultaneously, that this was a mine. I expressed a keen desire to open fire on it with the Oerlikon, showing tremendous courage when the target was not likely to fire back. Common sense prevailed and the captain exercised his veto, drily and tersely pointing out that the explosion would not only lift us out of the water and damage the machinery but would cause those on board other ships in the vicinity to have severe palpitations. The radio officer managed to clear a message to a small warship which was in sight and some time later there was a dull boom from far astern as he exploded it with small arms fire. In the Suez Canal there was a sense that the war had long since moved from that part of the world and that the piping times of peace were not far away. The bumboat men and the ghullie-ghullie men with their miserable chickens appearing from un-likely parts of their audience's anatomy were clearly practicing for the return of the big P & O passenger liners. But the old grey *Daldorch* still had a long way to go, down the Red Sea, through the Straits of Bab el Mandeb, into Aden for a short bunkering call and then along the coast of the Hadhrammut in the early part of the south-west monsoon - hot, sticky, uncomfortable with too much wind and sea and much reduced visibility. The Gulf of Oman and the Straits of Hormuz were strange waters to most of us on board. For me, at least, they were to become almost as familiar as the English Channel. At last, with our cargo of machinery, equipment and pipeline we anchored off the Shatt al Arab light vessel and awaited inward orders for Abadan. Eventually we steamed upstream to Basrah to discharge part cargo and then moved down to the refinery port with the bulk of it. Abadan was the main refinery of the Anglo-Iranian Oil Company, then the world's largest oil refinery with something like 26 berths along the two mile stretch of Bawarda Reach. Most were tanker jetties but there were three dry cargo berths at one of which the *Daldorch* finally discharged her cargo from Rothesay Dock. That activity was almost incidental, however, since the news on the radio was becoming more absorbing by the hour as the war in Europe moved into its closing stages.

Neither was attractive yet Abadan and the Shatt al Arab exer-cised an odd fascination for me. The mouth of the Shatt, the confluence of the Tigris and Euphrates, consists of featureless mud flats edging into low desert. Further up, towards Fao Reach in the river itself, date groves line the banks hiding the desert just

a few hundred yards beyond. The water is habitually a dirty cafe
au-lait colour from suspended silt and the first sighting of Abadan
steaming round a bend into Bawarda Reach, is of an incongruou
20th century intrusion upon a deserted wilderness. In 1945 th
world's largest oil refinery looked like a giant laboratory in th
sand surrounded by straggling townships of yellow brick bunga
lows. The towers, retorts, tanks and pipelines of the ubiquitou
refinery were silver-coloured or aluminium, the surroundings
the buildings, the desert, a dirty fawny yellow. And yet Abada
was pulsing with purpose and energy. Oil tankers, high out of th
water with a mimimum amount of ballast on board waited thei
turn to go alongside and load. With topsides painted in differen
shades of dark grey the lower part of each hull was a telltale of hov
long it had been since the ship was last dry-docked. Fresh, dark
red anti-fouling suggested a recent visit to the Mazagon Dock i
Bombay; off-white, streaked with rust and the dark tide-marks o
fuel oil indicated a great deal of sea time since the ship had last sa
upon the blocks. Each tanker, as it went alongside and pumpe
the last of its water ballast into the river, rose even higher in th
water its bow towering in the air exposing the curved forefoot
with the deck inclined at such an angle that it must have been
steady climb to move from aft forward. Once loading started i
seemed to take but a few hours to convert the balloon floating o
the water to a low sillhouette with most of the hull submerged an
the outline dominated by the bridge house amidships and th
funnel and superstructure aft. Seen across a convoy tankers ha
appeared strange and remote; seen close to they seemed mor
complicated and, in a way, more impersonal. Human figure
were usually conspicuous by their absence as one scanned th
deck of a ship loading at a near-by berth, imparting an air o
mystery. If merchant ships in general had suffered during th
war, the people who served in tankers had taken exceptional risk
and many had suffered dreadful deaths, blown up, burned
choked by their own cargo floating in the water in which thei
ships were sinking. Whether or not we had a lurking suspicio
that they were particularly courageous, the received wisdom i
ships like the *Daldorch* was that those who elected to go to sea i
oil tankers were an odd breed tending towards mental instabilit
and the demon drink. The ships themselves intrigued me for
after a few days in Abadan watching their comings and goings, i
appeared to me that everything on board an oil tanker happene

142

nore swiftly and silently than it did in a cargo ship.   Or so I
persuaded myself.

There was a general, hysterical and hedonistic loss of interest in
the pumping, refining and shipping of oil when, on May 8, VE-day
was announced.   A party was quickly organised in Abadan where
made my first acquaintance with the British who ran the Anglo-
ranian refinery and with the supposedly strange tribe who manned
ankers.   The first were embarrassingly hospitable; the second
urned out to be clones of ourselves, neither better nor worse.   My
inal memory of the VE-night party was of a vast gathering on a
awn near the bachelor quarters I was later to know as 'Slide
valve', singing all the British regional anthems and disposing of
vast quantities of liquor which mysteriously appeared.   Although
he outcome of the war had not been in doubt for a long time the
realisation that, at last, the fighting in Europe and the west had
come to an end reinforced our awareness of the Pacific war that
was by no means over.   For the ship's company of the *Daldorch* this
became a more immediate issue when she was ordered to Calcutta
o load, not a military cargo for the Arakan or the Far East as it
happened, but an UNRRA cargo of jute and other essentials for
southern Europe.   With the ending of the European war bigger,
faster ships were now available for seaborne military operations.
Lesser fry like the *Daldorch* could be returned to trade.

A few weeks later the ship was berthed in Salonika when the first
atom bomb was dropped on Hiroshima. The Nagasaki raid came
a day or two later, and the war in the east collapsed.   If the
celebrations in Salonika were more cosmopolitan than the Em-
pire-building British had managed in Abadan they were no less
boisterous and I cherish the memory of being taken back, with
three companions, to the jetty where the ship was lying, in an open
landau pulled by a very skinny horse urged on by a convivial
Greek with a splendid Viva Zappata moustache, who would take
no payment whatever.   Most unlike a Greek.

After a call at Safi on the Atlantic coast of Morocco where the
Daldorch loaded a cargo of phosphate as fast as any tanker had
loaded kerosine in Abadan, we headed north for Antwerp and
thence the Clyde.   And so, in September 1945, steaming back
through the English Channel with the navigation marks winking
brightly in the night, with the red, green and white of ships'
steaming lights all about her, past the dear, familiar names of
maritime England – the North Foreland, Dungeness, Beachy

Head, St Catherines Point, Portland Bill and Start Point, the Eddystone, the Lizard, Wolf Rock and Bishop Rock and through the St George's Channel to the coast of Wales, past St Davids Head, Bardsey Island and Holyhead, on to the Calf of Man and the North Channel, with the Mull of Galloway to starboard into Scottish waters, sighting Ailsa Craig and Pladda, the Cumbraes and Toward Point – the *Daldorch*, sturdy, unremarkable, weather-stained workhorse, returned from war.

Chapter 6

THE GREAT CRUSADE WAS OVER, the future secured. Yet for many it was a time of perplexity. Servicemen clamoured for demobilisation and a return to jobs, careers, education, family life. Merchant seamen were not servicemen but something called the Essential Works Order prevented many from seeking the equivalent of demobilisation had they wanted it. I was supposed to be well embarked upon my life's work which did not involve going home when the fighting was done. The *Daldorch* had revealed to me that not all ships were Blue Funnel ships and that my chosen profession might have to be pursued in humbler circumstances. Perhaps I had not impressed Captain Waiter much for my next appointment was to be as fourth officer in a Henderson passenger ship, a return to the situation I had avoided by resigning from Alfred Holt. Even less attractive was that the *Amarapoora* or the *Prome* were not in the same league as the *Priam*. Had I jumped from the frying pan into the fire? I started my leave in pensive mood.

Working life might be complicated, but not so private affairs. Some weeks after the *Daldorch's* return Cath and I became engaged to be married which concentrated my mind on improving my prospects while enjoying the raptures of young love. In the end I turned down the *Amarapoora* appointment to the justified annoyance of my sponsor, reported to the Shipping Federation and spent weeks standing by a variety of ships in a repetition of the previous winter's tedious Liverpool experience. But the evenings were free for Cath and me and the magic toils of courtship.

Early in the new year, I was interviewed for a berth in an American-owned, British-registered Socony-Vacuum oil tanker, the *Tamaha*, then lying at Greenock and bound for the West Indies. If the name was romantic not so the ship. Although applying for the third mate's berth I was instantly appointed second mate because the incumbent had fallen ill. Such accelerated promotion disposed me even more favourably towards the oil industry but my self-confidence was strained by the ship's apparent complexity. Tom Taylor the captain was a large, jolly, youngish man with a strong hearty face. Forty years on our paths still cross from time to time, to my great satisfaction. The chief officer, Curtis, came from London, had a large family and looked like my idea of a Balkan nobleman, even to the thin moustache. If Hopkins had been my mentor in early professional life, the infinitely patient Curtis introduced a tyro to the tanker trade in exemplary style.

The *Tamaha*'s hull was grey, her decks and superstructure dark red. The tall raked funnel, emblazoned with the Socony blue and white winged horse, was ungainly. Socony's American management processes were ponderous and demanding: everything which happened on board was detailed on forms calculated to leave no secret uncovered in a faraway office devoted to perpetual analysis. We seemed to spend as much time completing these forms as we did handling the ship; but the atmosphere was congenial, food excellent, Taylor a relaxed and well-disposed leader and the second stripe on my sleeve an undeserved encouragement to a young man approaching his 21st birthday. The *Tamaha* could be loaded in a day, discharged in two. The chief officer would calculate his cargo disposition in an afternoon and, having written it out on a blackboard, then ensured we followed his instructions precisely to make the ship do what he wanted. And she did, apparently by magic. Had she not been American-owned I would have been tempted to stay, but much as I loved the United States I thought my future lay in Britain and when we arrived home from Curacao in the spring I decided with some regret to pursue my new-found interest in the oil business with a British oil company, a more practical haven than an American corporation with one or two ships registered in the United Kingdom.

I knew three such companies: Cedric Hurt's Anglo-Sax, or 'Joe Shell' as he irreverently called it, Eagle Oil and the British Tanker Company which was associated with the Anglo-Iranian Oil Company and whose ubiquitous ships, with names prefixed *British*, had seemed present in every convoy and been the major maritime feature of Abadan. I wrote to all three companies on the same day. Almost by return I had letters from Anglo-Sax and Eagle Oil provisionally offering me appointments as third officer. Too late. The previous day I had received a telegram from the British Tanker Company whose need to recruit young officers must have been the most pressing. Before I knew where I was I had submitted a lengthy application, been vetted by a company doctor, pronounced fit and instructed to join the motor vessel *British Patience* at Thameshaven a day or two hence. From such simple beginnings can the blue-print of a lifetime emerge.

In the *Tamaha* I had become accustomed to the isolated dreariness of oil terminals, usually far from civilisation and often at the end of long, wind-swept jetties. Thameshaven, near Canvey Island in the outer reaches of the Thames estuary, was no less dismal and a grey late-April drizzle did nothing to enliven it. Before me lay what seemed an overlong oil tanker, her hull midgrey on top, bleached red beneath, her superstructure sparkling white in the rain and her black-topped funnel painted in the familiar pillar-box red surmounted by white and green bands. In April 1946 she was still fitted with three sets of massive booms I knew as Admiralty Net Device (AND) gear which enabled ships to stream heavy wire netting along each side as defence against torpedo attack. It looked complicated and the deck layout, too, was intimidating. I made my way to the bridge house to find someone to report to, hesitated at the lower bridge and looked aft. The main deck seemed to go on forever, even the funnel appeared to be several hundred yards away, and the tank tops were encrusted with a confusing pattern of vari-coloured valve wheels. At that moment, I would cheerfully have completed any number of Socony-Vacuum forms or languished for a month in the Gladstone Dock just to feel myself in familiar surroundings. However, it occurred to me then, as repeatedly since when over-awed by a novel situation, that some other mother's son had walked this way before and emerged unscathed. I was in with as good a chance as anyone else and so I entered the accommodation and reported to the mate.

A D R MacDonald was a suave, quietly-spoken Aberdonian, a senior chief officer, probably in his late 30s, laid back and delighted to have a third officer of any shape. One with a ticket was potentially even better, despite his limited tanker experience. It would not have mattered if the new arrival had been the man in the moon, the welcome would have been as genuine. He put me in the care of a gangly, smiling, ginger-haired second mate whose name, Stanley Eric Revelle Davison Smithson, intrigued me. A year or two older than I and about to be married Smithson years later became a Trinity House North Channel pilot. Between him and MacDonald I soon felt protected, the boy reasonably trustworthy and probably with a future provided he paid attention to what they told him. The captain, an Edward G Robinson type from Hull, dark of hair and visage was known universally, but never to his face, as 'Nigger' Kemp or the Black Abbot. Blunt, taciturn and not easy to impress he was a superb seaman and, despite his uncompromising Yorkshire manner, I liked him. I remember, too, with some affection George Bruce, a quiet self-contained man with horn-rimmed glasses and a neat moustache, more like a bank manager than a foreign-going chief engineer. The *British Patience* was well-found and well-run and I was sure that I had done the right thing in committing myself to this company – and would probably have felt exactly the same had Anglo-Saxon been quicker off the mark and I had become a Shell man. But the rub, the tiny maggot of doubt in my mind a year after the war had ended, was whether this was really the profession I wanted to pursue. On board ships in those days there was much dissatisfaction and disillusionment.   Perhaps there were better things to do in peacetime than accept an isolated, monkish existence divorced from the mainstream of ordinary life.   In wartime it had been different.   We had all been away from home; now it was only a minority who were wanderers, still at sea and likely to stay there. Much as I enjoyed ships, the closed introverted community of 50 men would always seem a group apart from the rest of humanity. And what kind of marriage would ours be separated for 11 months out of 12?   Although Cath had entered the compact with eyes open it would be no joke for her either. Should I not be trying to do something else?   Yet years before I had baulked at the patronising idea that being a milk roundsman's boy was a suitable alternative to being a Blue Funnel middie. Now the doubts were more complex.   I enjoyed what I was doing – when doing it.   I loved ships and the atmosphere of ships; but a lifetime at sea needed as much commitment as taking holy orders.   Torn between the realisation that my chosen profession demanded personal sacrifice, on my part and even more on Cath's, and the urge to get on in it, one thing was certain – unless I persevered we could not afford to marry, so I soldiered on.

And soldiering on had its compensations.   Outward bound from Thameshaven, through the Mediterranean, the Suez Canal, the Red Sea and along the southern coast of Arabia into the Gulf of Oman a route I came to know blindfold – I started to re-learn the tanker business in Anglo-Iranian terms.   The *British Patience* was a clean-oil ship, which is to say that her cargoes consisted of light refined fractions – gas oil, kerosine, aviation fuel and motor spirit in particular.   The time on passage through the English

148

Channel and across the Bay of Biscay was given over to cleaning tanks. Each cargo compartment was washed from top to bottom with a hand-held canvas fire hose through the wooden nozzle of which a sharply-focussed jet could be directed into any corner of the tank. Since petroleum gas was being displaced the seaman handling the hose had to be dressed in protective clothing and wear a helmet fed by an air pump operated by his two assistants. This, the accepted drill in 1946, was already archaic although I did not appreciate that for several years. Seawater in the tank bottom was sucked away by one of the cargo pumps and pumped overboard. The laws on oil pollution control then were simple and few realised there was even a problem, particularly for a clean-oil ship. Thirty miles offshore was deemed safe and every outward-bound tanker in ballast left a smoothed-out, iridescent wake from which the spirit quickly evaporated. When sufficient compartments had been washed, clean sea water ballast was pumped into them and the dirty ballast in the others, shipped at the discharge port before sailing, pumped out. The second group of tanks could then be cleaned. The routine was immutable – a certain stage in the exercise had to be reached before the Straits of Gibraltar, another before passing Cape Bon and the whole completed, with the ship gas-free and containing only clean water ballast, as Malta fell astern. In a clean oil ship this was easy; but in black oil ships – those carrying crude oil and heavy fuel – it was more difficult, as I was to discover. Whatever the previous cargo, the captain had to be able to declare a clean, gas-free ship on arrival at Port Said for the Suez Canal transit and no chief officer would risk humiliation by failing to report the ship in this condition several days prior to arrival.

The Canal was busier now that the old pre-war trade patterns were becoming re-established. The Red Ensign was ubiquitous, the funnels and houseflags of every eastern-trading British shipping company in marked evidence – P & O, Orient, the City Line, Clan, Blue Funnel, Glen, the Ben Line – and, of course, Anglo-Saxon and the British Tanker Company with their funnels aft and bridge houses isolated in the middle. One difference at Port Said, for me at any rate, was that the bumboat man preferred by BTC was a delightful, cross-eyed, honest rogue who called himself George Robey – or George Robbery to those who felt cheated. He, with a few helpers, brought a bumboat to the foot of the gangway where the crew could sign a chit for purchases. Near sailing time

George presented his customers' list which the chief steward paid in full, an appropriate deduction being made later from each man's account of wages. It was a time-honoured procedure no more abused by George Robey than by any present-day super-market cashier. It filled a need, for sailors had to buy tooth-paste, shaving soap, Turkish Delight, camel stools and brightly-coloured leather pouffes just like anyone else. Dirty postcards and blue books were also available from dubious-looking traders but never from Mr Robey.

In many years of passing up and down the Suez Canal I never lost interest in it and the world it opened up. I had found magic in the Blue Funnel names of my boyhood, the exotic places I had never reached – Penang, Singapore, Batavia, Hong Kong, Shang-hai, Kobe and Yokohama. Now, south-bound in a British tanker, I was entering a world with its own checks and choke-points. All ships passed through the Straits of Bab al Mandeb. Some called at Aden; but only the oil tankers, the BI mail and Frank Strick's turned east along the coast of the Hadhrammut, past the Kuria Muria Islands, Masirah and Ras al Hadd and into the Gulf of Oman, by Kuh i Mubarak and Jask to the Quoins in the Strait of Hormuz. The Persian Gulf, with Abadan at its head and upstream Basrah the only other port of consequence, was not then con-gested. In the south-west monsoon it would have been difficult, in any case, to see whether it was crowded or not for visibility at that time of the year is often poor. Nevertheless, the *British Pa-tience*, without benefit of radar, made her landfall at the an-nounced ETA and MacDonald set about having us load the ship. Smithson needed no guidance and I was learning fast.

Behind our tiny tactical decisions lay the parent company's com-mercial strategy and trading pattern. The *British Patience* had left Europe and made a four-week passage to the fountain-head. In the Red Sea her call-sign appeared one night in Portishead Radio's traffic list. The message, deciphered from the company's own code book, ordered us to Abadan to load kerosine and motor-spirit consigned to Land's End for orders, thus keeping the ultimate port of discharge optional. The ship had last been dry-docked eight or nine months previously and, as docking policy required this to be repeated annually, our cargo from Abadan would place her in home waters at about the right time for docking. A problem which took another ship out of service, or a sudden requirement for tonnage could postpone the docking for a few weeks; but those on board assumed it would take place and made preparations accordingly. Condition reports on hull and machinery had to be prepared for mailing from Abadan together with stores indents and applications for leave from those entitled. This all created an air of anticipation weeks before the plans could be implemented. The most obvious preparation, however, was the work to be put in hand as soon as our orders were known. The *British Patience*, already clean and tidy, was subjected to a spring-clean and repaint which the experienced hands had grown to expect. Starting at the trucks of the masts everything was washed and repainted as if the crews' lives depended upon it. What appeared at issue was the chief officer's reputation; for the marine superintendent's inspection he had to deliver a ship as near perfect as possible, a law under which I was to live for many years. At first I did not question it, and even when doubts about the system's logic began to insinuate themselves I asked no questions but lived by its decree. It was understandable from the chief officer's point of view. 'Inspect my ship, sir. Look how well cared-for she is. Aren't we efficient chaps?' would be in his mind. 'Hmmmm, seems to have kept everyone busy,' might think the marine superintendent. 'Wonder if it all works? Probably used more paint than his allocation. Expect he had it up his sleeve unaccounted for, anyway. Rascal - but seems keen. Eight out of ten for effort.'

The system was illogical since, 24 hours after the inspection, soot, grime and the shipyard workers of Tyneside or wherever would have undone the loving work of weeks and ruined the ship's appearance. The time for a repaint would have been in the first good weather after leaving dry-dock, but the marine super-intendent would not have been there to inspect and admire it.

The tempo increased as soon as the deeply-laden *Patience* headed downstream from Abadan low in the water and, in my view, the more elegant for that. Monsoon weather undid some of the good but the crew were deployed on equally important work inside until the ravages on deck could be repaired under the blazing Red Sea sun. Between Cape Bon and Gibraltar the funnel and finally all the steel decks were painted. As we rounded Cape St Vincent it was nobly indeed for the ship looked like something out of a Christmas catalogue. Even taciturn Captain Kemp had a good word for it and I thought the presiding genius, MacDonald, should have had a medal. His reputation was obviously safe.

Instead of a medal he was promoted when we arrived in Swansea, our sole port of discharge; little to do with the condition of the ship of course but the result of his seniority. Off he went to some humbler vessel to stand, at last, on that upper platform of his career to which he had been aspiring for more than 20 years. A good-natured, great-hearted professional his subsequent career as master was exemplary but sadly, after an early retirement, he died prematurely.

Dry-docking did not take place on this occasion. Instead, we made another trip to the West Indies which gave Cath and me a few more weeks to prepare for our wedding. To be strictly accurate it gave her more time for all I had to do was contrive to get back promptly and secure leave for at least a week's honeymoon. I had made plans without proper awareness of the British Tanker Company's leave system. Blue Funnel experience had bred the belief that a peacetime round voyage lasted about four months with a week's leave granted automatically when relieving officers would take over the ship during her turnround. But the tanker trade was different. Forty-eight hours was a long turnround, 36 more usual and 24 the ideal sought by the programmers. Activity was at such a level during these brief calls at a UK port that relief was not possible and the leave cycle coincided roughly with the docking cycle. It became clear to me that when the ship returned to dock in August I would be lucky to get a week off, my long leave being scheduled for the following spring. With the boldness and irresponsibility of extreme youth I allowed preparations to go ahead in Glasgow for what was to be a respectable suburban wedding of the sort normally planned at least six months ahead. Fortunately, the war-time technique of planning for weddings at short notice, knowing that one of the parties might be delayed, was well-remembered. Somewhere between Bishop Rock and the Windward Passage I announced to Captain Kemp that I wanted to apply for short leave on the ship's return to England to get married. He stared at me in disbelief for a long moment. 'That's a bold step at your age, laddie,' he said, finally. At 21 I did not have the excuse of the bomber pilot of two or three years earlier who felt he had better gather some rosebuds while he may. I was lucky and had a future; but I was impatient for life.

The ship was to load at Curacao, an island in the Netherlands Antilles almost entirely dependent upon the existence of a massive Shell refinery which processed Venezuelan crude oil for export to the USA and Europe. Like Abadan, the Anglo-Iranian refinery in the Persian Gulf and Perth Amboy the Esso equivalent in New Jersey, Curacao was one of the major oil terminals in the world. It was also a pleasant place to be, tropical, Caribbean, Dutch-influenced, clean and apparently affluent. Two nights in Curacao, one evening of which was spent on the verandah of a superbly comfortable club drinking Oranjeboom and putting the world to rights, gave me strength for the return voyage. Next morning Smithson and I did some pre-wedding shopping for he was getting married the same week as I. In the market I struck a bargain for a dozen pairs of American-made nylons, wealth beyond the dreams of avarice until Cath opened them four weeks later to discover that they were beautifully packaged seconds about three-quarters of an inch wide at the ankles!

The homeward passage was as idyllic as the outward except for a growing domestic problem the genesis of which pre-dated my joining the ship. For a year the captain had reared chickens on the monkey island, the open deck above the bridge on which the main compass platform was located. The carpenter had constructed an elaborate hen-house and pen where the Black Abbot spent happy hours persuading his 12 pullets to produce eggs. Now that we were homeward bound to dry-dock should the captain ship home a dozen year-old pullets with poor laying records, together with the complicated joinery work put together by the ship's carpenter, or have them slaughtered and despatched to his address in Hull? He was pondering this on the bridge one forenoon while I was on watch. Having established that I had once lived on a farm he looked upon me as his agricultural consultant. As we stood on the bridge there came to us the distant, slow croak-croaking of a broody hen. A chicken had escaped from the pen on the deck above and approached us, round the bridge house, in a slow, stalking gait, feathers fluffed out, eyes wild and unseeing, and suicidally bent upon maternity.

'God almighty! What's the matter with that thing?'

'It's only on the pook, sir,' I responded confidently.

'The pook!' he choked. 'What does that mean, for God's sake? What am I going to do with it? Catch the bloody thing before it breaks something!'

I stalked the chicken sure of what to do. In a moment I had it in my hands and ran to the row of firebuckets which decorated one side of the charthouse, thrust the poor bird's head into the water and held it there. Gradually the kicking subsided until a 15in ball of feathers had shrunk to a slim, fish-like shape with barely any life left in it whereupon I released it on the deck. With a shake of its head and hatred in its yellow-ringed eye it fled round the back of the bridge house, cured of all maternal instincts and brought back to its senses by the age-old method of taking it to the brink. The captain was impressed. He nodded his head sagely as if he himself had instructed me to carry out the act, but was generous – for a Yorkshirean – in his praise. It was a beautiful morning. We were homeward-bound. I could see a good report and perhaps, in due course, promotion. Then, first faintly, but getting louder, 'Cloa-a-a-ak, cloa-a-a-ak, cloa-a-a-ak.' The broody hen returned from behind the bridge house in exactly the condition it had started out. My stock fell, my hopes were dashed and the Abbot left the bridge in dudgeon.

Sadly, the day after the carpenter completed dismantling the coop, the captain decided that it would be cheaper to ship home 12 carcasses than live, ill-natured chickens. He sent for the steward who sent for the cook and the 12 apostles were despatched, plucked, drawn, trussed, packaged and frozen. Despite this mild eccentricity 'Nigger' Kemp was a consummate shipmaster who knew how a ship should be run and saw that it was so without raising his voice. I learned from him how to send a lookout to the lowest part of the ship to look underneath the poor visibility and pick up whatever was then to be seen which could not be sighted from the bridge. And I saw him turn the ship round, through 180 degrees, and steam back along exactly the line he had approached because he could not be sure of where he was. It was an essential first principle on which he had been reared and he was passing it on to his successors. Weather-beaten, tough little Yorkshire poultry fancier and master mariner - he was a born seaman.

Stanley Smithson and I were sent off from Swansea in style. However bold Captain Kemp thought it for so young a man to marry he was kind in his own gruff way. The day before our release I was told that I was being promoted to second officer in an almost new ship, the *British Major*, then lying in Queens Dock and undergoing repair following her maiden voyage. Progress indeed. I arrived in Glasgow on Friday August 9. On the Glorious Twelfth, Cath and I were married in Lansdowne Church which her mother and father attended regularly. Built in affluent late-Victorian times it was said of Lansdowne, 'This church was not built for the poor and needy, but for the rich and Doctor Eadie.' Cath and I were the opposite of rich but her parents were generous and the reception in the Grosvenor delighted the 60 guests to which postwar rationing limited us as much as it frightened the bridegroom. We spent our brief honeymoon in the beautiful, stone-faced, old-fashioned Aviemore Hotel which then stood on the lower slopes of Craigellachie looking towards the Forest of Rothiemurchus. Burned to the ground a few years later it was replaced, eventually, by the hideous breeze-block leisure complex which now occupies the site. By August 20 we were back in Swansea and I had taken up my new appointment aboard, two stripes on my sleeve, a wife on my arm and life in front of us.

Repairs to the *British Major* progressed slowly. Built by Laing's on the Wear and commissioned earlier in the year the ship was one of the first of the immediate post-war standard 12,000-tonners. If I had been impressed by the wartime-built *Patience* the *Major* was several shades better and I saw it as no drawback that she had developed boiler problems which the builders were putting right under guarantee. It should have taken three or four days but because of a strike and other interruptions it took six weeks! Our honeymoon was extended and living on board Cath began to learn a new way of life.

The master of the *British Major* was Captain Hugh McMichael, a member of a clever and successful family from Gatehouse-of-Fleet in south-west Scotland. One brother was a distinguished surgeon, a sister headmistress of a girls' school and Hugh himself holder of an Extra Master's certificate when few others aspired to that distinction. He was a joy to serve under, strict but humane, exacting but patient, intelligent and formidably competent – and determined to bring others along in his own footsteps. His chief officer, John Wilson, had grown up in Paddy Henderson's but had transferred to the British Tanker Company during the depression. A big, powerful man with a deep voice and dogmatic likes and dislikes he fortunately took an instant liking to Cath so I was tolerated. He and his wife, Isobel, became our firm friends for many years. Sidney Page, the chief engineer, was a small, affable, bespectacled native of Swansea who talked so much and so fast that his dentures, which clicked up and down, invariably seemed several words behind his conversation. The prolonged spell in Swansea meant that the ship's officers had come to know each other well by the time we sailed in early October. The crew, except

155

for petty officers and catering staff, did not then stand by the ship in a home port, being engaged from the local office of the Shipping Federation, the 'Pool', a day or two before sailing. The system suffered from all the disadvantages inherent in an industry content – or perhaps compelled - to depend upon casual labour. It is a wonder that, for the most part, ships managed to sail with competent and reasonably sober crews. It was not always so from some of the more notorious ports but Swansea seamen knew the tanker trade and were, essentially, a good-natured lot.

At first the *British Major* was deployed on short-haul runs delivering Iraqui crude oil from Tripoli in the Lebanon to the Haifa refinery. The Stern Gang's campaign of terror, or liberation struggle as they saw it, against the British meant that tankers in Haifa harbour were prime targets for limpet mine attack by divers. Every now and then we threw small charges into the harbour to discourage potential attackers and, whatever effect it had on them, it certainly kept everyone else awake. Trading over such a short distance meant that there was no time to clean tanks between the discharge of one cargo and loading the next less than 48 hours later. Iraqui crude deposited prodigious quantities of wax and sediment so that by the time we were ordered south through the Canal, the cargo tanks were in an appalling state. It took the entire 11 days between Suez and the head of the Persian Gulf to clean them adequately so that the next cargo, again for the Eastern Mediterranean, could be loaded at a place called Fahaheel in the sheikhdom of Kuwait. In late 1946 the Kuwait Oil Company's installation at Fahaheel consisted of two off-shore buoy berths served by submarine pipelines. Visible ashore was a single aluminium-painted tank peeping coyly from behind the sand dunes and one or two black Bedouin tents on the foreshore, a lonely, sand-blown, frontier wilderness.

Trade between this arid place and Haifa throughout that winter left me discontented. Despite pride in the *British Major,* and vaulting ambition, the old sailor's cry, 'This game's not for me,' had taken hold, a frustration I must have communicated home. As a result I knew that I could find a job, sponsored by my father-in-law, in the Singer Company. An indulgent marine superintendent in Abadan transferred me to the homeward-bound *British Pride* and by April I had left the British Tanker Company after barely a year, to become a clerk in the foreign shipping department of the Singer Manufacturing Company. So much for my single-mindedness.

Domestic life in our own home was a splendid revelation. For six years I had spent only a week or two at a time in various family houses, apart from the golden three-month spell at Queensborough Gardens in 1944. Now 'demobilised' Cath and I could set up our own establishment. We were lucky. Housing in post-war Britain was at a premium but Cath had managed to rent a so-called service flat in a large Victorian house looking over to the West of Scotland cricket ground at Hamilton Crescent in Partick. Our first home, 59 Peel Street, consisted of a single large room with a bay window, high corniced ceiling and a tiny kitchen which had probably been a butler's pantry. It had been the dining room of the original four-storey terrace house and, although we had to share a bathroom at the rear of the house with another tenant, we thought it palatial. In 1947 it could have been a great deal worse, for so many of our generation had to embark upon married life under a parental roof.

• *59 Peel Street*

157

If domesticity was idyllic it took but a few weeks, however, to realise that my change of career was a disaster. Clerking was not seafaring and I would not have believed that I could have missed, so soon, the ship-board environment about which I had rebelled. This I could not confess to Cath, at least to begin with. But as the year wore on and the work became even more boringly repetitious, I could not contemplate the thought that I should never again stand on the bridge of a ship, feel a deck rise and fall beneath my feet, give helm orders, take sights, lay off courses, plan cargoes, take charge of a mooring gang, or keep anchor watch on some balmy, tropical night. Could I reconcile the two worlds – be involved with ships and still enjoy the ordinary pleasures of home life which everyone else took for granted? How did one become a naval architect? Four years at university and no money coming in – out of the question. Become a Clyde pilot? All that was required was a master's ticket, luck and the patience to go on the waiting list for an indefinite number of years. What about journalism? Set out to become the shipping correspondent of the *Bulletin* or even the *Glasgow Herald*? Who would want a novice cub reporter far less a shipping correspondent? I thought of every conceivable, outlandish and impractical way out of my dilemma and grew to understand Thoreau's comment that 'most men live lives of quiet desperation'.

Respite came early the following year in two ways. Singers set up a Work Study Unit and appointed 20 young men, clerical and technical, as time and motion study 'engineers'. One of the chosen it did not take me long to realise that we were rate fixers employing a quasi-scientific method although it was, at least, more interesting than checking bills of lading. The Singer factory then employed 15,000 workers, a major name in light engineering, and its work study unit's mobility gave me an insight into manufacturing industry to be remembered with affection – and respect – for the sense of planned order, the smell of hot oil on metal, the indefinable flavour of a work-shop, the thunder of the forge, the scream of a circular saw slicing through balks of mahogany, and for the tough, warm-hearted citizens of Clydebank who weekly turned out thousands of sewing machines and shipped them to the corners of the earth. It was a bitter-sweet year, for our private life which should have been so happy was gradually overshadowed by my growing awareness that there was no career for me in the Singer Company, that I was only partly qualified and that, without proper qualifications of some kind, there was no advancement and a thin future.

Geoffrey David Watson King was born just after midnight on October 22, 1948. George Burnett, our doctor, encouraging Cath after 18 hours' exhausting labour, said to the midwife late in the evening, 'We'd better get this baby born before midnight. It's Trafalgar Day – and father's a sailor.' They didn't manage it, but it was a close-run thing. The infant looked exactly like my father and I thought him the finest child ever born. So did his mother and his grandparents. And his uncles and his aunts. But I suppose that is par for the course.

Father was no longer a sailor, of course, but three or four months later the dam burst and I set about becoming one again, the cruellest decision I ever made. To leave a young wife and tiny infant to return to a way of life which would mean months of separation every year of our lives was pure selfishness. Cath, not brought up to service life, was unhappy but resigned to the inevitable. I can imagine no contemporary young woman tolerating such a situation for a moment but the decision to return to sea and qualify in my profession was probably right, looked at dispassionately, although it was one of great personal difficulty and conflicting emotion. Furthermore, I did not know if the British Tanker Company were prepared to take me back. They were, although I had to revert to third officer being appointed to the *British Yeoman*, a new ship completing in the Furness shipyard at Haverton-Hill-on-Tees. During the fitting out period, I returned to Glasgow, a self-indulgent mistake making final parting from wife and chubby, handsome infant even more cruel. Eventually the wrench was made. There was no recrimination although Cath must have had her own thoughts about the perfidious nature of my actions. Whatever she thought then she supported me loyally for the rest of my career, becoming as immersed in the triumphs and tribulations of seafarers, ships and shipping as I. A Lowland Scot, she comes of a breed of honest, tough-minded, indomitable women. I often wonder at my good fortune.

The grey, tousle-haired, laconic and dry-as-dust master of the *British Yeoman*, Robin McLean from Kirkpatrick Durham in the Stewartry of Kirkcudbright, soon sorted me out. My three-year vacillation was over, mischief created by my own indecision. McLean knew nothing of that and would have cared less, but he certainly knew what to expect from his officers with a new ship to lick into shape. With domesticity behind me I re-entered the world I knew - the seven-bell breakfast before the forenoon watch, checking lifeboats or deluding myself that I was studying, bridge relief at five o'clock to let the chief officer go below for a Tyneside high tea - the last meal of the day, and the peace of the evening watch until midnight. Almost effortlessly I slipped back into the way of a ship. Our loading instructions, for a new ship, were extraordinary - Land's End for orders. Home so soon! In no time at all we seemed to be back in Grangemouth - and I was told to take two days leave and then join the *British Advocate* in Purfleet as second officer! All at once luck seemed to be running our way.

The *British Advocate* was a standard 12,000-tonner, similar to the *Yeoman*, of which more than 50 were built, design details improving as time went on. They were the workhorses of the post-war British Tanker Company fleet, supplemented by 10 American-built T.2 tankers which were, in fact, more efficient. The 12s were eventually overtaken by 16,000-thousand tonners then, in the early 60s, by a completely new design of 19,000- and 20,000-tonners. I joined the *Advocate* in a drizzle at eight o'clock one morning oddly reminiscent of my boarding the *British Patience* three years earlier. This time I did not need to look for the chief officer. Whatever problems Charlie Smith was wading through I walked right into them. Some 15-stone of puzzled good nature, and a native of Greenock, Charlie immediately recognized my Caledonian accent, made some rueful and disparaging remark but seemed relieved to have support. Early on he made it clear that he and the captain were not always in agreement. It was not surprising. Captain Surrey D Bumstead, OBE – he claimed he was called Surrey because that's where he was born and considered himself lucky not to have been born in Middlesex – could not have been a greater contrast. Surrey D, with groomed silver hair and neat white moustache had a presence, the image of the chairman of a successful family firm of high-class grocers and wine merchants. He had a habit of dropping his 'g's' and when he wrote – infrequently – to head office he started at the beginning and finished at the end without a hint of punctuation throughout. A very senior master it was said that he got his OBE when he tore the bottom out of a new ship leaving the Tyne, by driving her over an uncharted wreck and then getting her back into the river in a worse state than the *Kelly*. His first wife was a spiritualist and he communicated with her after her death until his second wife, quite reasonably, dug in her heels. His time at sea, since he was a most effective delegator, was spent doing the most beautiful tapestry and writing unpunctuated letters to the Malmesbury Girls' High School in Worcestershire, a school he had 'adopted', or which had adopted him. As always, on joining a new ship, one was mindful of the strictly hierarchical system until the glass had cleared. I walked cautiously round the master whose initial greeting was less than friendly since he thought he was entitled to a much more senior second officer. In time I grew to like Surrey D and even drew pictures and wrote letters to the Malmesbury Girls' High School at his bidding. But I liked the exasperating Charlie as much, even if he always seemed to be in a state of feud with his and my master.

The two senior engineers in that ship, Alf Hazlewood the chief, and George Johnston the second, were almost a Mutt and Jeff act or, more accurately, a Laurel and Hardy comic team. Hazlewood was stout, elderly (well, he was 50 which was elderly to me) and provocative. A good engineer he was an even better administrator adept at having everyone running to his beck and call. As I write these lines, I wonder who was the better delegator, Surrey Bumstead or Alf Hazlewood. One of the chief's foibles was to read up some esoteric subject in *Pear's Encyclopaedia* as he sipped tea following his post-prandial nap. Having marshalled his facts he would say at dinner, apropos of nothing, 'Do you know, captain, there were more people kicked to death by donkeys in Oklahoma in 1947 than were killed in aeroplane accidents there?' Surrey inevitably rose to the lure, never seeming to realise that he was being bated and that Alf had memorised only enough information to keep an argument going for half-an-hour. George Johnston was physically Alf's opposite being short, slight and myopic with thick horn-rimmed glasses and rather prominent ears. A superb engineer he would have been deeply offended had Hazlewood come near the engine-room, other than by appointment, an attitude which suited the chief admirably. One of Johnston's tricks was to change a fuel valve without stopping the ship. It was probably dangerous and contrary to regulations, but it meant that the logbook averages which Alf Hazlewood returned to the office were better than anyone else's. They were a curious pair, forever wrangling, always in each other's company, Hazlewood baiting Johnston as mercilessly as he baited the captain, and Johnston running his immaculate engineroom to suit himself. All three argued with Charlie Smith. Consequently, the *Advocate* was an extremely happy ship. We were long away that voyage making an intermediate passage from the Persian Gulf to Australia, the first time I had traversed the Indian Ocean since 1941. It was as peaceful and beautiful as I had remembered it but, from north to south, it is an extraordinarily long ocean, and the return distance is exactly the same! Charlie Smith's obsession with fresh water consumption I never forgot and developed my own phobia while serving in ships unable to distil their own potable water and dependant upon the capacity of the ship's fresh water tanks. As we sailed from Kuwait with crude oil, he had to bear in mind that the passage to Melbourne would take 30 days. The ship's fresh water capacity – which was all that would be allowed for in the deadweight calculations – was 90 tons, and the *British Advocate*, like all ships of her type then had sufficient distillation capacity only to ensure boiler feed water supplies. The crew of 45 was thus restricted to three tons a day on this passage, or about 650 gallons for cooking, cleaning and ablutions. 14 gallons per man each day sounds ample but it can be controlled at that level only by shutting off the supply to taps and showers for most of the day. Charlie was fanatical in his enforcement but, of course, the ship's company hated it and, with hindsight, it seems more appropriate to the 19th century than the 20th.

Early in the spring of 1950 the *Advocate* arrived in Grangemouth and then steamed south to the Tyne for dry-docking. Some of the officers' wives, including Mrs Bumstead, had been living on board during the turn-round in Grangemouth for the ship's accommodation was roomy, comfortable and quite as good as the passenger cabins in liners of that era. As we warped through the lock poor Mrs Bumstead was in tears as if her husband was off to war instead of a hundred miles to North Shields. There I left the ship for I had completed enough sea time to sit my next examination after the appropriate period at the Technical College. Cath and I could look forward to at least three months together. It is odd - the Second Mate's examination and sitting for my Master' certificate in 1952 I can remember vividly but I recall nothing about the intermediate First Mate's hurdle. Geoffrey I enjoyed enormously. At 18 months an active intelligent chatterbox, he was part of what I was missing at sea; but the die was well and truly cast and both Cath and I knew that I had to have a Master's ticket at least before there could be real advancement. Brave and resolute, she had accepted the life to which I had exposed her; but the spring of 1950 was sweet indeed and, inevitably, passed all too swiftly.

No sooner were the examinations over than I was appointed to the *British Dragoon* whose master, Donald Ward, had the florid features and slightly boiled eyes associated with high blood pressure. If he did so suffer it did not make him choleric. Indeed, he was rather placid, if worldly-wise. The *British Dragoon*, commissioned in 1942 for the Ministry of War Transport, was one of three sister ships referred to as the Norwegian design. The *Cavalier, Bombardier* and *Dragoon* were, at 14,000 tons, a little larger than standard ships like the *Advocate*. All three, however, had unreliable engines, were utilitarian and, to save steel, had been designed with fewer transverse bulkheads resulting in a smaller number of cargo tanks. The free surface effect of oil or ballast water in such large compartments made the ships roll heavily and they were uncomfortable and unhandy. My service in the *British Dragoon*, lasted for the rest of that year but has not left a deep impression on me although I do remember that the Korean War started as we were discharging in Durban and also recall, quite vividly, sitting in my cabin painting a picture for Geoffrey of the *Vital Spark*, Para Handy's notorious steam lighter!

When the *Dragoon* arrived in Falmouth for dry-docking in mid-December the local marine superintendent sent me home for a week's leave, starting on December 20, with instructions to report to the *British Councillor*, a ship barely a year old, on December 27 as chief officer. Home for Christmas, and a notable promotion into the bargain! I had no illusions about merit being a contributory factor in this advancement. The company was engaged in a massive post-war building programme of which the 12,000-ton all-purpose tanker was the standard unit. In the late 1940s men had given up seafaring in great numbers. Some, like me, had come back when the grass on the other side of the fence proved less than green but many never returned. With more ships and fewer qualified men the experience which pre-war officers had had to accumulate could no longer be garnered before young men were pitched into senior positions. Aged 25 I was typical of my generation – brash, bright enough, apparently self-confident but woefully lacking in experience and, privately, well aware of the fact. Only a few years before I had been serving as a midshipman in ships where the chief officer was in his 40s, the second in his 30s and perhaps only the most junior in his early to middle 20s.

Although elated, I experienced that frisson of self-doubt which so often accompanied promotion, a perfectly seemly and healthy reaction provided it is kept under control and displaced, fairly quickly, by the more optimistic view that, if the others can cope so can you.

On Boxing Day, I left home for Falmouth and the *British Councillor*. When the porter at Paddington lifted my trunk onto his barrow he remarked, "Whatcha got in there, guv - the Stone of Destiny?" Inexplicable, until newspaper headlines told of its theft.

For my first appointment as chief officer I was lucky to sail with a Cornish crew signed on in Falmouth. From that port, as with Swansea, the men were familiar with tankers as so many dry-docked there and signed on crews from the local 'pool'. The Cornishmen knew their trade and British Tanker ships well, an easy lot to get on with although not to know. They all seemed to be called Pascoe, Trevithick or Kneebone. As chief officer of the *British Councillor* I was going to be more closely associated with the deck crew, the biggest single group in the ship, than I had been since my years as a midshipman. Normally, the more junior officers dealt only with the three crew members on their own watch. Certainly the second mate had charge of half the deck crew when leaving and entering harbour, but that didn't last long and concerned only well-defined tasks. Now I was responsible for all of them and dependant on them for the upkeep and running of everything on board except the machinery.

The officer in charge of such a group is only as good as his petty officers in direct touch with the men all the time. In a merchant ship a good bo'sun can make a mediocre chief officer shine and the life of a good chief officer far easier. A poor bo'sun, in my day, was rarely seen and, if sighted, did not return next trip. A poor chief officer, of course, could ruin a good crew, and sometimes did. I was lucky, therefore, to start with an experienced crew and a first-class bo'sun who could save me from my worst excesses, at least in deck work. Until now I had been more concerned about who the other deck officers might be, and whether we were all reasonably compatible. The master, in particular, held the power of life and death and his style set the tone of the ship. Now, it was even more important that he be congenial. The chief and second engineers were likewise of great concern for one had to get along with them too to ensure the system worked. I could not have asked for a more amicable commander than Guy Attfield, the master of the *British Councillor*. He was an imposing, full-bellied, olive-skinned, patrician-looking man with flared nostrils and dark, amused eyes twinkling from under heavy black brows. Years afterwards he told me that, when I joined the ship, the chief engineer, whom I'd met on my way on board, had taken himself swiftly up to Attfield's quarters and said, 'Have you seen your new mate, captain? He looks as if he's just left school!'

I suppose I must have done, but Attfield showed no sign of distress and did not patronise the novice. Although he must have had to grit his teeth sometimes while I made mistakes, he steadfastly forebore from interfering. 'If you're worried, Mate, or in a fix come up here and talk about it. I'll probably have seen the problem before,' was all he said. I did climb the inside companionway to his day cabin to ask his advice - but not too soon lest he thought I was really worried.

The outward passage was easy for the ship, straight from drydock, was already clean and gas-free. In the four-week trip to the Persian Gulf, therefore, the main thrust of activity with the bo'sun and deck crew was to overcome the ravages of the dry-docking which normally took at least two months. It took little intelligence or experience to know what had to be done and to give the bo'sun appropriate instructions. He could have thought it out for himself, in any case, but it led me easily into issuing orders and planning for other people. The acid test loomed ahead – loading my first cargo. I had been lucky in that the senior people with whom I had served previously had taken pains to satisfy my curiousity about filling a ship rather rapidly with 12,000 tons of oil. Our orders were to load a full cargo of crude oil at Mina al Ahmadi for Australia. The calculations for a single-grade cargo were not difficult and I took them up to Captain Attfield who was gratifyingly impressed by the fact that I could use a slide rule. He suggested some minor adjustment and appeared cheerful and confident. In his shoes, I should not have felt the same.

Controlling fresh water consumption on the four-week passage south was my greatest worry. Guy Attfield, an old campaigner, knew the problem exactly. 'You filled the fore and after peaks in Falmouth, didn't you?' he asked. I assured him I had and it was clean, drinkable water. 'Right,' he said, 'don't discharge it all before we load. Keep some back and don't declare it. Load as if it wasn't there. You'll be an inch deeper than you ought to be but nobody's going to know. They can't read the bloody draft to an inch, even if they bother to look.' It was against the law, of course. Technically the ship would be overloaded by the fresh water we kept back, say 60 tons, which would sink her exactly an inch deeper than the properly assigned mark. But the captain was right. No-one could read a ship's draft or freeboard to an inch in an exposed sea berth. The crime, like the parlour-maid's baby, was only a little one after all and would ease the domestic water problem on the voyage. A few years later, in more up-to-date ships equipped with ample distillation capacity, such a silly subterfuge would be unnecessary; but on long ocean passages, in ships essentially of pre-war design, built to carry 12,000 tons of cargo at 11 knots on a consumption of 14 or 15 tons of diesel fuel per day, an inch overloaded in the Persian Gulf in the good weather season was a small price to pay for peace of mind.

Thus it was organised, and the crude loaded without incident at a thousand tons an hour. No-one hovered over my shoulder and when all was over and we were back at sea again, the captain's flared nostrils creased up towards his eyes, he sent for the chief engineer and the boy mate and poured us both a congratulatory libation. After this display of confidence and his willingness to keep a gentle watching brief on what I was up to, I would have followed him to the ends of the earth. On that occasion he made me think I was the cat's pyjamas; but, over many years, I never approached a loading port without a feeling of heightened tension before going into action – or onto the stage. Not a bad thing. Even in those days of small ships, modest loading rates and rudimentary instrumentation, loading a tanker, however carefully planned and controlled, was potentially hazardous causing the adrenalin to flow and sharpening the wit. My contemporaries, brought up in ships like the *Councillor*, would eventually have to learn to deal with loading rates of 20,000 tons an hour into ships 20 times the size. No harm in being at concert pitch for that kind of exercise.

From the beginning of a voyage to its end, the chief officer of an oil tanker usually went ashore only to look at the state of the ship from the outside or to check the draft the third mate had just read. Even that would have been an impossibility on that particular voyage since the ship discharged at an off-shore berth in Botany Bay and was back at sea within 48 hours. The return passage held fewer terrors for now there was no shortage of fresh water because a ship in ballast could carry as much as she needed. Tank cleaning on such a long voyage could be carried out at a leisurely pace

166

although heavy weather in the Australian Bight delayed the start. Ship's routine on an ocean passage, as seen from the chief officer's viewpoint, was enormously satisfying. The day started with a climb to the bridge just before four in the morning. In those days we still had a helmsman on the bridge, for such unsophisticated ships boasted no automatic pilot. A brief good morning to him, his face just palely visible in the compass light, a check of the gyro heading, the chart and night order book lying under the orange-shaded light over the chart table, and back to the wing of the bridge to finish a mug of tea in peace. An hour later the first signs of dawn, preparations for star sights and then half-an-hour's intense activity taking sextant altitudes of four or five favourite stars and calculating the position fix to be entered in the log and plotted on the chart. That would satisfy the Old Man when he surfaced. Almost six o'clock and time for the bo'sun to appear. A quarter-of-an-hour's quiet chat with him about the crew's work for the day and, as he disappeared below to muster his crowd, a young steward would materialise on the bridge with more tea and toast. Full light now and the sea a beautiful dove grey, never quite flat but, in good weather, with a barely perceptible heave. By quarter-to-seven sounds of activity from all around. The carpenter on the fore deck taking his daily soundings and coming up to the bridge to chalk the important ones on a status board. A brief session with him to establish his work for the day. Captain on the bridge at 0715, showered, clean, stinking of after shave, towel round his waist, well-slept, refreshed, genial, cognisant of the star fix in the log book and on the chart at which he'd glanced on his way through the chartroom. Smell of frying bacon wafting from the galley as the sun warms and the ship is bathed in its glow. New day in glorious, peaceful solitude on this painted ocean. Well-scrubbed third mate on the bridge at 0755. Ten minutes hand-over and a walk round the ship checking everything by looking. A shave and a shower and then breakfast. And, oh, what breakfasts, after four hours of the morning air, at sea when one was young.

Against form, for a ship so recently out of dry-dock, the *Councillor's* instructions as she approached the Persian Gulf were to load for Land's End for orders. We had anticipated another Australian trip. Instead I faced my next organisational hurdle - getting the ship tidied up for a superintendent's inspection when she reached home. There was no guarantee that she would be nominated to

167

a UK port but the drill still had to be gone through. I knew what to expect, as did Captain Attfield who had been doing it all his life, the bo'sun and the crew. We set about washing and re-painting the ship from mast trucks to deck. The side was touched up as she lay alongside when I was far too busy to pay much attention since I was loading my second cargo. It mattered not. The bo'sun knew what had to be done and did it, for his pride in the state of the ship was as great as mine, the captain's, or anyone else's. As we romped homewards, the *Councillor* grew shinier every day. The Gloucester Regiment fought its epic battle in Korea that spring while we were on passage and there was news from the BBC about the forthcoming Festival of Britain. The ship's company were more concerned about our final port of discharge and when we were ordered to the Mersey, there was a predictable outbreak of channel fever and a dusting off of suitcases as people prepared for home. I did not expect leave but got it. Delighted at the prospect of long leave, nevertheless I left the *British Councillor* with regret. She had been a happy ship and I appreciated my good fortune in having encountered Guy Attfield at such a crucial stage.

Cath and I decided to have a holiday in Arran, a cult with the aspiring Glasgow bourgoisie for generations. We were aspiring enough but had not been able to afford a holiday before. However, a chief officer's salary was a good deal better than that on which we had embarked upon married life so a good boarding house in Brodick, in the month of May, was within our reach. It happened that we chose the right week and enjoyed seven days of unbroken Mediterranean sunshine when we swam, rowed, walked and lazed, returning to Glasgow baked brown. There were no examinations to face since I had insufficient service in to sit for Master and when my leave was over I was appointed to the *British Pilot* dry-docking at Hebburn-on-Tyne. Cath and Geoffrey came with me as was permissible and expected. John Wilson, who had been chief officer of the *British Major*, was master of the *Pilot* so we had landed in friendly territory. This was some compensation for the ship was not a pretty spectacle. Built in 1943 as a merchant aircraft carrier (or MAC-ship) the *Empire MacColl*, with her sister ships, *Empire MacKay* and *Empire McCabe*, had been taken over after the war, had their flight decks removed leaving the tanker hull and accommodation structure beneath intact. Appropriately modified they re-entered service as near-standard oil tankers, but the joins tended to show and the *Pilot* was not the *Councillor*. A day or two after we arrived on board there was a flood of re-appointments and I was sent off, accompanied by wife and child, to join the *British Unity* lying at North Shields. Though a pre-war ship commissioned in 1939 and of an older design than anything I had served in recently she was a splendid ship with which I fell instantly in love. For almost a year I considered her my own and the *British Unity*, with her bone-white, teak-wood decks, varnished bridge front, solid, well cared-for appearance, polished and burnished by a superb Indian crew, still seems one of the brightest jewels in the collection. The so-called 1936-class of standard 12,000-tonners was the immediate predecessor of the type of ship I had encountered hitherto. The *Unity's* 'midships house was smaller, more uncompromisingly square and old-fashioned in an attractive sort of way. Her funnel was at the forward end of the engine-room fiddley since the boiler room was above the fore end rather than the after end of the engine-room. There was nothing utilitarian about her although her pre-war equipment was dating. That she was manned by a crew of Indian petty officers and ratings was novel in my experience. At that time about 20 per cent of the fleet, generally the older ships, had Indian crews signed on in Bombay but recruited in the province of Ratnaghiri. The cooks and stewards were Goanese. Geoffrey, not yet three, ash blond and talkative, was an instant talisman. On realising that the new burra sahib and his mem were approaching the gangway, the seacunny on duty sprang into action and within seconds the serang had been summoned and a dozen curious Indian seamen assembled to bring the luggage on board. They possessed both natural courtesy and an air of vulnerability making it almost impossible not to like them. The Goanese, being Catholic, usually devout and easily besotted by small children, were soon engaged in looking after Geoffrey and we settled in with a mounting sense of continuing good fortune. It was my first experience of Indians and I came to like them very much. Man for man a British sailor was better, tougher and more dependable in a crisis but in port the British sailor liked the fleshpots and was then far less reliable.

The *British Unity's* captain, John Murray, was a Border Scot married to a lady from Monkseaton and with a family of three. A short rotund man he was quite bald although only in his mid-40s He had a slight speech impediment but was a generous and warm-hearted individual who was friendly with everyone. Cath was made to feel at home and he handled Geoffrey with the confidence of experience. George Musther, the chief engineer, was dour, uncommunicative, difficult to know, but obviously competent as was the second engineer, a pleasant man called Sharpe who had only recently returned to sea. Sidney Garret, the second mate, some years older than I, was a victim of the depression who had never really caught up after losing his job in one of the P & O subsidiaries. The *British Unity* was one of the happiest ships in which I ever served and the officers truly became friends with each other. Many are dead but I still come across George Musther and I have to struggle to remember that he seemed dour, uncommunicative and difficult to know. Now he's just my friend, George.

We had certainly enjoyed the early summer of 1951 but sailing day arrived inexorably and we went through the usual parting agonies. It was even harder for Cath returning with Geoffrey to an empty flat haunted by memories and to bringing up a small child on her own. She used to say that the week-ends, when other wives had their husbands at home, were the worst. Her parents supported her wonderfully for many week-ends, which might otherwise have been intolerable, she spent with them. My own situation was different. I was occupied and in the company of people in the same situation as I. I had no reason, as Cath had, to compare my lot unfavourably with others. Straight from dry-dock an Indian-crew ship, normally trading in the East, could be expected to be away from England for at least nine months, so sailor's thoughts of home had to be suppressed quickly in order to settle down to that sort of programme. When loading orders came they seemed to confirm that we would be out for the full inter-dock period – Mina al Ahmadi for Fremantle. The great Abadan crisis had boiled up earlier in the year and the Anglo-Iranian oil fields and the refinery at Abadan were now in Mossadeq's hands. The European staff had been evacuated and sent home to England or distributed around associated companies in the Gulf. The tug fleet in the Shatt al Arab, operated by British Tankers, had been spirited away under the protective guns of *HMS Mauritius* and a price put on the head of Captain Dawson Johnson, the local marine superintendent who had engineered it. Abadan was no longer ours but Anglo-Iranian, with their American partners, Gulf Oil, had a major stake in Kuwait and from that time on our crude oil liftings from Mina al Ahmadi increased dramatically.

On passage to Western Australia the ship was diverted to Bombay as the Indian crew were due leave. The operation took but a few hours and by late afternoon of the same blazing Indian day we put to sea with a new crew whose first act was to conduct a prayer ceremony on the focs'lhead, seeking Allah's blessing upon the ship and the adventure on which they were embarked. It was touching, colourful and manifest of their devout Muslim faith. Their second act was similarly colourful, the delivery of enormous baskets of delicious tropical fruits to the captain, chief and second engineers and the chief officer. Having propitiated their God with prayer it made sense to propitiate the English demons with mangoes, a tradition which had lasted for years. It was harmless – well, reasonably harmless, for it took all the Europeans, eating madly, to consume the fruit before it went bad, after which the open nature of our bowels would have gladdened the hearts of whole legions of nursing sisters.

The serang – Indian equivalent of the bo'sun – four seacunnies who were quartermasters and did all the steering, and the seamen were as good as their predecessors. So, too, was the Chinese carpenter – all Indian crews had Chinese carpenters – who turned out, later, to be an excellent cabinet maker. It took little time for them to get used to the ship with whose type they were familiar. The Bombay 'pool' was supposed to be a general one but the bigger British companies recruited and then maintained their own roster so that the men sailed invariably under the same house flag to which they became fiercely loyal. They knew the ships, the company's rules and, after a time, the masters and officers with whom they had served. By the time we reached Fremantle it was as if they had always been on board.

Our visit to Western Australia should have lasted two days but, with cargo discharged, ballasting almost completed and the engine-room preparing for sea, the second engineer reported problems with one of the tie-bolts securing the main engine to its bed-plate. The tie-bolt, about five inches in diameter and 30 feet long, had fractured just below the securing nut at the top and had to be replaced. But no substitute existed in the whole of Australasia so a new one would have to be manufactured. With great difficulty, a suitable length of steel rod was located on the other side of the continent and the fashioning of a new tie-bolt put in hand. Six weeks later the repair was completed and the *British Unity* sailed again. The engineers had had a difficult time but for the rest of us it was a holiday. The captain had friends, the Pennies, who ran a hotel at Cottisloe, near Fremantle. John Murray and I, and the chief engineer when he was available, were invited to their parties at which sheep farmers from the outback and wool buyers from the big cities were heavily represented. Made honorary Members of the local yacht club, we enjoyed some marvellous sailing at the week-ends and were invited to the Saturday evening club dances.

The Pennies had a small holding 20 miles up-country and that gave John Murray and me an opportunity to see the countryside. Its predominant colour was grey rather than green – or, perhaps, the dust gave that impression. Among the Pennies' friends was canny old Dr Cameron, a Scot who had practised in Singapore before the war, suffered badly in Japanese hands between 1942-5 and had then settled in Australia with his wife. He took an avuncular sort of interest in me. Both John Murray and I were Scots but my home was still there and Dr Cameron liked to reminisce about the old country, although wild horses would not have dragged him back. He loved Australia, thought it the land of the future, for the young especially, and tried hard to persuade me to bring my wife and child to the land of plenty by the next P & O steamer. Enjoying the beautiful West Australian spring, sailing on the Swan River in a spanking breeze, eating crayfish on a golden beach, I should have been tempted. But I did not belong in Australia and would never have fitted. Britain, with all its faults – and in 1951 these were manifold – was what mattered to me, and not all the Foster's lager, crayfish, sunshine and outdoor sporting life of Australia could ever mean the same. I have never wished to live anywhere else but in the British Isles, much as I admire the USA, love France and Italy, am fascinated by India and China and impressed by the landscape of New Zealand. I think I disappointed Dr Cameron.

We returned to the Gulf and loaded for Sydney. One of the chief officer's responsibilities then, in an Indian-crew ship, was to administer the ship's rudimentary medical service. The deck and engine-room serangs made sure there was no malingering, the Goanese butler filtered the patients for surgery, and the crew loved this break in routine enjoying personal attention and being given medicine of some kind. It was usually a purgative, the dosage enough to produce action without turning the patient inside out. In the main they were healthy and certainly more robust than Indians of their class would have been at home in

Ratnaghiri. Nevertheless, one young seaman worried me a bit on the way south. At first I thought he was malingering because he looked well enough and had no symptoms other than a feeling of exhaustion. I compromised with the serang and put him on light duties until even that proved too much. The *Shipmaster's Medical Guide* was no help. On arrival in Sydney the doctor could find nothing wrong but hospitalised him for observation. Three days after sailing a radio message told us that the young man had died, to the consternation of the crew. I felt guilty because I had been treating him as a malingerer only a week or two before. A few days later the deck serang, a dear old man, died suddenly of a heart attack. Some 1,000 miles from any land, he had to be buried at sea which affected the crew profoundly. For a time it was difficult to make the look-out stay on the foc'slhead at night. When I insisted, I was suddenly faced on the bridge by the seaman who had deserted his post but had dutifully come to report the fact, grey with terror.

'Ghosts, sahib! I see ghosts,' he whimpered. 'Behind windlass, sahib. All round. They kill me.' He was almost out of his wits. 'What kind of ghosts?' I barked, rather unsympathetically. 'Hooman ghosts, sahib, hooman ghosts – maybe serang come to kill me.'

He had answered back to the serang a day or two before the old man died and it was sorely on his conscience, so he had to be put on day work for a while until his neurosis died down and he could face the dark.

King George VI died early in February as the *British Unity* steamed north through the Indian Ocean, and Queen Elizabeth was proclaimed. A week or two later the ship, now due for dry-docking, was on her way home to England. My seatime for Master complete I needed to study at the Technical College for my final examination. Homeward-bound the big paint-round had to be accomplished, of course. The ship did not really need it; but it got it and the crew would have been disappointed had it not happened. On board we had some beautiful American oak boarding scrounged from a Bibby liner where it had been used as dunnage. With some of it the carpenter built the stoutest doll's house in the history of the world for the captain's daughter and was then encouraged to make a small knee-hole desk complete with bookshelves, cupboard and matching chair which Geoffrey used until he grew out of it years later. Then it went the rounds of his cousins before coming back to roost.

Cath, with Geoffrey in tow, met the ship on our arrival in Falmouth. Having satisfied Captain Reay, the local Marine superintendent and a difficult man to please, it was time to go on leave. In company with Captain Murray we left the *Unity* to an emotional farewell from the crew. We caught the night train from Truro to Paddington, established Cath in the adjoining 'ladies only' compartment with Geoffrey stretched out on the carriage seat, and slept soundly, sitting upright, until somewhere near Reading. At Paddington Cath and I booked into the station hotel as I had instructions to report the following day to the man in charge of the company's training scheme, Captain Ronald Marsh. It was to be one of the more important encounters of my career.

Chapter 7

THE ECHOING, GRANOLITHIC-FLOORED corridors of the Royal Technical College were familiar and the mirror-backed half-models of ancient Clyde-built tramp steamers which lined them less than convincing in their dusty glass cases. I immersed myself in the syllabus rather enjoying my return to a student's desk. At that time I did not question the system which required a four-years' apprenticeship culminating in a rather basic test, followed by 18 months of watch-keeping, a more advanced examination and then two more year's seatime prior to the final for a Master's Certificate of Competency. It ensured a minimum of eight years' experience but little in the way of formal education. Attendance at navigation school was not obligatory and a few courageous and clever souls managed to pass the examinations without even signing on at the crammer. But, for the vast majority who went back to school, the excellent instruction was designed to satisfy current trends in examiners' questions. The examiners themselves were Board of Trade – or Ministry of Transport – surveyors, the responsible department seeming to change with every new government. Each had an Extra Master's Certificate but some were quite elderly and sometimes inexperienced in some aspects of the business in which they were examining – not absolutely necessary, of course, to decide if a candidate was fit to command an ocean-going ship. Naturally, no aspirant would have dared to voice such a heresy – at least not until he had been given a pass slip and was well out of earshot. For almost a century the system had ensured an adequate basic standard among British sea-going officers; nevertheless it was not the ideal way to train professionals, as the Germans and other north Europeans could demonstrate. But in 1952 I was not concerned with such flights of fancy. All I needed was a Master's Certificate in the minimum time, at least expense and without aggravation, as did my contemporaries. My concentration was broken a week or two after starting my studies by a summons to London for an interview with the chief marine superintendent, Captain William Hutchison, a great nabob known to the likes of me solely by name, and Ronald Marsh. The company had been asked to second an officer for a year to the cadet training ship *Conway*. My name had come out of the hat; did I want to be considered? It took little insight to know who had plucked out my name and less than a second to grasp the implications. *HMS Conway* was a name familiar to every British seafarer and I was being offered an irresistible opportunity. However, *Conway's* Management Committee had to vet the candidate who was proposed and the following week I absented myself from the classroom for another two days to present myself in Liverpool.

The *Conway* was a wooden wall, built as the 74-gun ship *Nile* shortly after the Napoleonic Wars, the third such warship to be loaned by the Admiralty to an organisation called the Mercantile Marine Service Association which had operated her for many years as a training ship. She had lain afloat in the Mersey off Rockferry Landing Stage for most of her life but had been moved to a mooring in the Menai Strait off Bangor in 1941. During the Liverpool blitz in March that year a German mine had dropped close to the ship but had failed to explode. The warning was enough, however, and the ship was towed away. After the war she was moved to a location further south in the Menai Strait on a reach opposite the Marquis of Anglesey's house, Plas Newydd. *Conway* cadets were highly regarded in most major British shipping companies, (not least by themselves). The only comparable establishments in the country were *HMS Worcester*, a steel-hulled, purpose-built training ship, in the shape of a wooden wall, berthed off Greenhithe in the Thames, and Pangbourne Nautical College in Berkshire, a public school - and a very good one - where the boys wore naval cadets' uniform and were subject to a discipline derived, approximately, from King's Regulations and Admiralty Instructions. But *Conway* as the oldest, thought itself the best and had nurtured John Masefield as a cadet - and a long list of distinguished seamen – to prove it. The Management Committee consisted of Alfred Wilson, general secretary of the Mercantile Marine Service Association, Captain Eric Hewitt, captain superintendent of the training establishment and two people who swam, without warning, out of the past - Brian Heathcote of the dark brown voice from my Blue Funnel midshipman days and, chairing the committee, Lawerence Holt, last seen following the Outward Bound School incident almost 10 years earlier. The interview was brief. Alfred Wilson explained the purpose behind the idea of a temporary appointment. Hewitt, a captain RNR and former Royal Mail Line officer had devised a system of borrowing

young officer from each of the major shipping companies in turn
to fill the position of second officer in the ship for a year. This
position he felt unsuitable for permanent appointment since he
wanted a young man, for whom promotion would be unlikely in
the near future, the senior officers being well-established and far
from retirement. It was a sensible idea and this year it was the
British Tanker Company's turn. Hewitt, himself a *Conway* product, took up the running. Heathcote said nothing much, nor did
Lawrence Holt for a while. Then he fixed me with an eye I could
well remember.

'Ever been up a mast, King?' he asked. He seemed to have no high
regard for tanker people but I confessed that I had served my
apprenticeship in his own company and considered myself well-
versed in masts – for a steamship man anyway. There was silence
for a second or two and some consternation. Either he hadn't read
the candidate's curriculum vitae or it was incomplete. He turned
to Heathcote who was as taken aback. The interview ended
shortly afterwards, without the murkier details of my Blue Funnel
career being exposed, and my appointment was confirmed. My
British Tanker salary would continue, the MMSA returning to
Anglo-Iranian what they would have paid a permanent second
officer. I should be on duty on board two nights out of three but,
if I wanted to have my wife and family with me, they could live in

HMS Conway

Anglesey or nearby. It was a wonderful opportunity, provided passed for Master, and I returned to Glasgow with a new incentive. Early in July three days of written papers were weathered without incident. The oral examination, usually feared by candidates and certainly by me, was conducted by a nautical surveyor from London with extensive knowledge of Indian crew matters as he had been responsible for setting up a ratings' training school in Karachi on behalf of the Pakistan government. Quickly he established the manning of the *British Unity* and my experience of and attitude to Indian crews. In retrospect it was more of an amicable exchange of experiences than the encounter I should have expected. It must have been enough to satisfy him for the following week, while I was taking over on board the *Conway*, I received a telegram from Cath telling me that I was a Master Mariner. Our year in North Wales was assured.

My predecessor, Eric Fowler from Shell, was most helpful. The cadets had left for summer leave so the ship was empty and quiet and he could take me round at leisure. Below decks the *Conway* bore an uncanny resemblance to a utility *Victory* without guns. When I first walked her decks with Fowler some ancient race memory stirred in the blood and I was delighted to be where I was. After a week Fowler disappeared south to his home near Dover and soon after he became a Trinity House Channel pilot. I never saw him again.

The great bonus of my appointment to the *Conway* was that Cath Geoffrey and I would have a year together. Accommodation was a problem but, with a hint from here and a word from there, one day I found myself standing on the 14th step of the approach to a tall terrace house almost opposite the entrance to the University College of Wales in Bangor. The house was owned by a spinster in her 60s who had inherited it from her father, one-time librarian of the University. Elunyd Shankland answered the door, a small rotund figure, a pale indoor face, large spectacles, short grey hair and a tight button-hole of a mouth dominating an expression of defensive aggression.

'Yes?'

I explained that I was attached to the *Conway* which information softened her a mite and I was ushered in. Half-an-hour later I emerged having secured a first-floor, almost self-contained flat for the weekly sum of £3.15s, a fortune as we had to maintain our Glasgow flat at the same time. When my leave ended the three of us trooped south to arrive on the steps of 'Bryn Awelon', 44 College Road, late one September afternoon. To this day I am not sure whether College Road was a good idea. Elunyd, who was a sharp little business woman, milked the relationship she developed with Cath. The rent was too high, the house antediluvian but comfortable enough in an old-fashioned way. The landlady gave us the impression that she was doing us a favour and promptly took advantage of Cath's good nature. I did nothing about it, however, and we stayed there for the entire year. And Elunyd kept in touch with Cath until her death many years later so presumably she had enjoyed the relationship.

Geoffrey's fourth birthday was imminent and he clearly needed to be with other children. Within a day or two, Cath had enrolled him in a local infant school in Bangor. On the first day she walked him down the hill to school and, with some trepidation, consigned him into the care of a junior mistress. Young as they were the infants had lunch at school and stayed until three in the afternoon. Later Cath slipped back and peered round the door at the group of tiny children lunching. Geoffrey happened to look up, saw her and exclaimed to his companion, 'Oh look, there's my mummy,' and went straight back to his plate. That was the first hurdle over. At three o'clock she returned to bring him home and was met by a flood of tears and protest. He thought that school was a one-day perfomance he would never experience again. Eventually, she managed to convince him that he could come back the next day, the day after and the day after that again. He was mollified, but alas this unusual reaction to a first day at school was no harbinger of a brilliant scholastic career. He grew into as reluctant a schoolboy as any other, but at least Cath had no problem with him when he was small. She, herself, continued to have problems associated with Elunyd Shankland who made her own rules. Before long it seemed as if it were Cath who ran the house while Elunyd entertained callers and thought out new regulations. She had an infuriating habit of breaking into Welsh when speaking to local friends in front of us. It was a lesson in the difficulties of being too dependant upon the goodwill of others, especially landlords.

Life aboard *Conway* was busy and fascinating and the return of 350 cadets at the beginning of term introduced a new dimension. About 150 juniors were accommodated in part of Plas Newydd house while 200 seniors lived on board distributed, like 18th century sailors, in every corner of the ship, their personal belongings restricted to what could be contained in a single wooden sea-chest. They slept in hammocks slung under the massive deck beams, cleared everything away when reveille sounded at 0630 and, after breakfast and morning divisions, dropped down wooden partitions, previously secured to the deck-heads, to create individual schoolrooms where they pursued their nautical and academic studies throughout the day. RNR cadets, they wore naval uniform and working dress and were subject to a naval discipline imposed by tough retired Royal Navy petty officers led by a commissioned gunner. Every day there was much movement between the ship and the Plas Newydd jetty 200 yards away. Cadets and staff were transported by two motor boats and the pinnace, manned and coxed by cadets. Fresh water was brought to the ship in a flat-decked motorised water barge, also with a cadet crew, which plied twice daily between the ship and Port Dinorwic, a mile away on the Caernarvon shore, where there was a handy jetty, a water fawcet, a length of hose - and a cafe.

On board, the day began at 0630 with the duty bugler sounding reveille. Cadet captains leapt from their blankets and punched the other hammocks with vigour. Breakfast of thick slices of bread and jam known as 'soddock', was at 0715 and then the day's work began. Hammocks having been stowed, the boats were lowered and by 0800, after 'Colours' (the hoisting of the ensign to the appropriate bugle accompaniment), the duty run to Plas Newydd was under way while the water-boat headed for Port Dinorwic where the crew could enjoy their first illicit cigarette. 'Divisions' took place at 0900 on the main deck and on the parade ground at Plas Newydd with drum-and-bugle bands in loud attendance. The captain, descending from his magnificent mahogany-panelled quarters under the poop, took Divisions on board with the padre reading the lesson. I watched it closely – a modest but effective imitation of Whale Island – warned by Fowler that it would soon fall to my lot to take this parade. Indeed it would be my lot, even sooner, to muster 200 cadets to hoist the boats to the davit heads in the evening and lower them in the morning providing the cadets with a twice-daily experience of what blocks, tackles, stoppers, fairleads and cleats were for.

By 0915 the last prayer had been said and the divisions marched off the main deck. The ship then settled to school and a similar hush fell over the Plas Newydd stables where the shoreside classrooms were located. Besides being divisional officer of the Main Top the second officer took elementary astro-navigation with the fourth termers, cadets 15- or 16-years old, with one year of *Conway* behind them and one to come. Their self-confidence had not yet been eroded by the searing experience of having to accept responsibility – like harlots they had power and influence without responsibility. They were not easy to control and I had no teaching experience. Collectively they were smarter than I if I didn't rise early to prepare for battle. Individually they were not too difficult, especially if they could be isolated physically, morally or philosophically, from their fellows.   The head of the navigation department, P P Murphy, an elderly, white-haired, blunt-nosed, clever little Irishman with an Extra Master's Certificate, had been an Orient Line officer before joining the *Conway* pre-war. He set the syllabus for all navigation teaching and I did my best with spherical trigonometry and solving the well-known celestial spherical triangle, PZX, by means of the haversine formula. It was fortunate that I had been studying throughout the summer. Most of my classes passed their examinations but, since I had set the exams and marked the papers, they would, wouldn't they? as Mandy Rice Davies so succinctly observed. Afternoons were devoted to seamanship, boat-work and rugby football in the winter or cricket and athletics in the summer. Boats ran continuously with seamanship parties, cross-country runners, backward swimmers, sick parade going to Bangor to see Dr Reid, and cadets pursuing other activities. The duty officer organised all this while finding time to bone up on the next day's lesson when, no doubt, Brown, D V, the clever little bugger, would pose another impossible question underlining the second officer's inadequacies both as schoolmaster and navigator. The day's work or play done, there was another flurry of boat activity before the evening meal, followed by prep, some free time for leisure pursuits and the final strenuous task of hoisting up and securing the boats.   At 2130 hammocks were slung and, just before 2200, the bugler, standing beside the duty officer, sounded off 'Taps', to me a haunting experience. After a lengthy walk around the ship with the chief cadet captain the duty officer might permit himself the luxury of sleeping the sleep of the just, or devote the night to preparing his next lesson.   And I loved every minute of it.   Not a natural pedagogue I sometimes found male adolescents a trial. Individually they could be intelligent, sensitive, likeable. In large numbers they sometimes gave the impression of being near-cousins to Genghis Khan's hordes, without the horses. Much was natural exuberance with little original sin but I would have made a poor dominie for, early on in the game, I would have taken to homicide although a still, small voice within reminded me, occasionally, that ten years earlier I would have been an active and vociferous member of The Horde. The ship's officers had an easier role than the academics for discipline was strict and the cadets knew where the line was drawn. In my case (and my predecessors') I was younger than the permanent officers and, at the end of my year, would go back to my real life at sea – for which all yearned.

Eric Hewitt, the captain superintendent, was a formidable figure. Captain RNR Retired, he had had a distinguished war. Slim, slightly above average height, sallow complexion, fierce eye, a thin mouth like a rat-trap, a highly-developed quarter-deck manner and the voice of authority, he was held in great respect if not universally loved. Under him there were a number of uniformed officers and petty officers. Geoffrey Drake was chief officer of the shore establishment. His opposite number on board, John Brooke-Smith, had been in the New Zealand Shipping Company and was still a Lieutenant-Commander RNR. An older officer, Lieutenant-Commander Lawrence, shared the burden on board. The petty officers were led by the commissioned gunner, Jackie Mayne, a small, parade-ground martinet but a great companion. 'Pony' Moore was the model of a long-service chief petty officer - tall, cadaverous, dry as a stick – 'The other left foot, young man - the other left foot' – and the third, John Oliver, was a local yachtsman with less naval service than the other two.

At the head of a larger academic staff of graduate masters T E W Browne, a middle-aged bachelor who had been appointed headmaster in 1934, was known irreverently as 'Tube' for obvious reasons or, alternatively, as Tom Trampoline because of his prowess on that equipment. Hewitt and Browne maintained an uneasy truce. Some bachelor staff lived in and took an energetic part in out-of-school activities. Others were married and, with one or two honourable exceptions, drove through the gates homeward bound in the late afternoon and were not seen again until the following morning. Except at the top, where there was a genuine problem – although kept well under control – there was great accord between the seamen and the academics. I grew to admire the dedication of both groups and became particularly friendly with the senior history master, Paul Kingsford, who had been captured on the eve of the Battle of El Alamein while serving with the Duke of Wellington's Regiment – the 33rd of Foot, as I well remember. My academic mentor, Pat Murphy, who taught the seniors navigation, was a much rougher diamond than most of the others, had no illusions about the cadets and, as an ex-Orient Line officer, could bridge the gap between uniform and academic gown and criticise both with impunity. His Irish wit helped.

The cadets came in all shapes and sizes, from every part of the country and most parts of the old British Empire. They joined as 'new chums' at 15 and left two years later. For the merchant service they were first-class material but lacked some of the fundamentals of ordinary secondary education. Any advantage they might have enjoyed over the grammar school new entrants had evaporated by the time they finished their apprenticeship. What they never did lose, though, was an identity. They left as proud *Conways*, and would so remain for the rest of their lives. Little of this was immediately obvious at the beginning of my first term. The experience was so new and exciting that I imbibed the atmosphere through a process of osmosis.

Expeditions into the mountains were a feature of early autumn term. Some cadets and a surprising number of the younger staff were enthusiastic about serious rock climbing and hill walking and their standards were higher than those to which I had been accustomed. For the cadets, rowing the ship's six-oared gigs was an important exercise, *Conway* pride in oarsmanship being second only to their justified conceit about their rugby prowess. The First XV were quite capable of taking on, and occasionally beating, first-class teams from the RAF station at Valley in Anglesey and the Royal Artillery establishment at Ty Croes. The great rival, however, at both rugby and rowing was *Worcester*, the other cadet training ship in the Thames. The annual rugby match, alternating between Greenhithe and Plas Newydd, was an event of more importance than the exams. From his tiny cabin at the after end of the maindeck Paul Kingsford edited a popular weekly wall newspaper in which these activities were faithfully reported and, on my nights aboard, I produced short pieces and a cartoon in colour which eventually became a weekly feature. It was all rather adolescent, but after all so was the school.

At home Cath did more house-keeping on behalf of Elunyd than she should and found herself entertaining the old lady most evenings for supper. Elunyd was lonely and Cath must have seemed a wonderful piece of good fortune to her. I am not sure that she took the same view of Geoffrey who was a healthy, boisterous, noisy small boy. Within weeks he had begun to develop a Welsh accent and, as the children learned nursery rhymes in Welsh at school, quickly came to understand that the baker, in particular, was good for a bun or a sweet cake if he performed in the shop.

On board we were soon at examination time and, shortly afterwards, at the stage of writing end-of-term reports, a duty which exercises the ingenuity of every schoolmaster in the land. Suitable phrases were bandied about, relished, rejected or copyrighted. My own favourite was one of Pat Murphy's – 'Effort negligible; results commensurate'.

The Spring term of 1953 was dominated by an event scheduled to take place during the Easter vacation. The *Conway* had last been dry-docked in 1941 and was overdue for another examination. This could be done only in Liverpool or Birkenhead and the task of towing the ship there and back was formidable. She drew 19 feet and, from her mooring off Plas Newydd, would have to negotiate the narrowest part of the Menai Strait between the Tubular Bridge which carried the railway and Telford's Suspension Bridge half-a-mile further north, which carried the main road. As the tidal race through the Swellies Channel could reach seven knots it was important to know the velocity throughout the entire range of the tide so that the most propitious time for making the passage could be selected. Taking soundings and current rates became part of the curriculum that term. By early March the weather had improved and preparations for the move became more urgent. Strangers from Liverpool came on board for conferences with Captain Hewitt - pilots, tug masters, nautical advisers from the offices of Alfred Holt & Company, and the local press. The date was set for around April 13 when the spring tides would give us the greatest depth. Term ended and off the cadets went again, a small number of volunteer seniors remaining behind to help with the move. The weather deteriorated around April 10 and, the day before the move was due to take place, the operation was postponed for 24 hours. By the evening of April 13 conditions had improved although there was still some wind from the northwest. Two tugs had arrived from Liverpool and at six o'clock next morning they were secured, the *Dongarth* forward and the *Minegarth*

aft to steer since the ship's rudder was immobilised and locked in the 'midships position. At 0730 in a gentle breeze the journey to Birkenhead began as the *Dongarth* took up the tow and headed for the entrance to the Swellies Channel and the passage under the two bridges. To those ashore it must have presented a brave spectacle and for those of us on board it was a moment of excitement and exhilaration.

I was in charge of the after mooring party which had secured the *Minegarth* by taking in her three-and-a-half inch wire through one of the aft-facing gun ports in the sick bay, passing it nine or ten times round the heel of the mizzen mast and then stoppering it off further forward. We could see little, having a view only through the two gun ports. At first the shore seemed to be slipping along nicely astern but an occasional plume of black smoke from the lead tug suggested the application of extra effort to get the ship through without further delay. Our lengthy observations had suggested that at High Water Springs we could expect a stand of tide of about 14 minutes, in that part of the channel between the bridges, before the south-going ebb started away. The tidal current built up rapidly in the Swellies Channel and it was vital for the ship to be north of the Menai Bridge before that happened. A speed of almost two knots was required between the bridges if that section was to be negotiated during the stand of tide. The ship passed under the Tubular Bridge a minute or two later than scheduled and the tugs urged her gently onto a heading towards the Menai Bridge. But the atmosphere was beginning to intensify. The Caernarvon bank, to starboard, was slipping past painfully slowly. The billowing smoke from the tugs was thicker and the *Minegarth* sheered from side to side, struggling to keep the *Conway* on a straight course for the bridge. The water was flowing swiftly past the ship but the Caernarvon bank was now stationary. The *Dongarth* could barely hold her. The ebb tide had come away already. Our calculations had made no allowance for the effect of a strong north-westerly wind blowing continuously for more than 24 hours. An estimated 14-minute stand of tide had been reduced to three or four and we were caught in the worst part of the channel with nowhere to go but ahead and insufficient power available to achieve that.

A breathless messenger arrived from the poop deck instructing us to let go the *Minegarth* so that she could tow in tandem with the other tug but that was easier said than done. Lacking direct communication with the tug it was difficult to peruade her master to come ahead and ease the tension on the wire so that it could be slipped from around the mizzenmast. At last we managed to cast off, the last turns smashing the sick bay into match-wood as they flew clear through the gun port. Eventually, the *Minegarth* coupled up in tandem with the *Dongarth* to double the amount of towing power but the rudderless *Conway* yawed wildly in the current. A hundred yards ahead the Menai Bridge, black with onlookers, loomed over the bow sprit. The two tugs strained on their wires, heeling heavily with the effort as the current caught them on one bow or the other. The ship continued to yaw, the stern swung wildly to port, the current took hold under the port bow and, despite the Herculean straining of the tugs, she could not be held. She sheered in towards the Caernarvon shore and, with a wild grinding, drove hard up onto the bank, her bowsprit penetrating the branches of the overhanging trees. At once the tugs slipped their wires and stood off in the stream leaving the *Conway* hard aground on a rapidly falling tide. Soundings confirmed the ship's parlous position. For almost half her length forward she was fast aground on what appeared to be a rock shelf. Abaft the mainmast the water deepened suddenly and it was obvious what would happen as the tide fell. High water had been at 0900: low water would be about 1500.

By 1100 the *Conway* was beginning to creak and groan as the strain came on the inadequately supported after end. We were frenziedly evacuating everything loose in the ship assuming she would open up with the next flood. Our three motor-boats and some local craft from Menai Bridge ranged alongside while our volunteer crew passed valuables and equipment through open ports and over the bow. By noon the noises from the ship were more ominous and, early in the afternoon, one of the steel pillars on the maindeck bent perceptibly and then sheared with a loud report as the deckhead dropped an inch or two. The ship's back was broken and the pressure of her own weight downwards had begun to pancake the decks into each other aft. At 1400 Captain Hewitt ordered everyone ashore until the tide began to make again after low water. Two hours later we were all back on board salvaging as much as possible before the next high water. Some 30 or 40 men and boys, with three or four motor-boats, might attempt miracles but they could not empty the ship of all her contents and by late afternoon the tide was rising again through the riven hull. In the early evening I remember passing over an original Russell Flint watercolour of the *Conway*. He had painted it many years before when his son, later a distinguished artist himself, had been a cadet on board. Wherever it hangs now, it must speak eloquently of that stout old wooden ship.

The struggle went on long after darkness had fallen. About 2100 a boat came alongside and three figures climbed slowly on board. Captain Hewitt, knowing who was expected, was at the brow. The leading figure was Mr Lawrence Holt who looked desolate. The ship had been a love of his life and he never really recovered from the shock of her loss. Soon we began to evacuate her for the night. The fuel supply to the generator was set with enough diesel to ensure that the gangway was cleared and we were all in the last boat before it ran out. With the boat punching into the stream the low hum of the ship's generator died away as the fuel supply was exhausted, the lights flickered, slowly faded to orange and then went out abruptly. The ship had died.

Hewitt would live with the memory of that day for the rest of his life. If the tidal information had been better the outcome might have been different. Had three tugs been engaged instead of two, or a further 24 hours' delay been accepted to allow the effect of the north-westerly wind to be dissipated. Men who must make decisions are hostages to fortune and the gods were looking the other way on that April morning long ago, but my sympathies have always been with Hewitt.

The next two days were days of salvage. We stripped the ship as clean as the time between high tides allowed: what was taken off ended up in half the church halls and empty garage spaces of the district; but with the ship gone we faced a daunting problem. In less than two weeks 350 cadets would return from Easter leave. They had to be accommodated and an emergency plan was drawn up to begin the summer term in an encampment in the grounds of Plas Newydd. I was not then aware of the power of the 'old boy' network, but watched the results with admiration. In less than a week we were unloading army vehicles from Ty Croes laden with sufficient Royal Artillery tents to house the 200 senior cadets who would normally have been on board. We strove mightily under the direction of patient army sergeants to pitch 22 large tents in a ten-acre meadow half-a-mile from the Marquis of Anglsey's house. The start of the summer term had been postponed for several days but, when the cadets eventually returned, it was to a well-ordered encampment. At the time I was proud of our achievement: the returning cadets thought less of it, at least to begin with.

At once it became clear that control of the cadets in camp would be difficult. On board, once 'Taps' had been sounded, there was little scope for getting into trouble. Under canvas the boundary to be defended by the authorities was infinitely greater and more easily breached. The encampment could only be a temporary arrangement and the cadets set about making the most of it. Meanwhile our tranquility was further disturbed by the elaborate preparations being made for Queen Elizabeth's coronation in May, 1953. I recall only three things about the coronation but I recall them clearly – it was raining most of the time, Sir Rhoderick McGrigor, the First Sea Lord, almost lost control of his huge black horse ('What price the cruel sea now, Roddie?' shouted some wag in the crowd) and Queen Salote, despite Noel Coward, did not eat her travelling companion in the landau for lunch.

I have the happiest memories of the summer of 1953. The sun shone a great deal; I fell in love with North Wales; I learned to drive and sat the test successfully in Bangor on early-closing day when we passed only one other car - which was parked! The encampment continued to be difficult to administer but there were compensations in the opportunity it offered to study nature. A group of cadets represented the ship at the coronation naval review at Spithead. After the review the Queen made a progress about her realm and, when she and Prince Philip came to North Wales, *Conway* was requested to mount a guard of honour on the Caernarvon to Bangor road along which she would drive. The exercise, organised meticulously, rehearsed until perfect, was over in the blink of an eye. Prince Philip acknowledged the salute but the Queen was looking the other way.

Soon the term would end but not without those tribal gatherings and ceremonies inseparable from Summer term at any self-respecting English public school. Prize Day was the major occasion and that year the guest of honour was Admiral of the Fleet Sir Arthur John Power, a splendid larger-than-life character fit to put the fear of God into everyone in the establishment. A day or two later my annus mirabilis came to an end. Cath was delighted to return to our much superior Glasgow flat and Geoffrey did not care where he went so long as there was diversion. By now his Welsh accent was marked and his repertoire of nursery rhymes in the language extensive. But Hyndland Primary School, for which he was destined in six weeks' time, would put an end to that although not before he managed to extract chocolate from Scottish shopkeepers by reciting verse in a Welsh accent in much the same way as he had taken buns from the baker in Bangor. I departed with mixed feelings about the value of *Conway* training. It was tough, traditional, well-tried and turned out useful sailors, but the educational level was not high and many of the boys would have learned more at an ordinary school. Nevertheless, it did mark a young man for life in the way that membership of any elite does - and none the worse for that, in my view. My own horizons had been widened and I was ready to return to sea more confident than had I never seen the Menai Straits. For that I have been grateful all my life.

Early in August I joined the *British Resource*, a rather smart 16,000-tonner, more luxurious and better equipped than anything in which I had yet served. Although I had enjoyed my year in *Conway* I was glad to be spared the pressures of controlling teenagers. An adult crew of 45 was easier and there were no new lessons to prepare each night. Ben Naylor, her master when I joined, was a sweet-natured, avuncular man easy to get along with. There was also a particularly cheerful second mate, George Buckenham – aptly known as Henry the navigator – later to have a distinguished career in the development of the North Sea oil fields. Sadly, Ben Naylor went on leave after only a month or two and was succeeded by a wild, larger-than-life character. Captain D for Duncan, C for Cameron, McIver, a squat pugilist of a man in his mid-50s, and from the Black Isle, had served his apprenticeship in sail, with hands like hams to prove it. His idea of discipline was that of the bucko mate dispensing fists and belaying pin soup to recalcitrant crew members stepping out of line. Unimpressed by the officers and crew he had inherited it was clear from the beginning that we had to prove something to him early in our relationship. His bark turned out to be a great deal worse than his bite, however, provided one stood one's ground and could justify one's actions. His 'hardcase' personality was at odds with a sophisticated approach to navigation for he carried with him some advanced astro-navigation tables unfamiliar to me. I realised I was being tested when these were slapped down on the chartroom table with the suggestion that I work my star sights by his methods. After a night or two the tables began to yield results and my stock went up half-a-notch. Gradually we got used to each other. His style of coastal navigation consisted of rounding every headland or turning point as closely as the depth of water allowed and taking short cuts through passages which, though safe, were normally circumvented by more prudent, or nervous, navigators. He was a bold one, was Duncan. Steaming eastwards along the South Arabian coast on one occasion, I went on watch at 1600 reaching the bridge by the starboard or off-shore ladder. Through the wheelhouse I saw the rim of a sand dune filling the entire bank of port-side windows. If the dunes were as close as that then we must certainly be aground. 'Christ Almighty!' I muttered, my heart missing several beats. I rushed through the wheelhouse, looking for the second mate. In the port wing of the bridge the captain was leaning on the forward dodger crooning softly to himself. The shore appeared to be about half-a-mile away and, through the binoculars, chocolate-coloured babies could be seen near the water's edge while their veiled mothers in black robes shaded their eyes to get a better view of the ship which was almost on their beach.

'What's the matter, Mate?' asked McIver.

'How did we get in here?' I stuttered.

'Ach, man - ye're timid,' he grinned, 'I've just come in here to show you young fellows what the coast looks like – so that you'll recognize it in the monsoon.'

'In the monsoon I'll be 15 miles off,' I said uncharitably.

'Timid, timid!' was all he would say, but we reset the course to a more respectable distance off the coast and he stumped away having enjoyed his afternoon joke.

The *Resource* I thought a first-class ship, soundly built by Hawthorn Leslie's on the Tyne – one of the better British shipyards – a year or two earlier. Having enjoyed Naylor's short sojourn and become accustomed to Duncan McIver's little idiosyncracies I looked forward to putting in a full year in her but, after only eight months, I was transferred in rather unusual circumstances. About that time Anglo-Iranian had sold a substantial tonnage of crude oil to Argentina, hitherto not an important market for us. This crude was being shipped from Kuwait to La Plata near Buenos Aires - known then as Eva Peron - in T.2s or in the deepest draughted ships, like the *Resource*, capable of entering the River Plate. Early in the spring of 1954, en route for the Gulf, we were ordered to load a full cargo for Eva Peron. When the captain passed on the decoded message I grinned and said, 'That's it then, I can't go.' 'What d'you mean, you can't go?' he growled.

I then had to explain that, having been born in the Argentine, I was liable for military service there at 18. Since reaching that age I had received one or two sets of call-up papers, which I had ignored, instructing me to report for duty in Buenos Aires. By 1954, therefore, technically I had been a deserter for 11 years. This amused DC.

'Och here, man - you don't want to transfer. Stay where you are,' he suggested. 'If there's any trouble you can join their navy and do your two or three years. God, lad, you'd be an admiral in no time at all.'

In the end he signalled London and in Kuwait I changed places with the chief officer of the *British Tradition* then lying at one of the seaward buoy berths. She was not the *Resource* and the man I exchanged with got the better of the bargain. Late that evening I set about loading the *Tradition* to the plan my predecessor had made, stipulating only that the shore controller start delivering at no more than 500 hundred tons an hour until I was sure the valve settings in my strange new ship were correct. The signal given, I checked the forward group of tanks with the pumpman to ensure they were receiving oil. After a minute only a trickle had appeared when, suddenly, there was a loud report from aft. Through the deck floodlights I saw a fountain of black oil erupting abaft the bridge and the pumpman and I raced to the seat of the disaster. The berthing master, who stayed on board throughout a sea berth loading, had already pressed the emergency crash-stop button and the geyser of oil was starting to subside. But the afterdeck had filled with crude, the ship having been sprayed with the stuff which was beginning to spew out of the scuppers into the harbour, despite the wooden plugs previously cemented in against just such an emergency. Hell was let loose ashore and the emergency drill activated in case of ignition of the crude oil gas from the spillage. This was a major incident and I wondered what I had done to cause such a catastrophic failure. The crew and the shore services were at work within minutes to clear the oil into empty tanks when it became possible to investigate the cause. The manifold connection on the ship's deck, to which one of the 10in cargo lines had been connected, had sheered. Further enquiry established that the shore controller had started delivering at 3,000 tons per hour instead of the 500 I had requested. The sudden stress had been too much for the manifold but it took all night and about 500 gallons of kerosine to clean the ship. Next morning we received a letter exonerating us, the only time I ever heard of a shore installation accepting responsibility for anything. It could have resulted in a major disaster and was an unpropitious start but the homeward passage made up for it. Captain Saunders was a sunny-natured soul; an excellent Indian crew painted the ship from bow to stern and by the time we arrived in England all traces of the incident had been erased. That was the sort of job they liked.

My arrival home was clouded by an enigmatic instruction to report to London, once the ship was safely in dry-dock, for interview. There was no pat-on-the-back session with the chief marine superintendent this time as I explained the hideous complications of my Argentine birthplace to Jimmy Aitken in charge of deck officer appointments.

'This won't do, Mr King,' he said disapprovingly, 'People have to be able to go anywhere at anytime – absolutely anywhere.' He was not impressed by my plea that the staff department had known my place of birth when I joined and had not then been concerned. He countered by telling me that the Argentine had not been important then, but was now! I thought it too bad that I couldn't change my place of birth as readily as the company opened up new trade routes and altered its priorities but that appeared to cut no ice either.

'You'll have to fix it up while you're on leave,' he said finally,

'Otherwise we may have to take you out of the main fleet.'

This sounded threatening until he appeared to have a brain wave.

'How would you like an appointment in the Gulf?' he asked with a curious look.

'What sort of appointment?' I asked shortly.

'Well, the *Relume,* the lighthouse tender at Bahrein, will need a new master shortly. That's a nice job,' he said persuasively. 'What about command of the *Relume*?'

I knew her, a fine if elderly little white-painted ship, rather like a pre-war steam yacht with lifting gear over the bow, a good deal of accommodation, a buff funnel and a busy schedule servicing the navigational marks in the Persian Gulf and the Gulf of Oman. For a second I was tempted by the idea of a command at 29, but I was not sure whether Jimmy was doing me a favour or filling an awkward slot.   Although an easy way out of my Argentine problem, I thought it unlikely to favour my long-term interests so declined, which ended the discussion. By late afternoon I was on the train for Glasgow.

My mother, who had been back in Ayr since the end of the war, was upset by the Argentine impasse, took the matter personally and got in touch with her own MP, Sir Thomas Moore, who, with the aid of the Foreign Office, persuaded the Argentine Embassy to waive my obligation to serve provided I agreed to being listed in their Naval Reserve.   Without hesitation I concurred and was issued with an Argentine serviceman's paybook while vowing privately that the shores of Argentina would never see me under any circumstances. I think Jimmy Aitken was disappointed at not being able to solve two problems with one brilliant solution, but we both lived long enough to become colleagues and friends in due course.

Soon after my arrival home I received a letter from a George Bonwick whose letterhead proclaimed him to be managing director of the Maritime Press. He wanted to publish a book on oil tankers, was looking for an author and his friend Ronald Marsh had suggested my name: would I be interested? I replied that it sounded challenging, I would give it some thought and, if I had any bright ideas, would send him a synopsis. I promptly forgot all about it in the process of enjoying my leave. One modest joy was to meet Geoffrey from school each afternoon. On the first occasion Cath and I waited outside the school while a mob of diminutive figures tumbled over each other squealing as they sighted the light of freedom. In the first half-dozen I spotted my own son, cap askew, coat half on, stockings crumpling towards the ankles, rubber overboots flapping because he couldn't fasten the press studs and his school bag flailing in some dispute. He looked like William Brown – they all looked like William Brown or his friend Ginger. Quite unconscious of our presence he continued laying into the other small boy until I called through the railing, 'Here, what's all this?' in a gruff voice. Five or six small heads swung round like startled rabbits. It took a second or two for Geoffrey to recognize us but, when he did, he broke into a shy grin, abandoned the fight and ran through the wrought-iron gates to greet us. It was all very satisfying which was why we contrived to be there most afternoons throughout my leave. Some part of that overlapped the school holidays so we all managed to get away together, no further than Ayr where I remembered the publisher and my promise to him. With less than a week's leave left I bought a notebook and, on impulse, a second-hand typewriter and started putting together my ideas. I had some notions of what I would want to read myself and I set these down under 14 chapter headings with a brief synopsis of each. This I mailed off to George Bonwick who responded at once asking me to go ahead as proposed.

My orders were to join the *British Piper* in dry-dock in Birkenhead. As she was not expected to sail for a week or ten days, Cath and Geoffrey came too. Geoffrey instantly struck up a friendship with Margaret Clear, the chief engineer's wife, a stout, motherly person who thoroughly spoiled him. She and her husband, Noel – or 'Not Too Clear' as he interpreted his own initials – were west country folk and our friendship was to last for many years. Clear's second engineer was a humorous, anarchical Ulsterman called David McCallum who claimed, among other things, that he had played the tambourine in a Salvation Army band outside the Belfast taverns until he discovered that there was more fun inside than outside whereupon he took up beer and abandoned his tambourine. If the two senior engineers were jolly and excellent company the master, Denis Ayres, a slim, dark Welshman with sensitive features, was more withdrawn and quiet, his most exotic affectation being a long cigarette holder which he manipulated in Noel Coward style although there was nothing of the queen bee about Denis. After sailing for the Persian Gulf I got down to

194

considering what I had let myself in for with George Bonwick. Since our first exchange he had told me that he was hoping to start a new technical magazine and would first like to publish what I wrote, if suitable, in monthly parts, republishing in book form on completion of the series. I saw no reason to object but noticed that no mention had been made of payment for either. From Bonwick's point of view I was an unknown quantity, but my early impressions of publishing were that the cards were stacked heavily on the publisher's side and certainly not on that of the author. The first two chapters of my synopsis covered the development of tankers and their physical characteristics but I decided to kick off with the third chapter, how to measure oil in a ship. This was something I did every day and needed no source material. It was a fortunate decision since I was able to write four or five chapters from experience returning, later, to the first two chapters which needed research. Immediately after lunch each day, when those not on watch took a nap for an hour or two, I closed my cabin door and wrote. After coming off watch in the evening I did the illustrations. Thus I managed to deliver two chapters in six weeks and then follow up with one a month thereafter so that the magazine series could be sustained. This discipline eventually became addictive. The book took 13 months to write by which time I had completed my tour in the *Piper* – not my favourite ship but the model for much of the contents of the first edition of *Tanker Practice*. Thereafter I joined the *British Cavalier*, sister-ship of the *Dragoon* in which I had served in 1950. The articles were published in book form the following year, but I always had a slight regret that they had been written on board the *Piper* and not, say, the *Resource*. Since it was essentially a practical hand-book the model on which all the calculations and descriptions were based was the *British Piper* whose vital statistics became those of the *Procyon* the name I chose for the book's sample ship.

A day or two before the end of that leave in 1955 Cath and I bade farewell to my brother, Terry, and his wife, Morag, who were leaving to try their luck in Canada where her brother was already established as an accountant. Terry had gone from Dumfries Academy to Southampton University in 1944, passed through Cranwell a year later and had been a pilot in the RAF until a short time before. Repeated short-service commissions, in the early 1950s, made for an uncertain future, hence Canada's attraction

The *British Cavalier* was lying in Falmouth. Her reputation, like her two sisters, was poor, principally because of her unreliable engines. She too had an Indian crew and a good one at that, despite the low opinion held of them by the chief officer I relieved, a miserable soul who seemed reluctant to leave the ship. Eventually, he disappeared leaving one of the untidiest and most uncomfortable cabins it had been my misfortune to inherit. The pilot's cabin on the bridge was my temporary quarter while he was on board and I decided to remain there, in the meantime. Sending for the deck serang and the Chinese carpenter I told them what was wanted – the cabin stripped, re-decorated from deckhead to scupper and then put together again properly. The work in progress would have to be kept hidden from the dockyard labour, of course, or we could have a strike on our hands. They entered into the spirit of the thing and took half-a-day to clear the cabin down to bare bulkheads. Less than a week later, I returned to an immaculate and comfortable abode which served me beautifully for a year. The final touches had to be done in a hurry because I had sent for Cath on discovering that the *Cavalier's* docking would be prolonged. Thus we had two weeks settling in, with two other congenial couples, the second and third mates, Peter Gladwin and Bill Barker, and their wives Pamela and Eileen. Some friendships are transitory – on board ship most are; but the friendships we made then, in the *British Cavalier*, have lasted all our lives.

Captain Karl Wood, a slight, fair-haired bachelor in early middle age, appeared to bear the burdens of the world upon his shoulders. This became easier to understand on learning that he had been a Japanese prisoner-of-war for three years and had suffered abominably. My two younger colleagues had great difficulty with him but even they eventually appreciated that the captain's wartime experiences had affected his whole outlook. Jim Johnson, the chief engineer, a Viking-looking Tynesider and a man with his own troubles in view of the vagaries of the Werkspoor engine, also understood Karl Wood and we quickly settled down into a cohesive group.

One other character among that ship's company remains firmly in my memory – the Chinese carpenter, Ah Tong. I do not know why Indian-crew ships like the *Unity* and the *Cavalier* carried a Chinese carpenter, although I am sure I should. The Mazagon Dock in Bombay must have turned out shipwrights as from a production line but the carpenter was never an Indian, always a Chinese. Ah Tong looked like one of Genghis Khan's fiercer warriors with a thin, droopy moustache and hooded Mongolian eyes. His speech was quick, guttural and aggressive. To understand him was a major feat but, with the exception of Leo Galvin in the *Asphalion*, he is the only ship's carpenter I can recall with total clarity, a superb and absolute original. He came to my cabin one morning while the serang and his men were redecorating it. 'Sir,' he roared, fierce eye flashing, 'no Sunderland water in the lumbertrees!'

I had not the faintest idea what he was talking about and Sunderland was 500 miles away.

'No Sunderland water!' he cried in mounting impatience, 'no Sunderland water in the lumbertrees!'

Eventually he persuaded me to come and see the lumbertrees without the Sunderland water. It was simple. For some reason the gravity tank on the upper bridge had not been filled. There was no sanitary water in the lavatories. 'All the same I speak you - no Sunderland water in the lumbertrees.' Oh well, his English was better than my non-existent Cantonese.

In the fulness of time we got the *Cavalier* to sea but in the next ten months she carried only three cargoes and spent much of her time under repair. She always looked smart, though, since there was plenty of in-port time in which to tart her up! By early May 1956 she was due for dry-docking once more, having been home in Falmouth over Christmas with yet another machinery breakdown. The Indian crew, who had spent almost a year polishing the ship, were putting the final touches to their work as we steamed up the Red Sea. I often used to spend half-an-hour, during the day, on the focs'lhead looking aft and admiring their handiwork or, occasionally, looking over the bow at the forefoot cleaving the blue water. It was a private pleasure and I have a vivid memory of enjoying it one afternoon, singing to myself the Hoagy Carmichael tune, *Meet Mr Callaghan* of which I knew only the first line, just like my father before me. I went 'midships again, well pleased with the ship, the serang, the crew, life in general, and even Karl Wood. I had just reached my cabin when the radio officer came to the door with a message form in an envelope and a very enigmatic expression. I opened the cable. Terry had been killed in a flying accident near Winnipeg while piloting an RCAF aeroplane. The bottom fell out of my world and the perfect day of but a few moments before had gone forever. There were no details in the message from Cath but I was to hear it all in due time.

Two aircraft piloted by RCAF pilots, both former RAF pilots, were returning from an exercise with four other RAF pilots in Canada for an advanced navigation course. One was above and behind the other when air traffic control talked them both towards the same runway. Neither was aware of the presence of the other and they collided two miles short of the perimeter. They crashed, exploded in flames and there were no survivors. Terry was 29 and had lived for flying all his adult life. My home-coming that year was the saddest I ever experienced, my mother inconsolable.

That summer Nasser nationalised the Suez Canal. The day it was announced an elderly lady, a stranger, stopped me in a Glasgow street and asked, 'Does this mean there'll be another war?' I made reassuring noises but was by no means convinced. The ominous beat of a distant drum was in the air and, by the time I joined the *British Maple*, the last and best of the post-war 12,000-tonners, the drumbeats had quickened. Until my eyes fell upon

• *John Terence King*

the *Maple* I was disappointed not to find myself in the super tanker league. Those ships, of 32,000 and 35,000 tons, were an enormous attraction but either I was not good enough or senior enough for one of them. The *Maple* made up for my disappoinment. I followed a chief officer with a reputation far above average, borne out by the condition of the ship. Ralph Maybourn was one of the few officers in the company in those days who held an Extra Master's Certificate. His other claim to fame was that he owned a Jowett Javelin motor car, a mark of his lengthy bachelorhood now about to end. The ship's arrival was delayed, Maybourn's wedding day loomed close and by the time I boarded he had gone. His virtues were diplomatically impressed upon me by Captain Thomas Govan who clearly thought the world of him. It would be an uphill task to match his prowess but Tommy Govan turned out to be a delight to serve under. A small, dark, Irish leprechaun with an attractive accent and bright, twinkling eye, he was badly crippled by arthritis and walked with a decided stoop which did not interfere with his capacity to command. Widely read he was an accomplished pianist and took a violin to sea with him which he also played competently but privately behind a closed cabin door. I knew I had made the grade a few months later when I was invited to listen to him play, the first anyone on board was supposed to know that he had a violin although its muffled notes could be heard most evenings as Tommy practised his repertoire.

We started with two consecutive trips to the Baltic and, while in Stockholm expecting to return to the UK, were ordered to Galveston, Texas to load clean oil. Since the *British Maple* had spent her life in the so-called black oil trade, carrying crude oil and heavy fuel, preparation for a clean cargo was a tall order for one transatlantic voyage in the late autumn. Tank cleaning on this occasion involved steaming out each compartment with a 40-gallon drum of caustic soda suspended within it, the steam jet delivering through the caustic. Then the compartment was spray-washed with first hot and then cold sea water until the steel work was cleared of every vestige of waxy, black oil. With half the tanks thus cleaned, the pipelines were washed through thoroughly and clean seawater ballast pumped into the oil-free compartments. The remaining tanks were similarly treated and the pumps and pipeline system dealt with. The consumption of bunker fuel and boiler water to accomplish this task in less than a fortnight was prodigious and when we finally berthed at Port Isabel, Louisiana, we were down to our last 20 tons or so of both fuel oil and fresh water having eaten far into our reserves. The reason for this emergency exercise had not been hard to divine. The closing of the Suez Canal was imminent; the long haul of crude oil from the Persian Gulf to Europe had already been initiated but, in the short term, smaller ships of not more than 30 feet draught were required to move refined products from the US Gulf ports to make up the short-fall in Europe. The Suez crisis had by now erupted into military action. On top of that came news of the Hungarian uprising. Listening to the BBC World Service and the increasingly hysterical outpourings of local US stations I came to dislike John Foster Dulles heartily and was sadly disappointed when the British and French advance along the Suez Canal was halted. If Eden's exercise had been a ghastly error, lack of resolution wrecked its chances. The baleful influence of Dulles on his master, Eisenhower, was an easy subject for blame.

Throughout that winter the *British Maple* plied to and fro across the Atlantic between the Gulf of Mexico and Rotterdam, three times steaming up-Channel past the English coast without calling at a home port, a strange and desolate experience and especially so because of the intimidating fragility of the international situation. The spring was well adanced when we received orders to load at New Orleans for a European discharge port to be nominated later, but with a clear indication that the ship would then dry-dock in the UK.

Having loaded a full cargo of gas oil, and with a Mississippi pilot on the bridge, the *British Maple* cast off from her loading berth about 0200, edged into the strongly-flowing river and headed upstream in the direction of the Huey Long Bridge, a mile or so away. Here there was a turning basin where she could be swung to head downstream towards the sea. On the focs'lhead the forward mooring party secured for sea, the carpenter readied the windlass to let go an anchor should the pilot require it and I glanced upstream ahead of the ship. I reported to the bridge the lights of a tug on the starboard bow, close to the near bank of the river as I thought, and then walked behind the windlass to see that the steel covers of the rope store had been properly secured. Returning to the bow I became aware of more strange lights nearer midstream and realised that something was not right just ahead. Shining a powerful torch over the bow I was appalled to illuminate a red and white DANGER sign attached to something afloat in the river, and shouted a warning to the bridge.   Stretched across the Mississippi River, borne down on a five-knot current, a string of three laden oil barges, secured in tandem, with one large tug at one extremity and a much smaller one at the other, lay dead ahead only yards away. I roared, 'Let go!' to the carpenter who knocked off the windlass brake and, with a tremendous thunder of cable, the starboard anchor fell to the river bed. At the same instant the ship's bow ploughed into the centre barge whereupon the lashings securing it to the two end barges broke and all three wrapped themselves around the *Maple's* bow.   Fortunately the anchor held and we brought up all standing, one laden 12,000-ton tanker embedded in a 250ft-long barge leaking aviation kerosine furiously into the Mississippi, with the two other barges, similarly laden, banging alongside on each side of the ship. The tugs had cast off and were now trying to re-secure. The carpenter and I picked ourselves up from the foredeck whence we had retreated at the moment of impact anticipating an explosion. Miraculously, there was none and to this day I wonder why not. The aviation fuel in the barges was a grade called JP4 which, at ambient temperature, gives off petroleum vapour in sufficient quantity to create an explosive mixture when mixed with air. One cigarette, one flame from the galley fire, one spark from rending steel would have been enough. Someone up there was watching over us that morning. We dowsed every naked flame and DC electric motor and awaited help. After a nerve-shattering six-hour vigil, two large tugs from New Orleans managed to get the barges under control, prise them from the ship's bow and tow them towards the river bank where the damaged one sank.

Long before then the proximate cause of the only collision in which I was ever involved, had become clear. The three barges, 750ft over all and unlit along that entire length, had been manoeuvered into the river from the Chaumette Cut on the north bank. The small tug was to assist in turning the barge train to head the Mississipi current so that the big tug could push it, in true American Inland Waterway fashion, to its destination upstream. Although two sets of tug steaming lights had been reported a long distance apart no-one, either on the focs'lhead or the bridge, had seen the 750ft of deeply-laden barges, with a freeboard of only a few inches, until it was too late. The ship suffered only negligible damage to the soft nose of the bow above the waterline and was repaired within three days. During that time those of us with any

responsibility in the matter had given depositions before attor
neys. If one had the misfortune to be involved in a collision
thought we, this was the way to do it – entirely innocently with th
other chap making all the mistakes. But that was not how it wa
interpreted. The pilot should have anticipated the likelihood o
barge traffic. The captain should have stopped him doin
whatever he was doing and I should have posted a proper lookou
on the focs'lhead and not divided my attention between river anc
deck. Nothing was said about an underpowered barge train ou
of control in a swiftly flowing river close to a major port. Tha
early morning on the Mississipi River, many years ago, the *Britis*
Maple came within a hairsbreadth of major disaster. But it hadn'
happened and three weeks later we paid off in the Tyne. After ;
winter of tension and North Atlantic weather no-one was sorr
about that.

Chapter 8

SIGNPOSTS ON ONE'S PASSAGE through this world are not always obvious. Had Cath and I but known it the direction of our lives was about to change slowly but inexorably. In 1957, at the age of 32, with six years seniority as chief officer, I still had another four or five years to go before I could look for command, the ambition of every aspiring deck officer. It was now a matter of putting in the miles on the long slog to the summit. George Bonwick had published *Tanker Practice* the previous year, a few weeks after Terry's death. Inevitably, a good deal of the gilt had fallen off the gingerbread. I received encouraging letters from Houston Jackson, managing director of the Tanker Company, and William Hutchison, the chief marine superintendent – God and the Angel Gabriel respectively, as far as I was concerned – but mostly wry looks from my peers who tended to mistrust colleagues with ideas above their station.

'Nothing in the bloody book we didn't know, anyway,' was the comment of one stalwart who felt that he could, and should, have written it himself. In fact the seven-day wonder lasted about three days which at first disappointed me; but I embarked upon a second book for no other reason than that I did not want to admit I was a one-book author. Besides, in a masochistic sort of way, I had welcomed the discipline.

If British Petroleum, as the company was now known, were not exactly overwhelmed, one or two others had had their interest aroused and, while on leave, I was offered a job by an engineering company in London. Tongue in cheek I rang Ronald Marsh and asked him what he knew about them. He said he would find out and let me know. Instead, I received a summons from Britannic House and was rocketed into the London office on a temporary assignment. The work consisted of combing the archives and drafting a skeleton history of the tanker company, an earlier suggestion of my own. Lacking an academic background and without the faintest idea of research methods, the job was taxing but absorbing. It also kept me out of mischief for some weeks while another set of gears were meshing.

I loved London, despite missing my family less than eight hours away by train. Separation is less difficult to bear on board ship where all are in the same predicament. My circumstances in London were made easier by living in an establishment called the Caledonian Christian Club. Run by the Church of Scotland for young men arriving in the metropolis without accommodation, it was located in Endsleigh Street two minutes from Euston station. It had been recommended by Robert Waistel Cooper, a former school friend, now a chartered accountant and himself a resident. The club, once a fine Bloomsbury town house, was full of Caledonians with hardly a Christian in sight! They were a congenial lot, ambitious and impecunious to a man. I fitted in perfectly and shared a room with a junior bank manager called Andrew McIlwraith. A hearty breakfast was provided at 0745 every morning, after which I caught the tube to Moorgate and disappeared into Britannic House or, more properly, River Plate House next door, to put in a day's work, lunching well in BP's excellent dining room and returning to the club at six. I was by no means starving but living in London, even under such circumstances, was not cheap so that my scope was limited; an occasional theatre seat or a weekend visit to friends in some outer suburb was about the limit. Weekends could have been dreary but I spent them visiting every museum and art gallery of which I had ever heard. I could scarcely believe my luck in finding myself living and working in London. To be honest, I was not interested in being in London on my own but, while it lasted, I made the most of it by familiarising myself with the geography of the city.

My career as 'historian' lasted some weeks but I knew that I was bogus. At that time Henry Longhurst, one time assistant librarian at the House of Commons, successful journalist, golf correspondent of the *Sunday Times* and marvellous raconteur, had been commissioned to write a history of the parent company which later appeared under the title *Adventure in Oil*. Introduced to him one day I kept my mouth shut about my own labours. It required no insight to realise that, if ever a history of the Tanker Company were to be published, I was unlikely to be its author. A return to nautical life was the future I would have chosen in any case, despite the offer from the engineering company earlier in the year. But that was not how it happened. One Thursday afternoon in the autumn I was summoned to the general manager's office. Denis Bean was a big man, quiet, self-contained, soft-spoken and enigmatic. His company career had been spent mostly in what was hen called Supply and Development, the logistical planning core of BP's oil production and trading activities. BP Tanker Company, immediately downstream of S & D, existed to move crude oil from production areas to the group's refineries and the refined products to marketing outlets. Bean had come into shipping only a year or two earlier and it was said that his broader view of the oil industry had been good for the more insular shipping people. I knew nothing of that, of course, since ships' people had no insight into what happened in the office.

Bean sat me down and then exploded a bombshell.

What I am going to tell you, King, is confidential,' he said. 'We're proposing to set up a new, small tanker company in Glasgow. Ten ships, perhaps 12, will be transferred and operated from there. The office staff are being appointed from London and your name has been put forward to be put in charge of the personnel department in due course.'

Good God! Most of my life I had looked upon personnel departments as the Great Enemy, their role to be cordially disliked or mistrusted by every pawn on the board they moved at whim. Now Bean was suggesting that I join the gamekeepers when I thought myself a poacher.

'Think carefully about it,' he went on. 'Bissell will be going up to begin with, but he'll hand over to his successor as soon as it's running properly.'

Bissell was a dour, austere individual whom I knew only by sight and reputation since he had nothing directly to do with the appointment of deck officers. The prospect of being his understudy, even if only for a few months, was less than appealing. Nevertheless, here was an offer out of the blue and not sought after by me – in a new office in Glasgow, home territory.

'Are you interested?' Bean asked. Of course I was, but staff work had never been an ambition and, more important, surely this appointment forfeitied my chances of a future command.

'That's why I say, think about it. Talk it over with your wife. Go home for the weekend and let me know next week.'

That evening I walked pensively to Euston Station, caught the Night Scot and presented the facts over breakfast next morning.

Cath made no attempt to influence my decision, knowing how much the idea of command meant to people like me. On the other hand we would not have been human had we not realised the different life we would lead once the satellite company was established in Glasgow and I was there as a founder member. If I turned down such an opportunity I could hardly expect to be offered another. So, yes, I would like to be considered, but it was disappointing to fall at the last fence. Bean was sympathetic but noncommittal. Two or three weeks later, with half-a-dozen others, I moved to the rear of River Plate House where the BP Clyde Tanker Company had offices pending its move north.

The newly-appointed general manager of BP Clyde was a suave, silver-haired Edinburgh man called Robert MacArthur, at that time a BP Tanker fleet manager in London. He was experienced, accomplished, energetic and, as a result of his former involvement with the French BP company, spoke impeccable French – not an attribute of commanding value in Glasgow. His deputy, Captain Dawson Johnson – he who had spirited away the Abadan tug fleet from under the noses of Mossadeq's men – was a handsome man of great charm and engaging personality, looked upon by most deck officers with affection and respect. MacArthur and he made a contrasting team; not entirely compatible, they did not let it show. The rest of us were younger. Arthur James, a rising star in the London company, was responsible for ship management, issuing voyage instructions, loading orders, bunkering and storing guidance and generally handling the logistics of our small fleet. He was assisted by Donald Gillespie, son of a former managing director, Robert Gillespie, now on the main BP board. The marine superintendent, Captain John MacLeod, a Skye man, came with a reputation for competence and calm and spoke in a gentle, attractive Highland accent. His technical assistant, Angus Murray, was a native of Stornoway whose sea career had been interrupted for a year or two by service in the Glasgow police. His Hebridean accent was more marked than John MacLeod's but he had a quiet voice for so rugged a man. Technical matters were the province of two engineer superintendents – Jack Dickinson, the senior, a loquacious Liverpudlian, unsurpassed as story teller and bon viveur, and a first class engineer; and Robin Stevenson, his assistant, brought up in Grangemouth, earnest, devoted, tireless and an even better engineer. The accountants, Bob Stevenson and Ernest Bailey, I knew less well since their office in London was in another building near Aldgate and our paths had seldom crossed. A F Bishop looked after ships' stores and Arthur Bissell looked after me and the young man nominated as my assistant, John Attwood, tall, bespectacled, amiable and able. By no means were we all first choice for the slots we were about to occupy in Glasgow as I learned later.   Certainly I was not, and Arthur Bissell's temporary appointment would not have been necessary had the senior staff man who was first approached been prepared to go.

We settled down quickly in our fourth floor eyrie and throughout the winter gradually took over the management of the ships allocated to us.   Their names were changed, the prefix British becoming Clyde so that the *British Pioneer* emerged as the *Clyde Pioneer* and so on.   The purpose in setting up the new company was two-fold.   First, the main fleet, with 130 ships, was thought too large to manage successfully as a single unit; secondly, at a time of manpower shortage, some advantage was anticipated for a company operating from Glasgow, potentially a good recruiting centre.   Shipmasters would come with the ships but we were encouraged to go out and find other ranks, calling for support from London only when we could not man a ship completely ourselves. We set to with a will, realising that this was an unusual opportunity.   Arthur James and I, both 32, must have been thinking similarly about the situation, and our part in it. One day he said to me that, in his view, if you hadn't made it by the time you were 34, you weren't going to make it at all, with which I agreed wholeheartedly! It is my distinct recollection that we raised the age limit by a year every 12 months until we were satisfied that we had made something, or were reconciled to the alternative – but that was much later.

Privately, Cath and I were excited at the prospect of becoming houseowners and putting the rent book behind us forever. On one of the *British Maple's* visits to Holland the previous year I had received a cheque for £250, my first royalties from *Tanker Practice*. I had never seen so much money at one time with my name attached to it. It became the down payment on the first house we ever owned, a modest, three-bedroomed semi-detached in Jordanhill.   Throughout the winter Cath watched a muddy field converted into a new housing estate of which one plot was ours. In the spring I was granted a week's leave to move in. The smell of newness and the pride of ownership were intoxicating but, when I compared our circumstances with those of my English colleagues, it made me realise that, in Scotland, we had always been far too timid about taking such financial risks. What was wonderful to me was taken for granted by them.

BP Clyde's new offices in Bothwell Street were being refurbished and MacArthur spent much corporate time selecting furniture and office fittings. When I was in Glasgow for our own domestic move I visited the offices and concluded that, if our personal circumstances were modest, my surroundings at work were going to be quite the reverse. The company was due to move north in July but, as I already lived in Glasgow, I was to be sent ahead in June as one of the advance party. My time in London was ending and I redoubled my efforts to know better the city I had come to love. Still a country boy at heart, I was overwhelmed at my own good fortune in being at the heart of what had once been the Empire.

MacArthur and Johnson, supported by the rest of us who thought we had worthwhile opinions to offer, tried to influence selection of the ships which would be transferred to our management. We did not always get what we wanted, but we finished up with a respectable-enough fleet, with its own name pattern, house flag and colour scheme. MacArthur's French exposure had involved him with the small tanker fleet of BP France whose ships had a rather dull colour scheme. He was not satisfied until he had redesigned the BP Clyde funnel, making it green with a yellow band below a black top. It was far from pretty and green, not a traditional British funnel colour, found little favour with seamen. But it was a small matter. We had our own ships, spanking new offices in the heart of Glasgow's shipping district and were issuing our own orders. In my little corner, under Bissell's watchful eye, we had set up a recruiting system, designed our own application forms - which we considered vastly superior to London's - developed an interview drill and already were getting results. Bissell, the hard, professional staff manager, years older than all of us except the two top men, turned out to be a first-class tutor, a dry wit, a good companion and, almost unbelievably, an accomplished clarinet player and saxophonist who had played with better-than-average dance bands. Appearances are not an infallible guide to personality and talent. After a few months I was pleased to be considered a friend by the forbidding Arthur Bissell who had the bearing and the clipped, military moustache of a regimental sergeant major. He was a model of painstaking accuracy to whom my more slap-dash, broad-brush approach must have seemed lacking in discipline. Perhaps we complemented one another, or else he was a great deal more tolerant than I would have given him credit for.

Life took on a different shape. A bus from Jordanhill College to Bothwell Street replaced the Northern Line to Moorgate. In the evening, going home to Jordanhill Drive was immeasurably better than returning to Bloomsbury and the Caledonian Christian Club, useful as that establishment had been.

Cath and I settled down to ordinary family life and Geoffrey, a sunny-natured boy, became used to two parents keeping their beady eyes on him. The pressure of new and interesting work kept me from yearning for the sea. I had moments of regret at having missed command but there were compensations and opportunities. I would rather have been doing John MacLeod's job as marine superintendent, for that was the summit of ambition for most competent chief officers and junior masters, but few were called and fewer chosen. I had opted for the staff appointment before having held command, a necessary qualification for promotion to superintendent; but the future looked secure.

Local recruiting now began in earnest. The BP Tanker Company, as BP's main shipping organisation was now called, had been incorporated as the British Tanker Company in 1915. Between the wars it had grown immensely, with a hiatus during the depression of the early 1930s. The first managers recruited came from Glasgow and Tyneside trampship companies and, able though they were, the Tanker Company inevitably took on some of their flavour and style. In its early years it was seen as a hard employer and only gradually did it develop into one of the bigger names in British shipping, employing men who were prepared to spend their lives in its service. By 1939 it was operating 90 ships of its own of which more than half were lost during the war. After the war there was a drift away from seafaring at precisely the time when such companies were rebuilding their fleets to pre-war level. For a year or two, therefore, there was some dilution in the quality and commitment of staff but, by the late 1950s, good employment conditions and an enlightened training scheme had created a highly professional organisation ashore and afloat. In Glasgow the other side of the industry coin was in evidence but I think we surprised London by the quality of people we engaged. We made mistakes but we learned how to deal with them and the young management team, given their head by MacArthur and Johnson, experimented with methods which would not have found favour in Britannic House. In my case this had to wait until Arthur Bissell completed his six-month tutorial and returned to

London permanently. John Attwood and I were then left to get on with it.

There was a social side too. The London company was in the throes of a major ship-building programme, mostly of bigger ships, a number contracted for with Clyde shipyards. From time to time some of us, accompanied by our wives, would be bidden to a launch party, ever a moving and exciting experience. Robert MacArthur also dispensed hospitality to other Glasgow shipowners and included his department managers in much of this. Once established in their own new homes, both the MacArthurs and the Johnsons had us all to dinner, Mrs Johnson, in particular, intimidating the younger wives by the sophisticated perfection of her dinner parties. To a woman they were afraid to invite the Johnsons back to their more modest homes. All this seemed to be rich living indeed, a measure of my own naivety and unworldliness. Until the previous year I had never attended a cocktail party in my life and I thought it very inside-track and important. Cynicism and déjà vu soon forced me to the conclusion that the cocktail party is the social gathering I can bear least. But it was all great stuff at the time. In any case Arthur James and I had a game plan and a schedule – to make it by the time we were 34. Time was getting short, a few cocktail parties might help.

At home we tried to carve a garden out of a quarter-of-an-acre of builders' rubble. Never having possessed green thumbs I admire the English passion for gardening without wishing to emulate it. I am one of nature's ground clearers, however, and in due time all the half bricks, debris from the concrete mixer, broken tiles, discarded rainwater pipe, assorted beer bottles and pieces of broken machinery had been removed and some semblance of order imposed upon the plot. A lawn – more accurately a patch of grass – was encouraged to grow. Our newly-married neighbours, Margaret and Munro Anderson, shamed us with their high-quality garden design, Margaret being a kind of female Capability Brown. Cath's mother and father had recently bought a small flat in a stout, mid-Victorian, stone building in Perth of which city her mother was a native. Within two or three years of retirement her father was content to live with us during the week and spend his weekends in Perth. Good-natured and easy-going he presented no difficulties, providing me, rather, with a gardening instructor of much experience.

Numerous visitors from London office passed through, curious to see what Robert MacArthur and his conscripts were making of their new venture.   Late that autumn Captain John Ross, now chief marine superintendent, was expected in Glasgow to inspect a new ship at one of the local yards. Captain Johnson warned me to be present on that day because Captain Ross wanted to see me. I took it to be a routine matter and thought no more about it but made sure I wore my best suit (the other one) on the day. At 0930 I was sent for. The 1400 appointment with Captain Ross had been cancelled as he had to return to London urgently. Instead, he saw me on number one platform at Central Station in the half hour before the mid-day train left.

'Want to see if you'd be any good as a marine superintendent – in London,' he announced.

I mumbled incoherently.

'You'll have to do some time as master,' he went on. 'I've spoken to Mr MacArthur and Captain Johnson who are prepared to let you put the time in in one of the Clyde ships. If you're suitable I want you in London a year from now.'

He boarded the train and I was left to collect my scattered wits.

Ross was an unusual man. He had achieved early promotion to chief officer before the war, was in command in his early 30s and had been appointed as marine superintendent in Liverpool by 1941. With intellectual qualities far above average he was a very different animal from his predecessor, William Hutchison, every inch a shellback, every finger a marlin spike. Hutchison was a bluff and colourful personality: Ross gave the impression of controlled intelligence and a strong will. Others argued with him only when they thought they had a perfect case. Inevitably one remembers affectionately, as I do John Ross, those who open up the great opportunities in life. Three or four years later he taught me more in four weeks than I might have expected to glean in the same number of years – but I must not anticipate.

The lights burned late in Jordanhill Drive that night. Cath was delighted if a little apprehensive. Early in the new year I would go back to sea in command of a ship, the goal at which I had long been aiming.   Ultimately, we would have to sell the house and settle down to a London life. Geoffrey would be 11 by that time, due to change from Hyndland School to Glasgow High, even the Academy if particularly bright and we could afford the fees. The future would be very different for us all. With luck it might be better, certainly it would be strange.   The rest of the year disappeared in frenzied preparation for the next stage.

I was concerned to leave a clear desk. Attwood could take over without difficulty. Nevertheless, he and I prepared a plan for the next 12 months. Fairly high on the list we placed – more properly, I placed - my appointment as master of the *Clyde Explorer*, from February until the end of the year, ensuring that the officers being appointed were congenial. Unashamedly, I took an inside track over a long bend in the road, but to me it seemed a defensible perquisite of the office I held, that I should arrange for compatible people in a ship so important to me. I am less sure now.

It was not until March that the *Clyde Explorer* arrived at Isle of Grain where her new master could join her, still recovering from farewell parties. Wearing a Harris tweed overcoat and grey felt hat – to add gravitas, I suppose – I took myself off for distant Kent. Saying goodbye to Cath just before the train left was like being back in wartime except that there was little chance of being killed. I was leaving to seek fame and fortune, not to fight for King and Country. I relieved a man called Candlish who lost no time in handing over and securing my signature against everything which had to be signed for. As we walked round the ship for an hour or so he told me about her idiosyncracies which were few and next morning a taxi arrived at the foot of the gangway and bore him away. I was Master under God and glad that I had made sure of a good chief engineer and chief officer!

That evening we sailed from the Isle of Grain, outward bound for the Hamble. Since Southampton Water is barely 150 miles to the west it was hardly like Christopher Columbus setting out to

• *The British – and Clyde – Explorer*

find his way to the Indies. Nevertheless, it was the first time I had been confined to the bridge with a pilot and expected to enunciate words of command. It had been easy to organise a ship from one deck down, to get everyone to where he ought to be, on time and capable of doing what was expected of him. It seemed quite different to be above the battle, to depend on others to look after the mechanical details and yet to take responsibility for all. At however humble a level, acceptance of ultimate responsibility is sobering. I knew the pilot was experienced and would get us to Folkestone without trouble, the chief engineer dependable and the machinery reliable. I knew the chief officer, Peter Nicholson, was first-class but, for the first time in my life, the buck – perhaps not a big buck but a buck, nevertheless – was going to stop here. And it did, at 0200 the following dark and windy morning as we approached the pilot cutter off Folkestone. The pilot bustled into the orange-lit chartroom and thrust a piece of paper towards me. 'Will you sign my chit, Captain? She's all yours. Quite straight-forward. Engines at dead slow, course from here is about 255°. Have a good trip.' And he was gone.

Check the course. 253° would be better. Get the second mate to lay it off – and the next course. Out to the front of the wheelhouse, check compass on the way past and look into the night as eyes become used to the darkness. Half ahead, port easy. Come round to 253°. The idling main engine throbbed more urgently, tiny rings of exhaust smoke blowing away into the darkness from the dimly discerned funnel as the foremast began to track across the night sky. Away to seaward the steaming lights of other ships marked the way. To starboard Folkestone's sodium vapour street lamps made an orange glow in the sky above the sleeping town and Dungeness light flashed powerfully to the west. Before noon we were berthed safely at Hamble Terminal on Southampton Water, my first sea passage in command of a ship accomplished. Hardly the stuff of legend but the first experience is the daunting one.

The *Explorer* had been nominated to load a rather complicated cargo of various aviation fuels being delivered on a NATO con-tract. Tank preparation would take some days so Cath came south and spent that time on board as we lay alongside at Isle of Grain. It was more fun together under the new regime in a master's suite that would not have disgraced a passenger liner. While the chief officer supervised preparations for loading the chief engineer saw to his engine repairs. My days were comparatively free to do as I pleased once the routine morning mail had been dealt with and I had paid a duty visit to the marine office in the refinery complex. The partially-laden ship was to sail to a US Gulf port, yet to be nominated, and complete loading with more aviation fuel for Mediterranean destinations. It seemed a long way round and an odd example of oil company logistics but all I had to do was follow orders and enjoy a springtime trip across the Atlantic. It was difficult to believe that I was being paid for enjoying myself! Cath had brought the four volumes of Churchill's *A History of the English-speaking Peoples* for my birthday, perfect for the next month or two. I felt I had found my niche at last – and all four volumes were finished in 10 days. The crowning moment of the passage, however, came when the lighthouse near the entrance to the Providence Channel in the Bahamas spiked the horizon in exactly the right place and on cue. The US Gulf ports had become familiar enough when the *British Maple* was trading there in the tense and dismal winter of 1956-7. Loading in Houston, at the inner end of a hair-raising ship channel from Galveston Bay, took little more than a day and we were at sea again, east-bound for Casablanca, Gibraltar, Tangier, Barcelona and Tripoli - which did not seem entirely NATO territory. Late in May we reached Casablanca and the next four or five weeks proved hectic. Morocco presented no problem but the receivers in Barcelona claimed that one parcel of their consignment was off-specification. It could not pass the copper test, whatever that was. I envisaged the fuel tanks of nuclear bombers being eaten away by our contaminated cargo and was chagrined. In such circumstances it is standard practice to blame the ship – inadequately cleaned tanks, water not drained from cargo lines, leaking valves permitting contamination between one grade and another, allocation of the same pump to handle incompatible grades – but Peter Nicholson I knew was meticulous. Without interfering too much – remembering Guy Attwood in the *Councillor* years before – I took a personal interest myself. My indignation must have burned through my diplomacy but still Barcelona refused the cargo. I was instructed to take the lot to the BP refinery at L'Avera near Marseilles, to have it checked and await orders. L'Avera could find nothing wrong with it, to the relief of Peter Nicholson and me; but authority in London decided not to risk Barcelona again so we carried 3,000 tons of aviation gasoline round half-a-dozen ports in the Western Mediterranean, trying to get rid of it piecemeal. Libya proved difficult. Customs in Tripoli wanted nothing to do with the stuff since it was not manifested to that port and was therefore an embarassment. I sat up half the night arguing about it but it was too large a consignment to be accepted for a small consideration of several packs of cigarettes which would have covered a minor manifest discrepancy. Off we went again, like a milk float on its rounds, to offload the gasoline ultimately in Piraeus – no surprise since the Greeks could be relied upon to prefer 3,000 tons of aviation fuel to an impeccable manifest. That exercise was a wonderful slice of experience which I should have missed had I been ploughing backwards and forwards round the Cape of Good Hope in a big ship carrying crude oil. It had been an advantage to know, as friends and colleagues, the head office staff to whom I had to explain my dilemmas and decisions. I realised, as it was happening, that I was more fortunate than other masters. They knew only names, their relations cordial or not according to personalities; but my contacts were my close friends. I had no need to impress anyone, hide anything or be devious for we were on the same side. It was a lesson I never forgot and it assumed greater significance later.

Throughout our Mediterranean trading we basked in continuous, glorious sunshine. It seemed more like a cruise in a private yacht – a rather cumbersome, utilitarian yacht, but well cared for, properly equipped and ably manned. Even in high summer fog is not unknown in the Golfe du Lion and, on one of her approaches to L'Avera, the *Clyde Explorer* ran into an extensive bank. Shortly before it came down the radio officer had been in touch with a Shell tanker some distance astern but within sight. As usual the radio officers exchanged gossip. The master of the Shell ship, also bound for L'Avera, turned out to be Robbie Lumsden, Fowler's predecessor in the *Conway*, a legend in my time. We exchanged civilities and then lost sight of each other in the fog. Lumsden had no radar and I had, but he checked his bearing and distance from me by radio and then we so manoeuvered ourselves that we navigated two ships on one radar. Fortunately there was little traffic; but courageously Robbie followed me for several hours until I told him I thought I was about a mile from the harbour entrance and proposed to anchor for the night. He edged in until he was half-a-mile from the *Explorer* and, faintly through the fog, we heard the rumble of his anchor cable. As dawn broke, clear as spring water, there we were, within a respectable distance of the breakwater, thanks to the application of one radar and two radios. I had a great deal of admiration for Lumsden after that as did our - and Shell's - agent, Maurice Pomme. So impressed was he that he insisted on taking both of us to a splendid fish restaurant where I met Robbie Lumsden, face-to-face, for the first time while we enjoyed the finest bouillabaisse I have ever tasted. Robbie eventually became the Commodore Master of the Shell fleet and I doubt if ever they had a better one. Maurice Pomme, too, a smooth, polished, beautifully-mannered Frenchman with a keen wit and a warm heart, was to become a personal friend. As I write this behind me rests a handsome little model of an 18th century bomb ketch, a gift from him and a memento of the beautiful summer of 1959.

The idyll had to end or, more accurately, enter another phase. Our last call in the Eastern Mediterranean was to the Turkish port of Izmir, once known as Smyrna. The complicated approach I made slowly and cautiously. About a mile from the oil jetty a tiny pilot boat stood out from shore and the pilot, more like a plump, moustachioed merchant from the suk than a seaman, boarded, roared 'Full Ahead' with astonishing bravura and berthed the ship in a flat calm after I had done my own pilotage over a good number of miles. So much for local knowledge. The game was up, though; our cruise was over. We had spent the summer on the wine-dark sea, shooting the Straits of Bonifacio on a Saturday afternoon and the Straits of Messina, 'twixt Scylla and Charybdis', the following week-end with a pleasant visit to Naples in between; lying along-side in Piraeus and, on my part at least, spending one whole wonderful summer's day at the Acropolis; arguing with Customs officials in Morocco; enjoying some of the simpler delights of the south of France in the company of a cultured Frenchman and a quietly-spoken British ship-master; following the milk run in response to Arthur James's intructions from far-away Bothwell Street. Now we were told to proceed through the Suez Canal where we spent a pleasant morning striking sparks off George Robey, making his normal mark-up in Port Said.

Our destination was Aden there to load feedstock for Grangemouth refinery. Horace White, the local marine superintendent was a genial host despite his notion that a good way to spend an afternoon, in a temperature of 110° in the shade, was to climb the Ass's Ears, a small mountain with a double peaked summit –

hence the name – which everyone had used as a navigational mark for decades. The voyage home was almost without incident apart from a single sticky moment off Cape Finisterre where again we ran into thick fog. I decided to pass about 15 miles off. So did everyone else so that, instead of having a concentration zone five miles off Cape Finisterre, the concentration was 10 miles further out and intense. Acutely aware that my future depended on staying out of trouble for another three or four months, I was perhaps over-cautious and obeyed the rules to the letter, no bad thing in the circumstances although not the way to discover the North-West Passage or get to the South Pole first. With the officer-of-the-watch plotting from the radar, the engines on Dead Slow and Stop, we inched through the fog in the manner prescribed by the collision regulations, aware of blips on the screen indicating ships obviously steaming more boldly. One echo, in particular, bore down upon us out of the north-east at a plotted speed of about 12 knots as if it were a clear summer day. Hearing what the second mate and I assumed to be a sound signal foward of the beam, I stopped and went astern to take the way off the ship. As we lay dead in the water, a vast shape loomed over the starboard bow and slid past only feet away, the wash from the phantom's bow-wave breaking over our own low foredeck. It was a close encounter I could well do without, the more so as half-an-hour later we ran out of the fog into a clear, starlit night when the steaming lights of other ships, like coloured jewels, could be seen for miles. In due course, we warped into the oil dock at Grangemouth to be greeted by a small welcoming party of wives, Cath at the head.

The *Clyde Explorer* was not to dry-dock until November so there was time for one extended Baltic voyage as Arthur James had arranged. But our stay in Grangemouth was prolonged by generator trouble which the chief and his people had unsuccessfully tried to repair. Robin Stevenson was despatched from Glasgow to take charge and, as usual, effectively did just that, overhauling the offending equipment in a couple of days. As it looked like being my final round trip in the *Explorer* Cath was on board for the voyage to Sweden. She had left Geoffrey in my mother's care and the sale of our house in that of the solicitors' for, unless something went wrong, we would soon be on our way south.

The machinery repaired, we set sail for Gothenburg, Malmo, Stockholm and points north. Our agent in Stockholm was a charming silver-haired lady-killer called Torsten Sparring, a man over-flowing with old-world courtesy. He adored ladies; ladies adored him and Cath had been a little under his spell since first meeting him three or four years earlier. He and his wife, Britta, invited us to dinner one evening at the Opera House after drinks at their own flat beforehand – and, in those days, breaking the barrier into a Swedish private home was unusual. From Stockholm we were bound for Sundsvall and Umea and, finally to the port of Lulea in the north-west corner of the Gulf of Bothnia, a few kilometers from the Finnish border. Though the late September weather was beautiful, already there was a hint of winter's onset. Torsten Sparring had telexed ahead to all his colleagues in the agencies further north and, on this final voyage, Cath and I enjoyed the most wonderful Scandinavian hospitality. When we finally turned south for the homeward run I savoured every lingering minute of the passage, past the Kvarken Islands and through the Aland Passage near to Mariehamn of the great four-masted sailing ships, south between Gotland and Oland, past Karlskrona and the island of Bornholm to the pilot station at Trelleborg, and through the Sound, with Malmo to starboard and Copenhagen to port and Hamlet's castle of Elsinore ahead, up to the Skaw and out into the North Sea. I concentrated because I knew that this was an experience which I might never repeat. I had navigated happily in the Mediterranean. I had enjoyed passage-making across the Atlantic, Pacific and Indian Oceans. Over the years the Persian Gulf had become Main Street, the Malacca Straits more mysterious and exotic. If the coasts of the British Isles bore the most beloved names and associations of all I had a special affinity for the cold, grey Baltic, for Scandinavia and the bleak shores of Germany, Denmark and Holland. This would probably be the last time I should navigate an oceangoing ship in and out of the Baltic, or anywhere at all for that matter, and I wanted to etch it into my memory.

With the lights of the Tyne Piers five miles away and dead ahead, St Mary's flashing on the bow, the visibility closed in suddenly and ships in the vicinity disappeared from sight, as quickly to reappear when the bank of fog cleared. Stopping the ship was easy for she was lightly ballasted, ready for the river. The astern movement of the engines to take off the way caused her to vibrate heavily and shake the teeth out of every one on board but the Tyne Piers were still where they had always been. From between their ights the pilot cutter appeared and the pilot boarded. He was probably called Purvis because all Tyne pilots seem to be called Purvis. An hour later the ship was secured alongside at North Shields, a gas-free certificate was about to be issued, I had signed the pilot's chit and we had shared the ritual small scotch. When Peter Nicholson came back amidships from the focs'lhead I poured him one too and then, at 0300, went to bed on my last day as a sailor. Although I had not completed the year Captain Ross had decreed, I was to report to Britannic House after a fortnight's leave. My appointment was probationary, of course; if my face did not fit I could be back at sea early in the new year. It had taken more than 18 years to get to this point, the peak of ambition for most seagoing deck officers, and I was not about to give up for want of effort. Besides, we had received a cable from my mother that the house had been sold - and, when a house is sold in Scotland, it is sold. There was no turning back. Our boats were burned.

Chapter 9

NO MATTER HOW WELL TRAVELLED and worldly aware, a provincial, newly-arrived at the beginning of 1960 in what was about to become swinging London, was an innocent standing on the lip of a volcano, but I could hardly know that.   What I did know was that a school had to be found for Geoffrey and that house prices were double those in Glasgow.   Cath and I had no conception of the social geography of the place but one thing quickly became clear. It would be difficult to find a house we could afford in a desirable locality.   Fortunately, through the company grapevine, I managed to acquire the lease of a modest flat in Wimbledon. From that base Cath spent several exhausting and frustrating weeks looking for a house within travelling distance of Dulwich where Geoffrey had a tentative place at Alleyn's School. She almost managed it but there was a difference of about £750 between the asking price of the only house we liked and what we thought we could afford.   'Don't buy what you think you can afford,' an old office hand advised me. 'Buy what you want. You'll be able to afford it next year.'

My caution in matters financial persuaded me to ignore his words; but he was right, as I realised too late.   In the end we gave up the idea of Alleyn's. Geoffrey sat another examination and was interviewed successfully for Merchant Taylors School in the north-west corner of the outer suburbs – Betjeman country.   Cath's target area changed. She eventually found a house in Hatch End, then a decent but unremarkable attachment to Pinner. After a term at the local school, Geoffrey started at Taylors in September. Meanwhile, I had begun the second but quite different half of a career spent in the service of ships.

At that time BP Tankers owned, manned and operated a fleet of about 120 oil tankers, employed 2,500 sea-going officers directly and twice as many ratings indirectly.   Its headquarters staff of about 400 was mostly based in London.   Some, nominally attached to Britannic House, were deployed in the group's refinery ports at home and abroad or in the major UK ship repair centres. Incorporated in 1915 as the British Tanker Company, a subsidiary of the Anglo-Persian Oil Company, it had come a long way in the

5 years of its corporate life from its simple, rugged origins. By 960 it had developed into a significant element in the British hipping industry. Within the BP group the Tanker Company, ccupying the slot immediately downstream from oil production, arried crude oil to the refineries either from the group's own roduction centres or from wherever it happened to be so trading. : was also the ocean link between those refineries and the group's arkets, delivering refined products in the fleet's smaller ships esigned for the purpose. BP Tankers took its instructions from le group logistics centre, previously Distribution Department ow Supply and Development, which controlled the pieces on the roup chess board. The BP Tanker Company had its own board haired at the time of my arrival by A E C Drake, deputy chairman f the parent company, a man whose name had been headline lews at the time of the Mossadeq sequestration of Abadan Refin- ry in 1951 when he was general manager of the entire Persian lulf operation. The managing director of the Tanker Company vas a Glaswegian called Houston Jackson who had joined the ompany as a young clerk just after the first world war, worked is way up through the organisation and succeeded another Scot, lobert Gillespie, now on the BP main board.

The headquarters staff, like ancient Gaul, was organised in three arts: the commercial and operational departments which imple- nented instructions from the group supply and development lepartment, ordered and operated ships to satisfy those require- nents and chartered supplementary tonnage when necessary; the echnical departments which designed, built, repaired, main- ained and husbanded the ships; and the service group which rovided staff, training, stores, spares, supplies and legal advice. lach group developed its own ethos and, dependant upon the ersonality and effectiveness of the robber baron heading its ffairs, devolved more or less power and influence. The commer- ial side possessed a certain cachet, its people more directly oncerned with the outside world and with the 'customer' up- tairs in the shape of the main company. The two technical lepartments, engineering and marine, contained the specialist rofessionals, ex-fleet seafarers almost to a man, conscious of their uardianship of the mysteries of their calling. Not invulnerable o criticism from the commercial people they had a history of onservatism, determination, and sometimes intransigency. The ervice departments had less influence, with the exception of

Legal and Claims whose maritime lawyers, most of whom ha
been called to the Bar, were well able to promote their own statu;
The staff department was necessarily larger since it was respor
sible for several thousand seamen, difficult to administer as the
working lives were mostly spent at the other end of the worlc
Ships' stores bought everything required by the fleet, no sma
undertaking for 120 widely differing ships. The training divi
sions, nominally part of the staff department, also owed allegianc
to the technical departments whose requirements and standard
they had to satisfy. Such an organisation differed then only i
nomenclature and detail from that of other big British shippin;
companies of the period. The closest parallel was with the Shel
fleet, the major difference being that Shell separated its day-to-da
fleet operation from long-term planning, ship design and ship
building programmes, port development and chartering. In Shel
Centre these latter activities were carried out by a separate organi
sation, Shell International Marine, which provided services for al
Shell fleets under a variety of flags. BP, on the other hand, ha
only a British fleet, apart from six obligatory ships under th
French flag, and all shipping activities were administered unde
the umbrella of the BP Tanker Company.

To a newly-appointed marine superintendent the organisation'
general shape had long been familiar. The relative weight of eacl
component part, however, was less clear and, with the exceptio
of the staff department with whom one had had the most direc
dealings, the cast of characters were names only. Fortunate i
having had a preview with my short apprenticeship in the B
Clyde Tanker Company, and thanks to my peers, I was no
entirely ignorant of who was who and what was what. But now
I was knee-deep in a bigger world and quickly began to under
stand office politics, not then a serious problem. Certainly, ther
was rivalry between the organisation's constituent parts. Ambi
tion, jealousy, intrigue of course existed but not to the extent o
warping judgement – so far as I could see. However, if a mariner
one strove to look like, think like and behave like a marine
according to the Head Mariner's Holy Writ, defending one'
corner until told to desist. As ship-board life had been hierarchica
and elitist so, too, was the office; but people like me, appointed
from the fleet, joined the scramble more than half-way up the rock
face and, by virtue of professional experience, had an edge. The
obverse of the coin, however, was that seafarers tended to be

nnocents among the street-wise. Some never lost that attractive quality of otherworldliness and remained professional experts all heir lives. Others learned the wisdom of the streets and were oon indistinguishable except when deliberately taking advantage of their specialism.

The 'First Sea Lord' was the chief marine superintendent, Captain John Ross, highly regarded by board, management and fleet. An astute politician, his department consisted of marine superintendents, some on fleet operations, others on research and development, port and hydrographic assessment, safety and anti-pollution measures and the promotion of company views and intentions in the debating places of the industry. The three senior superintendents, Bailey, Foster and Smyth, dealt with fleet matters. Two understudies, Finnis and Broad, handled complex cargo placements and stood in for the three seniors. Frank Broad was something of a legend. Not only was he the essence of competence and integrity, he had a sparkling technical imagination and was eventually to make a number of major and unusual contributions. A Mancunian with a ribald sense of humour he had one wife called Maureen, one boxer dog called Butch and one house in Coulsdon with one door only which John Ross called Broad's Igloo'. Frank liked large motor-cars with fat, twin exhaust pipes and was a great companion. I treated him with healthy respect and still do.

The three elder statesmen shared a large room separated from Ross's magnificent first-floor office in River Plate House by a cubby-hole where the chief's secretary, Olive Simmonds, wielded frightening authority permitting only vouchsafed visitors to enter. Finnis and Broad shared another office and, in an adjacent box overlooking the frosted glass window of the ladies' closet, sat the most recently appointed superintendent, Kenneth Nicholls. I was put under his wing and shared his office to learn the tricks of the trade. Accompanying him on ship inspections I now saw this sacred ritual from the other side. For years I had readied ships for the superintendent's inspection, donned my best uniform and smile for the occasion and tried to anticipate the probing to which the ship and I would be exposed. Now I was having to ask the questions and in Nicholls I had an ideal mentor.

The port information section was critically important since it maintained constant checks on more than 800 ports to which the ships traded. 'Limpy' Johnston, the man in charge, was nearing

223

retirement and was understudied by Stanley Mee, as broad as he was high and possessed of a solid reputation in and out of the office. A number of technical assistants completed the staff. One a talented Welshman called Hopkins, had been a personal assistant to William Hutchison, was a gifted artist and inventor of marine equipment. Something of a prima donna he needed careful handling. Amongst these fellow labourers in the vineyard I had to find my way.

I need not have worried. The atmosphere under Ross, if rigorous, was collegiate and comparative inexperience was no bar provided one's contributions were properly argued and presented reasonably. At the start I was too busy flitting to and from Southampton, Thameshaven, Hull and Liverpool with Kenneth Nicholls to become involved in matters of state about which my seniors pontificated. Nicholls and his ebullient Cornish wife lived in Stanmore and Nancy helped Cath find the house we ultimately bought. They became and remain close friends and I recall with amusement the first ship he and I inspected together, at Immingham one week-end. On our return home he described to our wives how we had spent an unblemished Saturday evening in Grimsby, weighing ourselves at the railway station and watching a grocer using a ham slicer in his closed shop, the limit of the entertainment available.

Within a few months I was deemed fit to carry out my own inspections since Kenneth had quite enough to do caretaking groups of ships laid up in southern and south-eastern estuaries. Well do I remember an early inspection. The *British Duchess* was quite new and at 42,000 tons big for the time. Commanded by a senior master, later to be commodore, he had complained about the quality and quantity of paint supplied to his ship. Prior to the inspection I was given copies of the corrspondence. One look at the crew list, at the head of which appeared the name of a chief officer I knew well, convinced me that there was more to this than met the eye. I also knew the master, an able but tight-lipped individual who occasionally liked to tweek the office's tail. The chief officer, equally efficient, knew how to get the most out of the system, on behalf of the ship of course. As a 'makey-learn' superintendent I had to tread warily into this situation. represented the establishment but must handle the master and chief officer diplomatically while conducting a proper investigation. In the end there was no problem. The chief officer had stowed away a proportion of his paint allocation – in this case more than was customary – indenting for new stock as if all the previous issue had been used, building up a surplus so that he was in a position to create an impressive display of well-kept ship by never running short of material. From his secret horde he had used some ancient stock about which he had persuaded the captain to complain. We resolved the situation. I reported a modest overlooked surplus and a mistaken stock rotation. The oldest paint went ashore leaving the ship with only what it should have had and no reputation suffered. Perhaps I had condoned the deception, but thereafter the two complainants walked carefully. For me it was an early exercise in the applied art of diplomacy. Brought up in a rigid system it takes some time to learn objectivity and flexibility in the face of complicated personal relationships. I saw the episode neither as an exposure of ship's malpractice nor as a triumph of management detective work. 'There, but for the grace of God, go I,' was probably nearer the mark. Now I sometimes wonder whether this sort of 'flexibility', the British talent for compromise, is always supportable. Of course, this would have been a non-event had the ship's people tweaked the office tail more astutely.

I now became familiar with a far wider range of the company ships than had been my lot when sailing in them. The earliest supertankers had been of 28,000 tons deadweight, impressive by the standards of the time. Next came 32,000-tonners followed by a batch of 35,000-tonners, six of them built in Italy - for the price of five, it was said - more handsome but less reliable than the British-built equivalents. After that came some fine-looking 42,000-tonners of which the *British Duchess* was the first, culminating, in 1959, with the *British Queen*, built at Vickers' Barrow yard, launched by Her Majesty and bigger, by 8,000 tons, than the earlier ships of the class. The *Queen* was an elegant ship. A photograph, taken of her as she ran trials in a force seven blow off the island of Arran, is surely the most impressive trials picture I have ever seen - the stately ship, solid in the water like the Rock of Gibraltar, is steaming away from the camera and a quartering wave has just

• *British Queen during her trials off the Isle of Arran*

broken over the port side of the maindeck giving an impression of dynamic force, wild nature and this beautiful man-made object designed and built to live with the elements. I imagine the lay mind finds it difficult to see beauty in an oil tanker - which is tough on the lay mind. Although my sea time had been in smaller product carriers I liked big ships and appreciated their improved design and new equipment. The American wartime-built T2 standard tanker had proved an important watershed in oil tanker design. By European standards it was over-equipped, too fast and used too much fuel. But it was a tough, reliable piece of equipment always capable of satisfying any demand and it out-dated our own standard 12,000-tonners. The new, bigger ships were very different, more in the character of the T2. They had power in hand and pumping machinery adequate to enable the ship to match the reception facilities built into post-war oil termi-nals and refineries, and they were superbly equipped.

Safety and the control of oil pollution were becoming significant issues in the late 1950s. Since 1956 discharge of dirty ballast and oil tank washings at sea had been drastically restricted by interna-tional agreement, and properly anticipated by Act of Parliament so far as British ships were concerned. In matters of safety several tank explosions at sea and in port had signalled a crisis in the operation of oil tankers, especially the newer and larger ships. In one notorious incident the entire 'midships bridge house of the *Esso Durham* had been blown off as the ship steamed in ballast from Bombay towards the Persian Gulf. Before that the *Atlantic Duchess*, on charter to BP, had exploded with loss of life while ballasting after discharge in Swansea's Queens Dock. The owners of the *Atlantic Duchess* sued BP for loading their ship with so-called 'spiked' crude outside the specification for which the ship was suited, thus contributing to the explosive condition. Dr Charles Sutton, although not a lawyer himself, had created a formidable legal department as a result of having been made responsible for insurance claims. A tall, bespectacled, silver-haired academic he was both visionary and philosopher with a searching, questing mind and steely determination once con-vinced that a cause was worthy. The *Atlantic Duchess* claim had to be fought he believed so he put together a team to investigate scientifically the nature of petroleum gas, its volatility in ship-board circumstances and what might have happened in Swansea. The scientist appointed to the team from the BP research centre at

226

Sunbury was a physicist, Dr Kenneth Brummage, later to make great contributions to international tanker safety. Brummage helped Sutton to win the *Atlantic Duchess* case with two important consequences; first, Sutton became convinced, and convinced others, of the need for a company investigative team ready at a moment's notice to go to the location of any incident, get there before the dust settled and procure the best evidence at once so that the incident could be understood and steps taken to guard against a recurrence. The second, more important, consequence was that Sutton became further persuaded of the desirability of blanketing ships' tanks with an inert gas capable of suppressing any tendency to explode. Sun Oil, a Philadelphia company with its own tanker fleet, had developed such a system in the 1930s when carrying casinghead gasoline, a highly volatile by-product of certain crude oil producing wells and one which needed delicate handling to prevent its running wild. John Ross and Charles Firman, a senior engineer superintendent, together with one of the naval architects, Ian Telfer, visited Sun Oil, sailed in their ships and were impressed. Under Telfer's leadership a BP version was designed and, by 1961, Sutton had persuaded the managing director, Houston Jackson, that a full-scale experiment should be carried out. I was to become deeply involved in the inert gas project but in the meantime I was visited by a stroke of good fortune, having been ashore for less than a year.

John Ross decided it was time for him to make one of his periodic visits to the Persian Gulf where immense developments in the maritime phase of oil exploration, production and transfer were taking place. As chief marine superintendent of one of the largest tanker operators it was incumbent upon him to keep abreast of what was happening in that most critical part of the oil world. Additionally, his own people were involved with off-shore exploration which, from its infancy in the Gulf of Mexico, had now spread to the Persian Gulf and represented the technological frontier of our operations. The visit was also a kind of royal progress round the installations for Ross's reputation was widely spread. Then in his mid-50s, Ross was well-versed in the politics of BP and the marine side, at least, of the whole industry. He had no intention of spoiling a good tour, showing the flag and getting up-to-date, by doing the tedious work himself. He would take a bag carrier and note taker as a kind of personal assistant. It was an enviable assignment and it fell to me. Aware of the shining opportunity I was equally conscious that others, many my senior, would feel they had more right to the limelight.

Bound for Aden by way of Khartoum, Ross and I flew out from Heathrow one evening in a BOAC Britannia. It was the start of a concentrated five-weeks apprenticeship. Twenty years, almost to the day, separated our ages, he nearing the end of a distinguished career, I a new boy with nearly 20 years sea experience behind me but with my way still to make in the highly-politicised oil industry. Like a good PA I walked discreetly behind, dictated notes on a portable tape recorder, wrote them up in the evening and had them edited by the Head Man. In public I kept my mouth shut but my eyes open, swam in the pool with the boss in the half-hour's leisure stolen between a day's work and the evening's engagement, and learned more about the company and its personalities than I had the right to expect. Ross paid me the compliment of relating confidentialities. If he had motives I did not know what they were, but I was flattered. Thus was I educated. We stayed in Aden with a friend of Ross's, a senior chemical engineer, Dr Allison, whose one-eyed Saudi cook had a single dinner party menu – fish and chips and baked alaska. We moved on to Abadan, Bandar Mashur and Kharg Island, names to become infamous 20 years on. We visited Kuwait with its vast marine installations built in less than a decade where we called on the English widow of a Colonel Boustead, a legendary figure in British relationships with the sheikhdom. She herself was an Arabist and a seasoned traveller through the Empty Quarter. Bahrein and Ras Tanura saw us, then we moved on to Abu Dhabi, a tiny Arab town on the southern shores of the Gulf in those days, its streets no more than sand-filled tracks between houses. Das Island was an off shore centre for the widespread drilling operations which had become so important in that part of the Gulf. Once it had been only a barren lump of rock, not much more than a mile long and less than that wide, inhabited by terns until the oil industry converted it into a driilling base. From Abu Dhabi we were driven along the sabbquat, the salty sand along the edge of the sea, for 100 miles or more in a long-base Landrover to inspect the site of what was to become the port of Umm Said. We saw the Persian Gulf in a way I could never have visualised and met the most extraordinary and dedicated people. After five weeks on circuit we flew home, sunburned and a great deal better-informed. I owed my permanent appointment ashore to John Ross who had not known me from Adam a year or two earlier. Now I was further in his debt for I had been exposed to an experience I was unlikely to forget. I suppose he was taking a chance on a young man, as older hands have done before and will do again, but this one would ever remember his indebtedness to and affection for John Ross, gentleman.

Each of six or so marine superintendents in the office had his special spheres of interest. As the junior hand my share of the action tended toward the odder or more transient things for which the others had no time. One such project took me to the Isle of Grain where the company wanted the marine operation to function for 24 hours a day while local interests considered that ship movements in and out of the Medway should be confined to daylight. After 10 days on site I returned to London as the instant expert bearing a draft set of regulations enabling the channel to be controlled and navigated by day or night. The peremptory, quasi-legal terminology in which I had couched the draft made Ross's hair stand on end.

'You can't lay down the law like this,' he said, 'not without an Act of Parliament, at least. You'll get us all hung.'

It was provocative enough to stimulate further discussion locally and our people on the spot duly negotiated an arrangement not spectacularly different, if set out more diplomatically. Through Ross I also became involved in a project sponsored by the Royal Institute of Navigation and associated organisations in France, Germany and Holland. These bodies were concerned about traffic conditions in the Straits of Dover. Governments did little. There were precious few votes in navigating the English Channel. Shipowners' representative bodies were less than interested. Either they did not acknowledge the extent of the problem or feared that any proposed solution would violate their ships' rights to freedom of navigation. It took a year or two to achieve but, in the end, we produced the first traffic routeing system for the Dover Straits, which was ultimately endorsed by the UN International Maritime Organisation. What we had designed for the Dover Straits became the pattern for dealing with other areas of traffic concentration throughout the world although it is my belief, now, that what was good for the Dover Strait may not have been ideal for other places, like the export of Westminster-style government to societies for which it is unsuited. Nevertheless, it was an achievement on the part of those institutes of navigation in which I was pleased to have played a small part.

London was stimulating. At sea I had not realised how circumscribed a closed community could be. Of course I had found kindred spirits who wanted to think and talk about matters other than their last ship – always perfect – or their last run ashore – invariably exotic; but the challenge of the task at sea was more to nerve and blood than to the mind and I suspected it might eventually become a frustrating routine. But I had been plucked away in time and pitchforked into a different world. By the time Ross and I returned from the Persian Gulf it was as if this were the only life I had ever known. The simple out-door life I had enjoyed as a young man was followed by something more mentally demanding. With a wider range of work and responsibility I had developed a detailed knowledge of the whole range of ships in the fleet and their crews without having served in the larger ones I had coveted.

Large tankers were now being built with the 'midships house removed, extra accommodation and the navigating bridge being located above the poop. The trend began with independent Greek shipowners, certainly not the British or the major oil companies. Two motives prompted them. The first was economic since it was cheaper to have one 'hotel' block aft with a single run of service cables and conduits. The second, and more important, was a matter of safety. The 'midships house, sitting over the centre of the tank range, had always been potentially hazardous, underlined by the *Esso Durham* disaster, so its transfer aft was a positive advantage. I had first seen a 'bridge aft' ship when serving in the *Explorer* in 1959. From a distance it looked like a gigantic canoe with an Indian brave crouching in the stern, smoke emerging from the top of his head. Whatever its appearance, I was persuaded by the safety argument. Predictably, there was opposition from those who believed that you could only con a ship properly from a point just forward of amidships where the ship was said to rotate under helm. Some vociferous British pilots claimed that accidents were bound to occur – unless of course two pilots were employed. Before BP commissioned a 'bridge aft' supertanker John Ross conducted a brisk debate through the columns of the technical press, defending the design. The Great Lakes steamer with its bridge almost overhanging the bow, and the aircraft carrier with the bridge on the starboard side of the flight deck were cited as acceptable configurations not presenting insurmountable difficulties. The first 60,000-ton bridge-aft ship to join the BP fleet was he *British Grenadier.* Accompanying Arnold Brereton, at that time deputy to the chief naval architect, on the acceptance trials off Arran I quickly became accustomed to the bridge location, as did every other mariner on board. These working trials lasted several days and culminated in an open day when the London brass were taken to sea and the ship put through her paces. 'Owners' day' was a jolly - provided the working trials had been successful and the ship had reached her contract performance. Usually, a group travelled from London on the night sleeper and were brought out by tender to the sparkling new ship lying at the Tail o' the Bank. A large breakfast was then consumed on passage to the Arran mile. That morning John Ross was the last mandarin to disembark from the tender. I hung back waiting for him.

Well - what's the bridge like?'

I waxed enthusiastic. Shortly afterwards the ship's master, Alex Henney, endorsed what I had said. Ross could see and feel for himself what it was like to be 550ft from the bow of a ship more than 700ft long, was relieved and then expansive. From then on no ship was built to any other general arrangement.

Charles Sutton's campaign for adoption of the inert gas system of cargo tank protection reached the experimental stage when the *British Skill,* one of the original 28,000-ton supertankers was fitted with such a system designed in-house. Boiler flue gas was driven through a vertical, multi-stage cooling and washing tower located inside the funnel casing. Split vertically it had been expanded to accommodate the gas- washing plant. Sucked from the delivery side of the cooling tower, the clean flue gas was blown along a header line extending the ship's length and delivered into each cargo compartment by way of a branch line entering the top of the tank. Each tank also had a length of six-inch diameter pipe, known as a purge pipe, extending from the deck to within a foot of the bottom. When inerting a compartment it was sealed except for the valve on the gas delivery line at the top and the cap of the purge pipe. The effect of this was that the inflowing inert gas, coming in at the top, displaced the air in the tank through the purge pipe leading from the tank bottom thus creating circulation throughout the space. By this means it was possible to replace the vapour content of even the largest tank in little more than an hour. The condition of the tank atmosphere was gauged by means of a hand-held analysing instrument to establish the oxygen content. Theoretically, a mixture containing less than 10 per cent oxygen is not flammable. The inert system was designed to replace the air in the tank with nitrogen and reduce the oxygen content to as near five per cent as possible. Regardless of what source of ignition might be introduced into the compartment thereafter, fire or explosion was impossible.

The *Skill* was fitted out in the Tyne and, since these new-fangled experiments were part of my business, I went off on the proving trip to Tripoli, Lebanon. The ship's young chief engineer, C F Day, got the inevitable teething troubles quickly under control and we reported progress daily. The design of the system was simple as it had to be. Telfer, the naval architect who had studied the system in America, and the engineers had satisfied the operators' requirement for rugged simplicity thus enabling us to load the ship in a fully-inerted condition and so maintain her throughout the return passage. By the time we reached the Isle of Grain Fred Day, the Chief Officer Tommy Mann, and I considered ourselves experts. On berthing, the ship was met by a party of distinguished visitors from the Chamber of Shipping Tanker Safety Committee led by its chairman, Lord Geddes, with his deputy Dr Sutton, John Ross and his engineering opposite number, Charles Firman. Fred Day and I did our stuff. Everyone seemed impressed by the experiment and authority was given for the next stage to go ahead. Wisely, the chief superintendent engineer had Fred Day transferred from the *British Skill* to the London office where he master-minded the practical side of the inert-gas experiments from then on. And never looked back. He was later appointed engineer superintendent, eventually engineering manager on special projects and new buildings and had a most distinguished career. He deserved his success for, had the *British Skill* experiment failed – and it was Fred who made it work – the project might have been abandoned, which would have been disastrous. Within a year it was decided to fit the inert gas system in all new large crude carriers. Later this was extended to the entire fleet following a tragic accident when the *British Crown* exploded and caught fire while loading at Umm Said.

A properly-ordered home life was one of the benefits of a transformed career. Our Hatch End house needed wholesale redecoration so Cath and I had to learn to do for ourselves what we could not afford to have others do for us. Kenneth and Nancy Nicholls, experts in the business, taught us how to hang paper, even ceiling paper! We had acquired for £475 a four year-old Morris Oxford

232

which lasted another four years and gave us both pleasure and service. Geoffrey was immersed in Merchant Taylors joining a number of societies and becoming a keen and properly warlike member of the Corps. Tough, resilient, stoical and possessed of a robust sense of humour I thought then – and still do – that he would have made a splendid soldier, borne out a year or two later when he won the pot for the best recruit of his year in the Honourable Artillery Company. Only when he had left did he confess how much he had disliked Taylors. Perhaps a contributory cause was the difficulty some children have in daily switching back and forth from the atmosphere of home to that of a public school. In retrospect, I should have paid a good deal more attention to him but, selfishly, I was too busy pursuing my own engrossing affairs to pay sufficient regard to his. That he turned out to be a normal, intelligent, successful business-man is an indication of his own resilience and no way attributable to any advice or guidance I gave him when he was a schoolboy. Telling a boy once every three months that he is an idle fellow fit only to be a butcher's boy does not measure up to the proper discharge of one's parental responsibilities.

Cath's father retired in 1961 thus ending his week-end journeys to Perth; soon he began to enjoy what turned out to be a long and happy retirement. Our Morris Oxford could almost take itself to Perth after a year or two although the journey time from North London was then lengthy, when the first motorway was still under construction. We would set out at 0600 and hope not to be held up too much by the road works in the East Midlands and Yorkshire; but we seldom arrived in Perth before 2100. Ayr was easier but only an hour or two shorter. Those were the two places in which we spent our summer holidays because, to begin with, we could not afford hotels and foreign travel. It caused us no distress at the time, as I recall, and Geoffrey quickly established his independence by spending his summer holiday each year with my sister Eileen in Ayr and her husband Tom who encouraged his latest entrepreneurial talents by employing him in his warehouse.

One simple pleasure we enjoyed was the company's annual dance, held in the Russell Hotel with Joe Loss's band in attendance and the maestro himself invariably putting in an appearance during the evening. During our first two years in London we saw a great deal of Nancy and Kenneth Nicholls who had been so supportive at the beginning. Their house in Canons Park was only three or four miles away and that helped to cement our friendship. Then John Ross sent for him one day. Kenneth was appointed resident marine superintendent at the company's refinery port of Kwinana, near Fremantle in Western Australia and everything changed. The refinery had been operating for seven or eight years and was an important terminal for our own ships with a marine and an engineer superintendent in residence since the start-up. It was a shrewd horses-for-courses appointment. Kenneth Nicholls was, by age, temperament and adaptability the most suitable man for the job, but the clincher was that, of all the company wives, Nancy seemed most capable of adapting to Australia. The appointment meant heavy expense for the company moving two people and their household to the opposite side of the earth. Whoever went had to accept that his tenure of office would be lengthy, albeit punctuated by home leave every two years or so. It turned out to be a 10-year stint and the remainder of Kenneth's career. We missed them.

It is a truth universally acknowledged that every person who was a sentient adult at the time knows where he was and what he was doing when he learned of John F Kennedy's assassination. The New Frontier had burned itself into the imagination of a generation under 40 when it happened. The Cuban missile crisis had been perceived as the nearest the world had come to the precipice since the Second World War and Kennedy was the knight in shining armour who had saved civilisation from the barbarians. I can remember, the day before Kruschev turned his west-bound fleet, deciding to buy my first new dinner jacket, which I could ill afford. My argument was that, if the bomb went off the next day, the cost wouldn't matter; if it didn't go off I could look forward to a lifetime's wear from the suit and the prospect of being able to pay for it in due course. Among profounder thoughts I was grateful to President Kennedy for having saved my dinner jacket from incineration. From that moment on, for many years at least, I was a believer in Camelot. The news of the assassination reached my ears as I lay sweating on board the *British Industry* in Bombay, recovering from a bout of recurrent malaria. Three of us had been rushed out to deal with a crisis following a cargo tank explosion on board the *Industry*, not dissimilar to that which had devastated the *Esso Durham* some years earlier. Fortunately there had been no loss of life but part of the ship's side, just below the starboard wing of the bridge, had been blown open by the explosion which

234

had occurred during tank cleaning. With a great, ragged piece of shell plating hanging down from the gap and extending below the ship's bottom, the *British Industry* was still limping gingerly back to port when our party arrived. This was the first occasion on which Dr Sutton's emergency investigative procedure had operated formally and promptly. The accident happened on a Friday. By Saturday afternoon three of us had been briefed and were en route to Bombay. Sutton's idea had been that the team should consist of a mariner, a marine engineer and a qualified lawyer to obtain prompt and accurate evidence while the incident was still vivid in the minds of witnesses. James Featherstone, the number two in legal and claims, was a history graduate who had spent a number of years in Abadan and had then read for the Bar after his return home in 1951. He was quick, clever and a splendid travelling companion. The engineer chosen was my former colleague from Glasgow days, Robin Stevenson. The Glasgow operation had withered on the branch following MacArthur's sudden death from a heart attack. The staff were now back in London where Stevenson had been recognized as a competent, innovative and dedicated engineer of great practical experience.

We established ourselves at the Taj Mahal Hotel and, with the help of the local BP representative, Captain Ian McCuaig, arranged visits to the Port Authority, the local administration and the Indian Navy. Until we could inspect the ship neither we nor they knew what to expect or how to deal with it. Captain Frank Wilson, in command of the *British Industry*, was steaming slowly towards Bombay not knowing how badly his ship was damaged below the waterline and what further mischief might occur were he to increase speed. It took him another two days to arrive off the port. We boarded at once accompanied by a hull surveyor from the Board of Trade – or was it the Ministry of Transport in those days? – called Charles Smith who had arrived from London the day after us. In the anchorage Indian Navy divers helped establish that a piece of jagged shell plating, hinged to the side like the lid of a half-opened food can, hung about 15ft below the keel. This meant that the ship had an effective draft of between 35 and 40ft and could not be dry-docked until the damaged piece had been cut clear.

First we had to complete tank cleaning and gas-freeing. The crew were nervous, as well they might be, but they buckled to. Giving evidence to James Featherstone, who had a calming influence on them, restored much of their confidence. By dead of night, with no-one around, Stevenson and I finished cleaning the last tank, the port wing tank opposite the damaged compartment. The Port Authority were nervous of what we were doing, fearful of another explosion and the risk of oil polluting the outer harbour. Daily, we kept them informed of our progress but we were an embarrassment until the ship could be declared gas-free and something had been done about the damaged shell plating hanging so deep in the water. We retained the tank washings in a separate cargo compartment and then slipped quietly out of the anchorage, steamed 100 miles off the coast before dumping the lot and then cleaned out the slop tank. Returning slowly to Bombay we prayed that the damaged shell plating would drop off miraculously as the ship rolled easily in a gentle swell. Alas we came to anchor off the port again, clean and gas-free but still encumbered. Stevenson, using a large hacksaw and hanging precariously tried but failed to cut a notch near the top of the hinge in the hope of inducing a tear. The plate would have to be burned off while supported by a dockyard crane barge and, with some difficulty, we arranged for these things. In the meantime a marker buoy had been secured to the damaged plating in case anything should happen. And it was just as well. About 0200, five hours before the crane barge with burning equipment was due alongside, there was a faint crack and a rumble. Hearts leapt into mouths and legs into action. Scrambling on deck we were overjoyed to see that the damaged plating had at last torn away and fallen to the seabed, its marker buoy bobbing innocently up and down a few feet away. A prudent Captain Wilson hove up and shifted berth. At daylight a diver's inspection confirmed that the ship was clear with no other observable damage. She could now be taken into the Mazagon Dock since it seemed unlikely that there would be further structural collapse when she landed on the blocks. But several days were to elapse before the dock was clear. I took the opportunity of having a short, sharp malaria attack - legacy of wartime West Africa – while poor John Kennedy was done to death in Dallas.

As the ship waited to enter dock Featherstone, Stevenson, Charles Smith and I discussed with the crew possible causes of the explosion. Had one of the washing machines, suspended on the end of a thick rubber hose, run wild – perhaps as a result of a burst hose? If so, could it have thrashed about in the tank and knocked one of the magnesium anodes, which provided cathodic protection, into the bottom while the atmosphere was in an incendiary condition? We could prove nothing about the atmosphere, but set up an experiment to test the plausibility of a machine running amok. An outrigger was secured over the ship's side and a washing machine suspended from it on the end of a hose with a small hole in it, heavily bandaged with insulating tape. With a cine-camera aimed at the rig, water was turned on the hose at full pressure. Within 30 seconds the insulating tape was blown clear of the hole in the hose and the washing machine ran wild, thrashing about in the most convincing manner. It was a neat theory nicely demonstrated. But a more likely cause was the build-up of static electricity through the unbonded hose inside the tank resulting, eventually, in a heavy electrical discharge through the water and gas cloud. It was a condition not fully understood at that time but Kenneth Brummage in London had been questioning us by cable. A square search of the damaged tank, once the ship was docked and dried out, might provide supporting evidence. Four or five of us searched before anyone else was allowed inside the tank. Featherstone elected himself recorder and kept a meticulous diagram of all our finds as if we had been clearing an archaelogical site. We boxed up the damaged machines, the rubber hoses and anything else we could lay our hands on and consigned them to the research centre at Sunbury. With a repair contract negotiated and our reports half-written Featherstone and I left for London leaving Robin Stevenson behind to supervise repairs. It had been a thorough investigation, and was followed up scientifically by the research centre, the manufacturers of the machines and hoses and by the Ministry of Transport. But no firm conclusion could be reached since most of the important evidence, as always, had been destroyed in the explosion. Nevertheless, it was a triumph for Charles Sutton's investigative system and a valuable experience for those involved in it.

Bombay is hot, stinks and the poverty of its streets is horrendous; but I have always been drawn to it and to the very idea of India and the Raj. Our small team had been there on a wholly demanding mission, but there had been moments of relaxation at dinner in Jeanne and Ian McCuaig's flat or drinking secretly in the 'permit' room of the Taj. Bombay State was officially dry and only foreign visitors could obtain a modest allowance of liquor for consumption behind closed doors on the premises or taken off furtively to private establishments. Featherstone, a soft-hearted fellow, was easily put upon by the young beggars who besieged us whenever we ventured out. His petty cash disappeared instantly, but the rest of us were harder and could enunciate 'Imshi' with a few suitable curses. Dealing with Indian officials demanded the patience of Job but, however difficult, devious or stupid they were, invariably the soul of courtesy. When the task was done and James Featherstone and I were on our way to the airport for the flight home my eagerness to be off was tinged with regret to be leaving unexplored, beckoning India. I have never been back.

The following spring John Ross retired as chief marine superintendent, Smyth succeeded him and I was put in charge of a new group entitled the marine development department. We were concerned with new projects, the marine input to the shipbuilding programme and what we were pleased to call research and development, better described as evaluation. Much of our effort was devoted to safety, including the inert gas system, and to pollution control. Shell had developed a method of tank cleaning in crude oil carriers involving no discharge to sea of dirty oil and water mixtures. Instead, the tank washings were retained in a slop tank and allowed to settle so that the oil floated to the top leaving uncontaminated water underneath. This, if handled carefully, could be pumped over the side without causing pollution. Using such a procedure a ship could arrive at her loading port with clean tanks, apart from the slop tank which, typically in a 100,000-ton ship, might contain 500 tons of water-contaminated crude oil. The ship could then be loaded with fresh crude including the slop tank whose contents, in any case, would be passed through a desalination process at the receiving terminal. This method, which became known as 'Load-on-Top', looked like a winner in the oil pollution battle and my new group carried out preliminary trials. It soon became accepted practice in the major tanker fleets despite the loading terminals' initial wariness, accustomed as they were to pumping only into certified clean tanks. Refineries likewise were unenthusiastic about having to process excessive quantities of salt water in order to get at the crude oil with which it was partially emulsified. Such development work was absorbing particularly as the majors were becoming increasingly conscious of their public image and social responsibilities. While BP was happy enough to copy good ideas emanating from the South Bank, where Shell Centre lies, our friends there seemed

238

reluctant to accept our arguments about inerting large tankers until convinced by their own experiences a year or two later.

A rising star in the office in the early 1960s was a young man called Peter Cazalet, son of a retired admiral, scholar of Magdalene College, Cambridge, lately of the Dreyfus Corporation in Paris and their London associate, Buries Marks, whence he had come to the BP Tanker Company as an assistant manager in the late 1950s. The company had few graduates and Cazalet was clearly top management material the moment he walked through the door. At that time much of his work concerned shipbuilding contracts, negotiations beforehand and the splendid arguments afterwards when any shipbuilder worth his salt fought every inch of the way to avoid the penalties for late delivery or inadequate workmanship which an equally determined shipowner was trying to exact. Cazalet was answerable to an assistant general manager called Peter Medcraft who was appointed general manager in 1961 and thus the likely man to succeed Houston Jackson. But the person most deeply involved in the new building programme was the technical manager, Commander Edward Platt, who had retired from the navy early in order to take up that busy and prestigious appointment. At that time the shipbuilding programme was immense, but it was running in parallel with the disposal of the wartime and immediate post-war 12,000-tonners. Thus, the number of ships in the fleet remained between 100 and 130 although the total deadweight rose dramatically as more big ships were commissioned. It was a time of enormous confidence in the oil industry. Crude oil was cheap and demand high. It seemed, in the mid-60s, that progress meant going on forever getting bigger and busier. Occasionally, a still, small voice might whisper that the bubble would have to burst one day, only to be dismissed as preposterous. Samuel Smiles had nothing on us in that great high noon and my personal fortunes flourished in company with the general trend.

In 1965 I was taken out of my niche, dusted down and told I was to be converted into a manager. The following year I would be appointed operations manager – a title new to the Tanker Company. Meanwhile, I had to become more familiar with the BP group as a whole and attend management courses to round off corners or paper over cracks until fit to exercise judgement in fields outside matters nautical. It was exhilirating – and sobering – for I discovered, in double-quick tempo, that the group was full

of ambitious talent. Although not directly competing – for few
wanted, or were ever likely, to operate ships – being judged
alongside them stimulated the adrenalin. In those days there
were three major management courses – Stages I, II and III. Stage
II, for 35-45 year-olds thought to be capable of going on further in
the company, was the one I attended in The Old House on the river
bank at Windsor, nigh unto Eton. I enjoyed the three-week stint
hugely and the friendships cemented during that short but intense
period were to last for the remainder of our careers, in some cases
for the rest of our lives. I went back to shipping with a better
understanding of how the great company worked and of the sort
of people who made it tick. For this experience I am sure I owed
a debt both to Medcraft and Cazalet who, between them, were
taking thought for the future.

The fleet was stricken by another disaster in August 1966 when
the *British Crown* exploded and caught fire from end to end in the
final stages of loading crude oil at Umm Said. Some 15 people
were killed in the holocaust and the fire burned for several weeks
before it could be extinguished. This time the investigating team,
on the spot in less than 24 hours, consisted of Featherstone the
lawyer, Brummage the scientist and Broad the experienced mariner who had dealt with a number of other tanker incidents which
had happened outside the company. A board of investigation,
chaired by Edward Platt, was set up in London and ultimately
recommended, among other modifications, fitting inert gas sys-
tems in all existing crude carriers, a policy eventually applied as
well to the new product carriers which presented more complex
technical problems. Meanwhile, Broad, on the spot in Umm Said,
had to devise a means of discharging that part of the crude oil
cargo, still in the ship, which had not been destroyed by fire. The
wrecked *British Crown* was dead and had no resources whatever
but Broad's fertile imagination was a match for the problem.

Immediately prior to that calamity the National Union of Seamen had staged its most effective strike ever to bring most of the
British merchant fleet to a halt for weeks. In BP we were too eager
to resume play and jumped the gun in the final hours of the strike.
As a result, Jerry Taylor, head of the staff department, and I had
to eat humble pie in Maritime House, Balham and plead forgive-
ness from the NUS nabobs, an experience which underlined for
me the bitter, adversarial nature of industrial relations in major
British industries resulting from stupidities on both sides of the

divide and a contributory, but by no means the only, factor in the national decline at the time.

Geoffrey had left Merchant Taylors the previous year and was articled to a firm of chartered accountants in the City. Cath and I were delighted that he had elected to pursue some kind of professional career although, in my heart, I could not equate such an outgoing and ebullient personality with my perception of the dry accountant. A year or two later he was wooed away by a firm of stockbrokers with whose audit he had been assisting. I was dismayed but have to acknowledge that, as things turned out, his judgement was a great deal better than mine.

In my own organisation change was afoot, the most conspicuous manifestation of which was the transfer of the company in its entirety from Lutyen's splendid 1925 Britannic House at the corner of Finsbury Circus and Moorgate to the new Britannic House, a glass shoe-box standing on end behind Moorgate Station. Accounts and stores were exiled to a satellite office in Harlow, Essex; but the majority of us ended up in identical hutches in the modern building. The new Britannic House was certainly functional and we saw more of the other tribes who ran different parts of the organisation, but it lacked the old style. The only window in the building which could be opened without calling in the security services was in the office of the chairman, Sir Maurice Bridgeman, who had insisted on it. About this time Houston Jackson retired as MD and was succeeded by Peter Medcraft, general manager since 1961. Jackson was a quiet, sincere – not to say dour – Scot. Medcraft was more hawkish and, with Cazalet as his general manager, set about restructuring the organisation. Management consultancy was the fashion of the day and McKinsey its high priest. Shell sought their advice as did P & O who later implemented what appeared to be a Night of the Long Knives, referred to around Leadenhall Street as The October Revolution. Seeing blood pouring from beneath so many doors on the advice of clever outsiders – and sometimes, perhaps, because the advice had cost a great deal – was not an impressive spectacle. It certainly did not impress Maurice Bridgeman and Eric Drake, the deputy chairman. They resolved to approach reorganisation differently and Drake, particularly, was credited with the view that any McKinseying that was to be done would be done inside, under his own steady gaze and without outside interference. The cynical – including me – concluded that a great

cloud of dust would obscure everything for a while after which
normal life would resume. Nothing could have been further from
the truth, for the inside group given the task were totally objective
and infinitely better informed than any outside consultant would
have been. They could be just as ruthless in presenting their
solutions but were more open to debate. Fortunately, the Tanker
Company had already examined its own navel and was preparing
a streamlined organisation. Cazalet, of infinite charm and persua-
sive ways, was our spokesman and as a result our own proposals,
more or less intact, were knitted into the general pattern for
implementation, although organisational changes in the group
would alter the Tanker Company's reporting relationships and
invade its apparent autonomy.

Cazalet had now emerged as the day-to-day leader of the team.
Medcraft was interested in the business side, in chartering, industry politics, wheeling and dealing in the shipping and shipbuilding world and in picking safe citizens to tend the shop. Cazalet
had been his obvious choice for general manager, and he was good
– a little inclined to want to be told everything and do it all himself,
I sometimes thought – but as a terrier who liked to be off the leash
I was bound to think that. I enjoyed working with him. Many
years later he became deputy chairman of the BP group. As the
eldest of four sons of Vice Admiral Sir Peter Cazalet, who had held
some interesting commands while Peter was growing up, he
understood ships. His wife, Jane, was a striking-looking young
woman with a vivid personality and great charm. When their
house in Wimbledon was featured in *Homes & Gardens* every other
company wife poured over the photographs to comprehend how
Jane did it. As operations manager I answered directly to Cazalet
for what went on in the ships. Our partnership had its most
dramatic moment in March, 1967. One Saturday morning Cath
and I returned to the house where Geoffrey was waiting impa-
tiently. Swansea office had been on the telephone, followed by
Peter Cazalet who required me to call him urgently. A voyage-
chartered ship with 100,000 tons of BP crude was in trouble off the
Scilly Isles. For the first time I heard the name, *Torrey Canyon*.
Fairly new, the ship was registered in Panama and demise chartered to Phillips Petroleum, an American secondary oil company
which had rechartered her to BP for a single voyage. We bore no
responsibility for decisions which the owners, demise-charterers
or master might make and, at this stage, the magnitude of the

disaster about to engulf that sorry ship was not evident

She had struck rock near the Seven Stones in the Scillies that morning, inward-bound to Swansea from the Middle East. Aground, she was beginning to leak crude oil. The naval authorities at Plymouth were in control and looking for support from the owners, the charterers or any identifiable commercial interest. In default of any useful communication from the US, Medcraft and Cazalet thought we would have to involve ourselves. Clearly the most vital task was to do something about controlling pollution. For the rest of the day I lived on the telephone mustering local tugs, fishing boats and a small coaster and arranging for Grangemouth refinery to ship south large quantities of the industrial detergent they manufactured. In Plymouth the Staff Officer, Operations, Commander Michael Garnett, had similarly gathered together naval resources. Little information was forthcoming from the ship but, by early Sunday morning, we learned that the Dutch salvage company, Wijsmuller, had been engaged as salvors by Phillips Petroleum who were sending an executive from the States in a day or two. Meanwhile the Government, dreading a pollution disaster, acted swiftly. The prime minister confirmed that the navy was in charge and the junior minster for the navy in the Ministry of Defence, Maurice Foley, was ordered to Plymouth to take political charge of a deteriorating situation. Early on Sunday morning Cazalet rang me for about the 40th time and told me to get to Northolt airfield by 1500 that day to accompany the minister to Plymouth. There his team and I were stuffed into a small RAF aircraft. At Plymouth we were accommodated in Admiralty House and were swept into a series of meetings with Foley and the Commander-in-Chief, Plymouth, Vice-Admiral Sir Fitzroy Talbot. I was instantly impressed by the style in which an admiral lived. My room had good antique furniture standing on a royal blue carpet extending, seemingly seamlessly, into the adjoining bathroom, a touch of comfort I had experienced only in hotels and was not slow to adopt at home when funds permitted.

Sunday evening was taken up by a counsel of war attended by about 30 people not one of whom really knew the *Torrey Canyon's* condition. Earlier, a young lieutenant had been put on board by helicopter which had fuel to stay in the vicinity only a few minutes before taking him off again. He had been surprised by how few crew were on board and had discovered nothing about the nature of the damage. The oil leak was so heavy, however, that dealing with it was at least as important as salvaging the ship. Late that evening Foley asked the prime minister, Harold Wilson, for £500,000 to guarantee the supply of detergents and ships capable of spraying it. He then suggested that I might be able to make a more accurate appreciation of the position if I were put on board by helicopter in the morning, a sensible idea since I was Jack-on-the-spot most familiar with oil tankers and their problems in a way that the ordinary naval officer could not possibly be.

At 0530 on Monday, I was delivered to the helicopter pad by the admiral's car, kitted out in survival suit and white flying helmet to take off into a watery dawn. On the flight to Culdrose, where we refuelled for the sortie, I was alone in the vibrating, noisy cabin of the helicopter with the winchman who much admired a hole in one of my socks as I was putting on extra gear. After refuelling at Culdrose we boarded again and were joined by two others dressed in our rig of the day. I had not the remotest idea who they were and was unlikely to find out above the noise, so intense that communication was possible only with the cockpit through the intercom. We could listen to the crew but were unable to communicate among ourselves. The Wessex swept over Land's End at about 200 feet and out towards the Scillies. Visible to starboard through the open door were a landing wheel, a strut of the undercarriage, the sea beneath and the distant horizon abeam. From time to time the pilot would pass a message, almost unintelligible to one unused to earphones and the jargon so laconically expressed. But, all at once the message was clear.

'Ship right ahead – one mile,' roared the winchman through cupped hands.

The helicopter banked to port, swung into circuit and there was the *Torrey Canyon* framed in the doorway, gigantic, impressive, like a ship at anchor, the only evidence of trouble a sinister oil slick extending away downwind and spreading wide across the sea. The ship's domed funnel bore Phillips Petroleum's logo, the numerals '66', and she looked surprisingly normal. The pilot made one wide circuit to starboard and then closed in from the port quarter as I hooked onto the wire to be lowered on deck. Skilfully he brought the aircraft down until the starboard wheel was just touching one of the weather shelters on the after flying bridge. As I prepared to launch myself through the door one of the two strangers bellowed in my ear a request to accompany me. I didn't know who he was but I had been warned that I had only

15 minutes in which to remain on board while the helicopter circled slowly conserving its fuel for the return to Culdrose. In that time I had to find out as much as I could. It didn't matter whether the strangers came or not as long as they kept out of the way – and down I went to the deck, unhooked, ran clear and was greeted, rather abruptly, by a lean bearded man looking strained and exhausted and speaking good English with a Dutch accent. He turned out to be the salvage master, Stal, representing Wijsmullers who had a small craft alongside delivering a compressor for use in his salvage attempt. The two Culdrose strangers had now disembarked and were closing in to hear what was going on. Stal and I made for the bridge. To begin with, he was reluctant to say anything but once he was aware that I represented the cargo interests and was a marine man he hesitated no longer. On the way to the bridge we were met by a forlorn little man in open-necked shirt and woollen cardigan with an expression of total bewilderment in his haunted eyes. The Italian master, Captain Rugiati, clearly had a lot to be haunted about. Stal had the soundings of every compartment in the ship and the sea-bed depths at 50ft intervals round the hull. It took only a moment's study of his diagram to realise that the *Torrey Canyon* was hard and fast aground forward on the starboard side, and probably across the complete breadth of the ship amidships.

With the minutes ticking away, I copied the soundings and known damage and then ran round the ship from bow to stern with Captain Stal. There was some swell over the Seven Stones and the ship's movement was unnatural. A small roll would come to a halt with a gentle shudder before it had been completed, rather like the effect of stabilisers in a ship underway but more marked and accompanied by the ship's hull grinding and grating ominously far below. The engine-room was partly flooded with seawater on top of which crude oil floated, the stench of petroleum gas a warning against naked lights. The pumproom, just forward of the engine-room was worse. Not only was the ship aground on hard rock but had been deeply penetrated in a number of places. Hurriedly, Stal explained his intentions. A confident optimist, like all salvage men – although tight-lipped and tired – he intended pressurising the damaged compartments by pumping in air through the hatch-coaming connections, thus reducing the level of oil and water in each tank. Having regained buoyancy he believed he could lift the ship clear of the rocks. His soundings suggested that he would have to lift her about 20ft since jagged rocks appeared to have penetrated the hull almost that far in several places. I was far less sanguine than he but made no comment. I was not a salvage man and perhaps salvage men like him could work miracles. It seemed to me divine intervention would be needed if he was to have half a chance. With that the helicopter closed in to hover over the ship. Our time was up. My mysterious companions were still with Rugiati to whom I bade a rather tense farewell. We hooked on and were lifted, one by one, into the helicopter. The pilot peeled away, made one more circuit and headed for Culdrose. On the return flight my companions revealed their identity. They were national newspapermen. Resourceful buggers, thought I, and refused to say more in case the *Daily Express* knew all the answers before Maurice Foley and the Ministry of Defence knew the questions.

In Plymouth my information and views were received glumly. They tended to confirm what had been suspected, that the *Torrey Canyon* was a major disaster and the salvage team would need phenomenal luck to save the situation. Foley decided to return to London and take me with him once I had arranged a Britannic House substitute. I asked for Frank Broad who knew more about crisis management on board ships in trouble than anyone else. No miracles were vouchsafed to poor Hans Stal. An explosion occurred in the *Torrey Canyon's* engine-room the following day, probably as he pressurised the cargo tanks with the compressor I had seen lifted on board. Stal was killed, a brave and resourceful professional facing an impossible task.

For a few days the weather held and the little ships spraying detergent did some good, but not a great deal. There was a hiatus after Stal's death until Wijsmullers sent a replacement. In London, industry and government circles debated how to deal with the ship if she could not be manoeuvered from the rocks. Brummage and I were summoned to the Cabinet Office where Solly Zuckerman chaired a meeting to explore setting fire to the ship and burning the oil or, alternatively, breaking her open with explosive charges and dealing with the oil on the surface of the sea. Experiments at the Government Research Centre in North London suggested that firing the oil on the sea surface would be almost impossible. Our own experience with the *British Crown* disaster at Umm Said, when the ship burned for two months and only a third of the cargo was consumed, did not augur well for destroying the cargo on board. Rumblings from Downing Street increased and the prime minister, with a holiday home in the Scillies, went to see for himself.

Then the weather deteriorated and the ship broke her back. Oil gushed from her torn hull. Calls for action became more strident. Eventually, 10 days after the *Torrey Canyon* had grounded, eight navy Buccaneers from Lossiemouth and three RAF Hunters armed with bombs and rockets were despatched to destroy her. Broad, who had been a tower of intelligent, informed strength to the Plymouth team, was ordered into a helicopter. Seated between an air marshal and an admiral, he had a ringside view of the attack from a mile off, advising the pilots where they should aim their missiles. Some hits were scored despite the first runs coming in too high. Broad was reputed to have remarked, 'It's all right. She won't fire back,' which I hope is not apocryphal. There was little success on the first day but a sortie next day supported by navy Sea Vixens coming in low with napalm after some oil had been released by the high explosive bombs and rocket fire, managed to start a major fire. A huge column of black smoke was visible from the mainland nearly 20 miles away but the fire was extinguished a few hours later when the weather freshened. A third attempt was made the day after, but the ship was now fast breaking up so the attacks were abandoned. Miles of the Cornish coast had been devastated by the released oil, a major ecololgical disaster. The whole dreary process of dealing with the pollution dragged on for weeks until, in the end, the ship broke up completely and released the last of her oil.

The *Torrey Canyon* was the classic tanker disaster, the seminal event in changing perceptions of the devastating effect of a major oil pollution incident. Although international agreements on the control of oil in the sea had been entered into in the mid-1930s and upgraded several times thereafter, the *Torrey Canyon* catastrophe galvanised governments into formulating new international legislation and provoked the oil industry into setting up organisations to hammer out common problems and form insurance co-operatives to meet the enormous clean-up and compensation costs. Early in the 1960s I had been involved in a Chamber of Shipping initiative to introduce safe operating procedures in oil tankers. I could not have known, as I ran about the decks of the *Torrey Canyon*, that for much of the next decade I would be immersed in the control of oil pollution and the alleviation of subsequent loss and suffering. Much of the work would concern itself with trying to ensure that accidents bearing a risk of oil pollution did not occur, a counsel of perfection unlikely to be achieved. But it seems to me that such disasters would have been more frequent and their effects more devastating had Captain Rugiati not driven his ship ashore that March morning in 1967 and set off a train of events which unfolded for years afterwards.

Later that year the Middle East erupted in the Seven Days War and the Viet Nam conflict escalated. My friends and I continued to struggle with more mundane matters, trying to do better the things which we felt were not being done properly. In the fleet we had manning problems aggravated by the 1966 seamen's strike. It was a time when unions appeared to be an arm of government settling disputes, if not setting policy, over beer and sandwiches at Number Ten. Medcraft, Cazalet and, to a lesser extent, some of the rest of us were involved through the Chamber of Shipping. It had always seemed to me a solid and 'establishment' organisation, self-assured and a trifle pompous. The council chamber then was laid out with semi-circular banks of seats facing a dais. The front rows were invariably occupied by those generally known as 'the liner knights' whose acknowledged leader, when I first entered the place, was Sir Donald Anderson, chairman of P & O, a tall, silver-haired patrician. It has always struck me that great swells whose forefathers had been Highland crofters – Harold MacMillan and Donald Anderson, for example – took but a few generations to develop an aristocratic style. Perhaps their great grandfathers had been aristocrats in their own habitat. The oil lobby, represented by John Kirby, the managing director of Shell International Marine and the group's marine co-ordinator, and Peter Medcraft, our own MD, were accepted in the inner circle because their huge fleets contributed substantially to the Chamber's financial well-being; but one had the feeling that the 'real' shipping men, third or fourth generations of family firms, had to struggle hard even to see tanker operations as legitimate. John Kirby an Englishman with rimless glasses, a mid-Atlantic accent and a large house on the edge of Wentworth Golf Course, was a match for the others, however, and eventually became president. Much good work was sponsored by the Chamber of Shipping, especially in technical and safety matters, and it was my lot to become more heavily involved. Despite a prejudice against committees, I enjoyed the cut and thrust of it all, particularly under a quick and intelligent chairman. In our own office I held the view that a committee of more than five wasted time. Meetings, if possible, should be restricted to one hour. The structure of Britannic House allowed easy access between offices and lengthy meetings, with great numbers of people, were unnecessary except over big issues once or twice a year.

About this time BP were developing a system of crewing which we called general purpose manning. For decades ships' companies had been divided into three departments - deck, engine-room and catering. Between them there were barriers for which no password existed. At least in the case of officers this was understandable. Training for professional qualifications of deck and engineer officers differed so much that there was little chance of cross-fertilisation. It had occurred to many, however, that in the modern merchant ship this need not be so with ratings. Every ship carried a deck crew large enough not only to man the bridge watches but also to handle the mooring and unmooring tasks, to deal with the preparation of holds for cargo and to carry out essential maintenance. At times the ship was over-manned on deck. In the engine-room manning was based on the watch-keeping requirements with little allowance made for the support ratings gave to the ship's enginers in carrying out repair and maintenance. If these two departments, each with differing peak loads, could be combined, a smaller group – a general-purpose crew capable of working on deck or in the engine-room – would suffice. The unions took some persuading but, to give them their due, they eventually agreed to let us experiment, exacting a price for the privilege. From a sticky start, and with many a hiccup on the way, the trials ultimately succeeded and the departmental divide, at least in the ordinary bulk cargo carrier, is now but a memory.

With an owned fleet of 100 ships and many more on charter management control had become more involved. The manpower study group – our internal McKinsey – gave us the opportunity to put forward radical ideas on restructuring. At the end of the 60s the BP Tanker Company was still structured in four sections – operations, technical, financial and services which included personnel. The first three were headed by assistant general managers; the last consisted of smaller specialist sections. Now, on the operations side where the burden of a 300-unit fleet was heaviest, we aimed to divide the ships into four separate fleets, each with about the same number of ships, both owned and chartered. The first fleet would consist of very large crude carriers (VLCCs), the second of medium-sized crude carriers, the third clean oil product carriers, and the fourth black oil carriers. Each fleet would have its own management structure under a fleet manager supported by those who planned the voyages, marine and engineering technical experts, a stores and supplies group and a personnel man with access to the general staff pool. Thus, 70-80 ships would be allocated to each fleet – substantial enterprises in their own right but more manageable than running the entire company as a single unit. The separate fleets did not control their own financial destiny, of course. Each had a budget but could not negotiate its own freight rates or make major capital commitments outside its operating budget. Indeed, this was the position of the BP Tanker Company itself inside the group. Its affairs were not monitored in terms of its balance sheet because that document was almost meaningless. The freight which the owned ships 'earned' from the group in any year depended upon the group's tax position and what suited the consolidated accounts best. I see nothing wrong with that in financial and accounting terms; but in the early 1970s we were operating a fleet valued at cost at well over £300m and with an annual expenditure, including chartering, of about £350m. An independent trading company of that magnitude would have depended upon its balance sheet and profit and loss account as its most important control mechanisms. Such controls were not available to us in any realistic way and we had to gauge our efficiency differently. Ship performance was the obvious starting point. Historically, our own fleet compared poorly with the best of the Scandinavians and Greeks. We obtained fewer effective days a year out of our ships than they did from theirs, our fuel costs were higher and we pumped cargo less expeditiously, at least in the smaller, older ships. Why did these differences occur? A small team, led by Ronald Ilian, an astute ship manager recently returned from a successful year in New York, went the rounds of those owners from whom we chartered ships to flush out our rivals' methods. In retrospect it seems courageous for a leading company in the industry to admit that it could still learn from others. But we confessed, Ilian listened and the results – which could not become clear until several years later – justified our investigations. We developed a creed – 'make it simple' – and it worked. To implement some of the ideas which came out of Ilian's work we set up a three-man team to create a ship performance monitoring system. The leader was a young Cornishman named Jewell. When taken off his normal management duties and told to produce a blueprint in four months, he almost resigned. 'Impossible,' he said. 'Couldn't be done in the time.' In fact, Mike Jewell and his two companions took only three months to produce a simple, straightforward system based on a weekly, coded report from every ship, translated onto a large condition board in the control room. It worked like a charm. Each ship was set norms for speed, fuel-consumption and cargo-handling performance. Whatever it was doing during any week was reported cryptically on its reporting day. If its performance in any category was better than norm a green button was stuck in the appropriate box on the condition board; if the performance was below par a red button, and if marginal or there were some odd circumstances, a yellow button appeared. With 300 ships listed on one wall the red buttons initiated remedial action at once. The system required no computer, merely a code book and radio communication. Later, as we needed more information and better analysis we modified and refined but did not lose sight of the value of simplicity. Mike Jewell never master-minded a more effective project.

About this time I was appointed an assistant general manager responsible for operations and operational departments. Edward Platt, the technical director, was another AGM as was Charles Fratson, chief accountant and head of financial and legal services. Oddly enough, the personnel manager, Frank Fowler, was not accorded this status depite the fact that he controlled a sea-going staff of 6,000 and an office staff of 500. Fowler, a former wartime intelligence officer in Persia, was charming but elusive. He had a small, dark moustache, vaguely pointed at the ends one of which he twisted as he listened, peering through half-closed eyes and thinking up a reason for disagreeing. When agitated both hands flew to opposite ends of the moustache which he twirled furiously. I enjoyed his company and he never seriously demurred when it was suggested that thumb-screws were a tool of his trade. He was succeeded by a short, sharp, ginger-haired Scot who had started off life as a Marks & Spencer trainee after graduating from Glasgow University, and almost ended it by being hanged by the Algerians from a lampost. Tom Murphy later became an AGM before moving on to greater things, first in BP and later in the Civil Aviation Authority.

As the 60s decade moved towards its close we believed our problems in the immediate future to be those associated with continued expansion. Our business would get better and bigger. Medcraft and Cazalet had negotiated contracts in Japan for the first of the company's real VLCCs, four 200,000-tonners to be built by Mitsubishi in Nagasaki, two by Mitsui with a seventh from Kawasaki. The first, the *British Explorer*, was named by Princess Chichibu, the Japanese Crown Princess, but before the ship was delivered and started her long voyage home profound changes had been put in train in our London administration. The four-fleet concept had been accepted and become part of the manpower study group's grand plan for the entire organisation. But Cazalet was destined to leave the shipping scene later in 1970 for wider experience in the mainstream world of the oil company. David Gresham, an AGM from supply and development department, had been appointed to succeed him. I hardly knew Gresham, but he seemed both civil and receptive, eager to pick up the details of the shipping business about which he knew little except as a customer. David Gresham was a crusader of impeccable character and excellent report in the oil company. He enjoyed the confidence of the main board directors and was a shrewd choice to succeed Cazalet. At first he did not know one end of a ship from the other but he was surrounded by people who did. What he brought to the job was commercial sophistication which could not be matched by anyone in the shipping operation and credibility outside the Tanker Company's barbed wire. Inevitably, David's new broom raised some dust but he did not see fit to apply the brush to the operational plans we had been at such pains to formulate and for which Cazalet had been such a potent advocate.

• *British Explorer, launched by a Japanese princess*

We entered the 1970s with high hopes, the best of intentions and a shipbuilding programme which, within a year or two, would give the BP Tanker Company the largest and most efficient fleet it had ever had.

Chapter 10

RONALD FRIENDSHIP WAS COMMODORE of the BP Tanker fleet in 1970. Appointed to the first of the Japanese VLCCs, the *British Explorer*, he flew to Nagasaki with his officers and senior ratings early that year. The Japanese Crown Princess had been invited to name the ship so Sir Eric Drake, now group chairman, and his wife did the honours. The day after the ceremony the *Explorer* sailed for the Persian Gulf, our first experience of Mitsubishi's capacity to deliver a ship in full running order on the contracted day. Two months later Cath and I drove to Milford Haven to meet her and, for the first time, I trod the deck of a VLCC. It was impressive. Seamen reckon that all ships are the same size after two days. For me it is not so for I am always impressed when I step on board a VLCC and familiarity has done nothing to diminish this feeling. Ronnie, a small, neat man with a highly-tuned sense of humour was justifiably proud of his ship. Unfortunately, the pounding the *Explorer* had sustained as she rounded the Cape of Good Hope had distorted her soft-nosed bow. Ronnie had no idea that damage had occurred until he arrived in Milford Haven, although he had slowed down prudently during the heavy weather. Eventually the ship had to return to Nagasaki to have a redesigned bow fitted and the rest of the class were similarly modified. This exemplified Mitsubishi style, a revelation to those accustomed to arguing every penny, every extra and every inadequacy. At that time I had not visited Japan and I had the usual reservations of my generation about the Japanese, but their business integrity was beyond question.

Cath had undergone a major operation at the beginning of the year and was convalescent early in spring. Peter Medcraft suggested I take her off in one of the ships and, without giving him time to change his mind, I arranged for us to take passage to Copenhagen and Gothenburg in the *British Mallard*, a Bird-class product carrier. Captain Malcolm Edge, recently appointed, I had known for years. An ex-*Conway* cadet who had played fierce rugby for the first XV a year or two before I joined the staff, he was married to a witty, vivacious ex-school teacher who had spent most of the five years of their married life accompanying her husband to sea. Anne was with us on the Scandinavian voyage and a delightful party it turned out to be. Her father, an executive with Ocean Fleets, had been unravelling some problem with one of his ships in Gothenburg when the *Mallard* arrived alongside and the convalescent trip turned into a family reunion. Any shipmaster's first command is dear to his heart, and so it was with Malcolm and the *British Mallard*. I can see him now, standing on the jetty at Copenhagen, looking fondly at her.

'Doanit myke yer prahd!' he said in a mock Cockney accent which ill became him. Now the Deputy Master of Trinity House, he still remembers that bustling, busy ship with great affection. So do Cath and I.

The *Torrey Canyon* disaster in 1967 caused the major oil companies – the Seven Sisters – to ponder how to minimise the risk of further accidents and how to deal with them when they occurred. In the US the Exxon Corporation took the lead as did Shell and BP here at home. From those discussions a self-regulatory agency was created, the Oil Companies' International Marine Forum, known more readily by its acronym OCIMF. Its membership consisted of the chief executive or deputy from each participating company. Kirby, the Shell Marine Co-ordinator, Peter Medcraft and Austin Pearce of Esso were the European founding fathers. In due course OCIMF spawned two more bodies, TOVALOP and CRISTAL. The first was a mutual insurance agreement between the oil companies, shipowners and P & I clubs – protection and indemnity mutuals – created to ensure that the cost of cleaning up oil pollution could be met by the industry on behalf of the owner whose ship had been involved. CRISTAL was an agreement between the cargo interests – primarily the parent oi! companies – pledged to top up any national or international funds available for sufferers of pollution damage resulting from tanker accidents. The agreements, partially interlocking, came into existence before the International Maritime Organisation set up its own schemes.

• *British Mallard*

If this seemed no more than enlightened self-interest there was nothing wrong with that. At least the majors had recognized their responsibilities and were prepared to pay up when things went wrong. After all, their good name would be at stake if any more *Torrey Canyon* incidents were to occur. To the general public the oil companies' image was never particularly high. Profit-seeking without social conscience was imputed to the industry and throughout the 1960s the profit motive, in Britain at least, had been made to seem immoral. International organisations cannot inspire public love so whatever we did was always closely scrutinised and often adversely reported. I can recall no sleepless nights on that score, but I am sure that those of us involved were not complacent, realising only too well that the spotlight would inevitably be directed upon our misfortunes. That made us wary and cautious; but the major oil companies were continually extending the frontiers of science and engineering and their shipping sectors followed suit.

This underlined the difference between traditional shipping companies – with one or two honourable exceptions – and the oil companies, as observed in the Chamber of Shipping, the shipowners' own forum. By the 1970s the oil companies had achieved respectablity in that august assembly although never wholly accepted by some as 'real' shipowners. It always amused me to be referred to, usually by trades union officials, as a 'shipowner'. I was a functionary with neither the hope nor the intention of owning any 64th parts of a ship. But there were still many of the real kind about who naturally adopted a more cautious approach, especially to problems involving the outlay of money. It is easy to have a social conscience and do all the right things if your income is higher than your outgoings and your good name depends upon your being seen as a responsible citizen. It is more difficult for smaller organisations suffering a downturn in their trade.

Many older British companies had continuing powerful family connections – the Andersons in P & O, the Geddes family in the Orient Line, the Cayzers who owned British & Commonwealth, the Denholms, the Commons, the Weir family, and so on. Their directors and managers were often scions of the founding families. Some were first-class but others shone less brightly. That is not to say that the aspiring plebeians of the oil companies were superb to a man – far from it. They threw up their share of ndividuals who should never have got through the flour grader, but for the most part such men were rapidly moved to posts more appropriate to their talents. But perhaps the greatest difference was that, enormous as the BP and Shell fleets had become, the companies operating them were still only parts of much larger groups whose chief purpose was finding, processing and marketing oil. In the BP Tanker Company we exercised no independent control over capital exenditure but had to fight our corner against the equally legitimate claims of explorers, refiners, engineers and marketers. We lacked a real bottom line and as students of that cult know it doesn't matter how smartly you do a thing, it's how much you make that counts. Perhaps the family-owned companies were more 'legitimate' than the oil tanker giants who were not masters of their own destiny.

By 1972 our allocation of ships into four autonomous fleets was a proven success. I had been appointed to the board of the BP Tanker Company in the autumn of 1971 and as assistant general manager (operations) had overall responsibility for the four fleets each of which was managed by an executive supported by his own management team. Ronald Ilian, fleet manager of the 'A' fleet of VLCCs, was a natural leader, knew his business inside out and took an intelligent interest in the development of his staff. He had an acute mind, a dislike of slow thinkers, a short fuse and a heart of gold. Above all, he was decisive. Robin Stevenson, my engineering colleague of many years before, was responsible for 'B' fleet which operated the smaller crude carriers. He insisted on knowing everything about everything and, in his canny Stirlingshire way, how much it would cost. Ted Chambers managing 'C' fleet of clean product carriers was another excellent executive with a well-developed love of his fellow-man which enabled him to rule by charm. The black product carriers of fleet 'D' were managed by Frank Broad who fitted the job as a size seven foot does a 10in sock. When he retired some years later, by which time he was chief marine superintendent, he confided that the happiest time of his career was his thousand days in control of his own fleet. I knew exactly what he meant.

The marine and engineering departments which supported these four fleets were now under the leadership of younger men. Smyth and Firman had retired and Ralph Maybourn, whom I had relieved in the *British Maple* years before, my close colleague when we set up our marine development group in the mid-60s, was now

chief marine superintendent. Austere and tough-minded, May
bourn was head and shoulders above most of his generation o
shipmasters. Like Ilian he had a clear mind and expressed h
views incisively. Stewart Speed, chief engineer superintenden
was a barrel-chested native of the north-east coast, had served i
the RAF as a fighter pilot during the latter part of the war an
embraced a sea-going career only after his demobilisation. /
cheerful, ebullient soul with an expansive personality, a great flo
of talk, technical and otherwise, Speed had a talent for getting th
most out of engineers by bluff or domination, whichever was th
more appropriate.   He had an uncanny flair for engineerin
diagnosis and, on the scantiest information, could sense wha
might be going wrong in the engine-room of a ship 10,000 mile
away and how to put it right. Like Frank Broad he was a first-clas
trouble shooter and, as I was to discover, an excellent travellin
companion who could get as much attention from a Britis
Airways stewardess as most film actors.   As the professiona
heads of the two departments which set the operational rules an
standards for all four fleets these two were effective in their quit
different ways.

It was a time to be alive. This way of running a vast shippin
operation so that it was kept under control and, at the same tim
humanised was an exhilirating experience. Years before I ha
day-dreamed about influencing the way ships were run, the type
to be built and how to encourage, cajole and persuade others t
feel involved. Now, in the early 1970s, with the oil world at rip
roaring full speed, a small band of brothers were realising suc
aspirations. Most of us shared Frank Broad's contention that i
was the apogee of our professional lives.

Charles Fratson, AGM in charge of financial matters, had retire
and been succeeded by a clever Scottish accountant lately re
turned from a senior appointment in Italy. Gordon Bissett wa
cosmopolitan, sophisticated, a first-class negotiator and smoot
Edward Platt continued as technical director and AGM in charg
of technical departments, most importantly those responsible fo
ship design and construction. As worldly-wise as Bissett, some
times irascible, his energy and ambition enabled him to leave hi
mark by building the best ships – VLCCs and a new class of super
25,000-ton product carriers – that the company had ever owned
He had fallen in love with Japan – easy enough as a feted custome
more difficult as a salesman.   But 'Commandaplatt-san' wa

ighly regarded by all his Japanese friends who were particularly
ntrigued by his monocle. Tom Murphy had succeeded Frank
'owler and, now an AGM, was in charge of all personnel ashore
nd afloat. He had a charming auburn-haired wife, Sheila, and
our titian-headed children with IQs of about 180 and associated
alents. Thus, each phase of the company's activities - operations,
inance, technical matters and staff – had an AGM in control. The
our fleets were operated by professional management teams
nswerable to the assistant general manager (operations), and the
ystem worked like well-oiled machinery. It was indeed a time to
e alive.

Under the general group re-organisation, however, the Tanker
Company had acquired a new set of upstairs masters. An execu-
ive committee of the BP Trading board linked the main BP board
nd its operating companies. Each member of the Trading board
executive committee – all potential main board directors – ac-
epted responsibility for several important group functions. Ship-
ing fell into the portfolio of Christopher Laidlaw, a successful
narketing man and later deputy chairman of the whole BP group.
aidlaw had a sharp tongue and a reputation as a holy terror.
Medcraft, MD of the Tanker Company, and several other senior
executives in charge of their own slice of the oil company's trading
effort, attended his weekly meetings which controlled the acqui-
ition, shipment and refining programmes. This was a vast im-
rovement on the indeterminate methods formerly in vogue.
Nonetheless, Laidlaw's robber barons, individually, had lost some
f the autonomy they had once enjoyed. Medcraft found this hard
o take. Gresham, who later took over from Medcraft, had less
roblem. On the few occasions when I stood in, I found Laidlaw
easonable if sometimes acid. If you were part of Laidlaw's team
nd were not a complete idiot he would defend you to the death.
f you were an idiot, complete or incomplete, you would not
emain on the team.

That spring the Palace suggested that, if the company had a
aden VLCC passing through the English Channel on a convenient
late in the summer, the Duke of Edinburgh would like to see the
Dover Strait problem for himself from the bridge of a ship draw-
ng more than 60ft. The honour fell to the new *British Surveyor*
vhose master, Captain Leonard Pugh, was about to be appointed
ommodore. Because it was a royal occasion it was proper that Sir
Eric Drake, the chairman, should be on board with Lady Drake.

259

Accordingly, the Drakes and I flew to Las Palmas in mid-July and joined the *Surveyor* as she steamed past the islands. After an excellent passage we encountered thick fog rounding Ushant the day before we were due to embark Prince Philip. Fortunately Lennie Pugh had left some slack in the passage plan and, when the fog lifted early in the morning of 'HRH Day', managed to reach the rendezvous, 30 miles south of Beachy Head, dead on his ETA announced weeks before. Seconds later, the vermilion helicopter of the Queen's Flight, escorted by an RAF machine, circled the ship once and landed on the foredeck. The Duke of Edinburgh is an exacting inspector who, in the few hours at his disposal, wanted to see as much as possible. He wasted no time in drinking coffee and was off round the ship in minutes. With the crew he was marvellous, with the officers searching. We ate on the bridge as Pugh took the ship through the narrowest part of the Dover Strait and, about four o'clock, the Queen's Flight helicopter and its escort reappeared to lift off the Duke and Lord Rupert Neville, his equerry. While on board HRH had given us his views on the design of ships' bridges wanting them more like the flight decks of large aircraft. Some disagreed but were either circumspect or kept their mouths shut. As Master of Trinity House and Patron of the Royal Institute of Navigation the Duke of Edinburgh had taken a great interest in the traffic routeing debate a decade earlier Now he had taken the trouble to see for himself how it worked.

That summer we moved house and, in the early autumn, when the dust had settled, David Gresham, who had become MD on Medcraft's retirement earlier in the year, sent me on an extended tour of the Pacific Basin. Historically, Singapore had figured in frequently in the BP itinerary. It was Shell territory and our trade routes seldom touched the Straits of Malacca; but the group had now acquired a small refinery there which fed the Malaysian market. More crude was being shipped to Japan from the Middle East and our new ships were often in the vicinity. Singapore had become important. Lee Kuan Yew's flock had prospered by their own initiative and hard work, and shipbuilding and ship repair were among their succesful ventures. We welcomed their workmanship, low prices and guaranteed delivery. It was appropriate, therefore, that Stewart Speed, the chief engineer superintendent, and I should spend a day or two there acquainting ourselves with the facilities available. We also visited Kuala Lumpur, BP's Malaysian headquarters, and saw something of that beautiful country, but Singapore was really what we had come for and it was an exciting place to be. One evening Stewart and I gave a presentation on our inert gas system about which the Port Authority was ambivalent. He dealt with the technicalities, I with the philosophy. The audience must have numbered 100 or more, the average age not above 30. The enthusiasm and comprehension London would have found difficult to match.

Our business in Singapore completed Speed and I parted company, he to Brunei and I to Western Australia where Kenneth Nicholls, once of Stanmore, had been the resident marine superintendent for nine years. I had a hectic time getting through the business in three days before leaving for a five-day visit to Melbourne from whence I flew to Wellington, being regaled with the New Zealand gossip by the lady sitting next to me. Coincidentally, she turned up with her husband at the welcoming cocktail party to which I was invited that evening. I don't know whether she or I were the more taken aback. The small New Zealand shipping operation required the services of only five ships each of about 20,000 tons. BP ran it on behalf of the other oil companies as Shell ran the refinery at Whangerei, north of Auckland, the source of most refined products locally consumed. After a day or two in Wellington I enjoyed a fascinating weekend being driven the length of the North Island by Alan Berry, the BP New Zealand shipping operations manager. We stopped at Lake Taupo and experimented with a fast, jet-propelled speedboat, admired the trout looking like 15lb salmon and spent the night at Rotorua, visiting the hot springs next morning before taking off for Whangarei. I had visited New Zealand only once before, in 1942, when Conrad Hopkins and I had admired the *Pamir* berthed just ahead of the *Asphalion*. I have never been back but retain a fond memory of that lush, green, beautiful country whose society seemed to me, then, still part of the 1930s.

From Auckland I flew to Hong Kong and my first experience of the hair-raising landing at that fabulous place where the pilot seems to stick the starboard wing into a convenient chimney in order to spin round quickly and face the main Kai Tak runway. After two days with the executives of the Y K Pao and C Y Tung shipping empires I was off to Tokyo for my first meeting of the OCIMF board which I was attending on behalf of David Gresham. It was an impressive gathering where I said little but paid great attention. Another new boy was also sitting in for the first time, an

Exxon man from New York called Christopher Carven. He was there in his own right and had more to say than I. What was good for General Motors was good for America – provided they both cleared it first with the Exxon Corporation, seemed to be at the heart of his message. Carven became a close friend – an all-American boy, brash, opinionated, abrasive, sometimes given to supporting lost causes, but perfectly briefed and prepared. He was a thorn in the flesh of less competent rivals and a good and true friend – except when playing golf. Homeward bound, as I looked down at the River Ob and the Yenessi veining the frozen Siberian land for what seemed like hundreds of miles, I was glad my lot had been cast among such interesting matters. Furthermore, I would be home for Christmas!

At the beginning of 1973 the international oil industry was riding high. Demand seemed set to extend forever onward and upward. Securing building berth options for new VLCCs meant a frenzy of activity, especially for Gresham and Bissett. Making the best use of what we had was my business. We had adopted what we thought were the proper techniques gleaned, mostly by hearsay, from the Harvard Business School, Stanford University and the London School of Business Studies. Management by Objectives was the current buzz word and we thought it worked for us. For a year or two we had set ourselves a series of operational and management objectives and had presented an analysis of the results annually to the entire staff. Similar techniques were introduced in the ships where the idea of a committee of five or six seniors sitting down each week to plan the ship's programme initially met with a cool response. Not surprising - no clipper ship was ever sailed by committee; the ethos of the seaman's life argued against such bureaucracy. However, by not pushing it too hard or expecting full cabinet government overnight, I believe we succeeded. No master or chief engineer had his authority diluted yet everyone knew what was expected of him and why. Our office scrutiny, initiated by Ilian's earlier study, uncovered some odd quirks in the way the company functioned. We discovered, because Bill Pond the stores manager brought it to our notice, that we were warehousing ships' stores and machinery spares in some 60 locations throughout the UK. A vast quantity of boiler tubes for ships long out of service were unearthed in a store at the Isle of Grain and another cache had to be removed from Aden and lost at sea. Pond, promoted over the heads of senior but slower men, was a great driver. His dream was to locate everything in one place and cut down the inventory tying up less capital. We found such a place in Harlow, not far from the BP satellite office, when Tesco vacated a modern warehouse and leased it to us. There seemed nothing we could not tackle and that year the company commissioned 14 new ships, a phenomenal programme even for a large organisation. Edward Platt was achieving his ambition in lordly style.

David Gresham, functioning both as managing director and general manager for over a year, acknowledged that there was too much in both jobs and that the earlier arrangement of separate appointments was necessary. As a result I was now appointed general manager, being succeeded as AGM (Operations) by Ronald Ilian. The changes had not been long in effect when Gresham was taken ill. Then in October 1973 the great oil bubble burst when the OPEC countries took over control from the international groups which, hitherto, had found and produced the oil and paid their hosts a modest royalty for the privilege. An era had ended and, though we did not then appreciate it, the maritime world would be transformed. The death knell of 20th century British shipping had sounded had we but heard the tocsin. Middle East crude oil was then trading at about five dollars a barrel: a year later the price was nearer 20 and going up inexorably. The developed world was in recession, the under-developed world near bankrupt: oil demand slumped and the need for huge fleets of large tankers contracted almost overnight. That autumn the Heath government was locked in conflict with the trades unions, an overmighty crew then holding every other citizen to ransom. Managing anything in England was difficult and the oil crisis compounded our problems. However, there was a shaft of sunlight for Cath and me. One Saturday morning that summer she had received a rather important-looking envelope. It was from Sir Eric Drake inviting her to launch a ship then building at the Rijn-Schelde-Verholme shipyard in Rotterdam.

The launch of the *British Patience* took place on December 22, 1973. Official company occasions were always superbly organised and the big shipyards also knew how to make a ceremony memorable. The Tanker Company used the group's public relations department for such events and they were excellent. Ship namings were an opportunity to extend corporate hospitality to a range of people associated with the group business. Furthermore, when properly organised, a launch is as enjoyable as a wedding, an emotional occasion and great fun. Our London party of 20 or so couples met in the VIP lounge at Heathrow at 0900 on December 21, a Friday. Several litres of coffee and magnums of champagne later we landed at Schipol and were whisked off to the Amstel Hotel in Amsterdam. In addition to our own party, headed by Geoffrey, the BP guest list consisted of colleagues from other shipping companies, the Department of Transport, Lloyds and the marine insurance and ship-broking worlds. After lunch we boarded an excursion craft alongside the Amstel's private landing stage and enjoyed a conducted tour of the city by waterway before being driven off to the Hilton in Rotterdam. That evening the shipyard entertained 200 people to dinner at a beautiful country hotel outside Rotterdam and we eventually got to bed in the small hours of the morning.

About 1100 next day a cavalcade of cars delivered us to a jetty on the banks of the Rotterdam Waterway where we boarded the rivercraft *Pieter Caland* which cast off on the stroke of 1200 and proceeded sedately downstream towards the distant shipyard and the *British Patience*. On the way the guests sipped a few of what Harry Truman described as libations and ate an enormous buffet lunch handsomely displayed in true Dutch style. Unfortunately, Cath , too concerned about the imminent ceremony, was unable to do justice but the rest of us made up for her. At 1400 we nudged gently alongside the yard's fitting-out berth, dominated by the vast hull towering over the intervening workshops, and disembarked in a drizzle which died away as we walked. A local band, mostly tall, blonde, 19-year-old Dutch girls with short, sky-blue skirts and long, bare thighs purple with cold, played, *When the Saints come marching in* over and over again as we walked towards the launching platform.

The *British Patience*, with a deadweight of almost 250,000 tons, was about 1,200ft long, 200ft in beam and 90ft deep, a bigger piece of steel construction than the largest passenger ship or any aircraft carrier. She looked her size, too. The yard was a seething mass of workers and their wives and children, for a launch is almost more important to the people who have built the ship than it is to those privileged to play a part in her naming. Van der Meer, the shipyard managing director, had taken charge of Cath who was pale but composed – not quite a tragic queen on the scaffold but a woman deeply concerned to do the right thing on a spectacularly

ublic occasion. But she was surrounded by friends and goodwill
nd, in the background the band still played, *When the Saints . . .*
) encourage her.   From far below came the sound of mallets
striking wooden wedges beneath the ship.   The bow towered
most 100ft above us, black above what would be the waterline,
broad band of bright red below that and the paler red of the anti-
ouling round the bilges to the keel.   The ship's enormous beam
lotted out any view down the slipway and, as the hour drew
earer, the tension mounted as always at a major launch.   Now
ommitted, Cath clutched the silver-headed axe with which she
as to sever the cord restraining the magnum poised over the bow
nd kept the gloved thumb of her left hand ready to press the
utton which would release the launching triggers.
The microphone crackled into life and Van der Meer spoke a few
vords in Dutch and then, in perfect English with a lovely, round
Iollander accent invited, 'Mrs King to name the new ship.' Clear
s a bell and sounding to me like royalty with a Scots accent, Cath
nunciated the hallowed words,
'I name this ship *British Patience*. May God bless her and all who
ail in her.'
The axe flashed, away went the bottle to crash against the bow
hampagne foaming white, down went the thumb on the button
nd, far away, the thuds and crashes of shipwrights' mallets
gnalled the last of the chocks being knocked out to free the ship.
or . . . it seemed an hour . . . nothing happened until, almost im-
erceptibly, the ship began to move, the bow now a foot or two
way and then, with gathering speed, yards further and acceler-
ting.   From the slipway came the crash of falling timber and the
athering thunder of anchor cables dragging along the ground
gainst a background of dockyard cheers.   The further down the
ipway the ship moved the bigger she seemed.   Her stern was
ow in the water and, as it became buoyant, the bulbous bow was
ressed on the ways throwing up clouds of blue smoke as the
ibricating grease burned away.   Gracefully the *British Patience*
ntered her element, dropping a curtsey as the bow dipped on
ntry and sliding away towards the opposite bank to be taken in
harge by the attendant tugs.   There was hardly a dry eye in the
ouse as kisses and congratulations were freely exchanged.   The
olemn playing of our two national anthems turned a party into an
npressive and noble occasion and we lingered awhile on the
latform, each with his private thoughts, as the tugs manoeuvred

...e great ship into the fitting-out basin.

I cannot tell how proud I was at that moment. Cath had launched the *British Patience* regally, a ship which bore the name of my first ship in the company 27 years earlier. It had been a coincidence that the ship Sir Eric invited her to sponsor was to carry a name so important to me. He certainly did not know that, nor did anyone else. It must have been the proudest moment of my lifetime in ships. Shortly afterwards, in the shipyard dining room, I had further cause for pride and admiration. Van der Meer included a pretty speech by presenting the sponsor with a gift, as usual; but the magnificence of the diamond ring rather took away the sponsor's breath. Getting it back just in time, Cath made an even prettier speech, concluding with a few sentences in Dutch which she had been coached by my secretary's mother, a native of Nijmegen. The Dutch was understood perfectly by the audience who cheered her to the rafters. At the end of an emotional and exciting day our party was driven through the gathering twilight to Schipol and were back in London by mid-evening. Cath's mother and father were staying with us at the time but had not been fit enough to travel to Holland. Her home-coming was triumphant and the launch of the *British Patience*, in the dark days before Christmas, 1973, is one of her most cherished memories. Malcolm Edge was given command of the ship and long afterwards, when she had been in commission for over a year, I decided to make a short passage in her, a practice the senior staff adopted from time to time to keep in touch with the fleet. Cath and I, with Anne Edge in tow, flew out to Las Palmas and joined the *British Patience* by helicopter for the passage to Taranto in southern Italy. The first sight of the great ship, swimming into view through the open door of the helicopter as the pilot made his circuit before landing, was inexpressibly moving. The godmother was near to tears. Thereafter, we tried to visit the ship once a year, as did so many sponsors.

Cath's mother had been far from well and the burden on her father eventually became too much. They had to be persuaded to give up their flat in Perth and move south to where we could keep an eye on them. Sometimes Kate Irvine's health would seem to improve and then she would have a relapse with the result that Cath worried about undertaking her first representative trip abroad in the spring of the following year. The second group of Mitsubishi-built VLCCs, the 260,000-ton 'R' class, were now emerging from the Nagasaki building bays and Lady Greenhill, whose husband was one of the two government-appointed directors of BP, had been invited to name the *British Renown*. It was the practice for a director of the tanker company and his wife to act as hosts at such ceremonies and to support the sponsor and her partner throughout the visit. Dennis Greenhill, whom I knew only slightly from board meetings, had recently retired from the Foreign Service as Permanent Under-Secretary of State and Head of the Diplomatic Service. He was a mandarin I could admire and his wife, Angela, promised to be a congenial travelling companion. Early in April Cath and I boarded a Tokyo-bound British Airways flight routed by way of Anchorage. It was her first major foreign trip as a representative of the company and it was likely to lack nothing in glamour and excitement; but she left England in some trepidation. Only the doctors' assurance that her mother's condition was reasonably stable and could remain thus for a long time persuaded Cath to make the trip for there was nothing she could do by staying at home.

Nineteen hours out from Heathrow we landed at Tokyo. There a friend from the Eton management course of long ago, Dick Bridgen, met us – he was deputy to Lynn Gardiner, the head of the

* *Slowly down the slipway . . .*

okyo office and BP's representative in Japan. It was about five the afternoon. Darkness comes quickly in Tokyo at that time of the year and it was neon-lit night by the time we checked in at the Okura Hotel, weary but exhilarated to find ourselves in exotic, fantastic Japan. Glad to be in bed by ten our sleep lasted no more than four or five hours. From that moment on we were to be engaged in a constant round of activity, business meetings with shipbuilders in my case, the sights of Tokyo for Cath. Gardiner and Bridgen looked after their visiting firemen superbly but two days later, now accompanied by Arnold Brereton, the naval architect, we left for Nagoya on board the Shin-kan-sen – the Bullet Train – and had 24 hours' sight-seeing in Kyoto, escorted by a diminutive and delightful lady, Misao Kumashiro, dressed in traditional Japanese costume. From Nagoya we flew to Takamatsu so that Arnold and I could visit the Kawasaki shipyard at Sakaide where the *British Scientist* neared completion. There we were joined by John Orpe, Edward Platt's chief technical manager in Japan, who had flown up from Nagasaki.

The Kawasaki people were as friendly and helpful as their Mitsubishi rivals. Japanese hospitality – to customers, at least – is lavish and the arrangement of hotels, entertainment, travel and provision for one's creature comforts are impeccable. I still find it hard to reconcile my wartime image of the Japanese with their competence, acumen and courtesy 40 years on. They were building better ships for us than we had ever had before, and at truly competitive prices. They delivered on time, the quality irreproachable. To do business with them was stimulating but I have never doubted that they see the world differently from westerners, influenced by another set of ethics.

From Takamatsu we flew to Omura, the airport closest to Nagasaki, spending a night at the hot-springs mountain resort of Unzen before driving down to the port. It was cherry blossom time on the island of Kyushu and the countryside was like a Japanese print come to life. I was persuaded to boil myself in the communal sulphur bath there and was astonished to find that, after a few moments, it was possible to move around and even swim a little although I feared that, on emerging from the water, all the bright red flesh would fall from my bones. Next morning we drove to Nagasaki, a beautifully situated city spreading upwards from its magnificent harbour through five valleys separated by low hills like the fingers of an outstretched hand. It was impossible not to shiver at the memory of August, 1945 but I found myself strangely unmoved by the Peace Park and the monument to the victims. The horror is in the air, and my generation need no reminders.

Lord and Lady Greenhill arrived from Tokyo by train the following day and the Japanese welcoming ceremony at the station was reminiscent of foreign royalty arriving at Victoria. That evening we gave a Japanese-style celebration dinner, in a splendid old guest house and restaurant called the Fukiro, to the Mitsubishi top brass and their wives. The seating arrangements, cross-legged in front of tables no more than a foot above the floor, were traditional Japanese and we English were glad to rise in due course, stretch our legs and try to emulate our guests in performing the Nagasaki Dragon Dance, a local piece of pantomime. The dragon, manipulated by six stalwarts hidden underneath, is led by a figure bearing a golden ball on a staff to represent the sun which tails behind a parody of a European foreman wearing a false red nose, a bowler hat, a happi coat, waving a flag and blowing a small, shrill whistle. The gales of Japanese laughter which normally greet this performance are calculated to blow the rice paper windows out of any geisha house, their sense of humour after plentiful wheesky and saki, being basic fourth-form. Talented geishas then sang sad traditional songs and played plangent music on stringed instruments accompanied by small drums. Earlier I had found Japanese music difficult to listen to. In the end I was captivated for it seemed to reflect the tragic side of the Japanese soul.

Another aspect of their nature, love of ceremony and ritual, became gloriously evident next morning when at precisely 0930 a fleet of limousines transported the launch party to the shipyard landing stage, a mile or two away, alongside which lay a splendid white river steamer. We were taken out to the *British Renown* moored in mid-stream dressed overall in coloured signal flags. We climbed a covered companion-way to the deck of the ship in order of precedence, Dr Takezawa the Mitsubishi managing director leading Angela Greenhill. Near the centre of the main deck, a marquee had been erected complete with red carpet, microphone and a small table with two chairs. Our hosts arranged us under the canopy which was a relief since the sun was overpowering. The shipyard band, in immaculate fawn drill with black half-boots, white webbing and white safety helmets, played the two national anthems. As the last note died away the head foreman marched across the deck, wheeled to face the platform party, took two paces forward and saluted Dr Takezawa reporting that all was ready. It was done with impressive military precision and perfect timing but in our society it would have been ludicrously out-of-place. In Nagasaki it seemed natural. Dr Takezawa turned to Lady Greenhill and invited her to name the ship. She stepped to the microphone, said the time-honoured words and pressed a button on the table. To a wild cacophony of exploding fire crackers, a white banner draping the front of the bridge house fell away and a flock of small doves burst out and wheeled round the ship almost as if they had been under training. A moment later Dr Takezawa and I sat at opposite sides of the small table and formally signed the take-over documents transferring ownership. Naturally, the new pen used for the signing was pressed upon the 'shipowner' as a memento! Then, led by the head foreman, the shipyard workers, uniformly dressed, roared out three 'Banzais' and the short, impressive ceremony was over. We toured the ship, which was beautifully finished, and then were led ashore to the company guest house for lunch and the ritual exchange of presents and speeches. It had been different from the *British Patience* launch but, in its own way, impressive although the sight of a big ship taking the water for the first time is the most unforgettable feature of a traditional launch.

Next day the London and Tokyo parties were driven to Fukuoka airport whence we flew to Tokyo and a rather splendid dinner at the British Embassy in honour of Lord and Lady Greenhill who were staying with the ambassador. Two days later, our pleasant duty done, we saw off the Greenhills on their journey home and ourselves boarded a flight for Hong Kong. After three days of business and pleasure – including the obligatory Sunday picnic cruise to the far side of the island in a rather grand motor yacht belonging to Y K Pao as he then was – we left for Singapore which had become, by this time, an important dry-docking and repair centre for BP Tankers. Cath fell in love with Singapore and was well looked after by a bevy of hospitable wives while I did the necessary rounds of the shipyards and government offices.

I had business in Bahrein and there we duly arrived in the small hours only to be roused at 0530 by workmen apparently demolishing the hotel but, in fact, repairing the plumbing on the floor below. At 0730 we gave up, arose and wrote the night off. My business took a morning after which we lunched on board the

Relume – the command I had spurned so many years before. An hour's postprandial nap was all we could afford before having to dress for dinner at the bungalow of Michael Kyrle-Pope, the retired admiral who ran the Persian Gulf lighting and navigation aids service. About to go down to the hotel foyer the telephone rang. It was Geoffrey. Cath's mother had died peacefully that morning. By 0200 we were on a London-bound flight and landed at Heathrow before breakfast, a sad homecoming after the most wonderful trip.

Despite the glamour and excitement of commissioning new ships acute depression in the oil industry was having a serious effect on the international tanker fleet and, not least, upon BP's perception of the future. We were already reviewing forward tonnage requirements and it was clear that, in our fleets, there were a number of middle-range ships which would never again freight economically. They were too big for the products trade and too small for long-haul crude carrying. Most critically, they were driven by steam turbines, the natural choice of power unit at the time they were built when there was a glut of heavy fuel oil and bunker costs were marginal. They would have to go. Other changes were in the wind too. In the late summer David Gresham, now back in harness, told me that he was to be appointed group director of personnel and thus would be leaving the shipping scene after four busy and successful years. Instantly, I wondered whom we might get from the mafia upstairs and was taken aback, but delighted, when the chairman, Sir Eric Drake, sent for me and announced that I was to be David's successor as managing director.

On January 1, 1975 I moved along the corridor to the MD's room and my place as general manager was taken by a tough, energetic and ambitious whizz-kid in his mid-30s called Robert Horton. An alumnus of the Sloan Programme at Harvard Business School Horton had joined BP from St Andrews University in 1963. It was said of him that he brought his own timetable for becoming chairman of British Petroleum. The Tanker Company was thought to be a stage in Horton's development, for it deployed a staff of 7000 and was a neat, self-contained management package with its own set of problems. A more important reason, never hinted at, was to stiffen a management which might be too conservative and insufficiently objective to deal with the mounting problems of over-tonnaging. What we needed, and knew we needed, was a well-thought out corporate plan and Rob Horton was the man to devise it. In his day David Gresham had put together a simple one but, by 1975, the international tanker industry was in deep crisis as a result of reduced demand for ships aggravated by the runaway success of Japanese shipyards. By our estimates there was a tanker surplus of about 100 million tons. The market was still falling, our problem acute. Inevitably, I found myself, during a spring week-end, presiding over my first major planning meeting with Horton and the four assistant general managers. Whatever others were doing, we had to face a programme of ship disposal and staff reductions.

Later that year we concluded an agreement with the National Iranian Oil Company to sell them five ships – two VLCCs and three 25,000-ton product carriers – and place a similar mix of our own ships into a 10-ship, joint-venture company to be manned and operated by BP Tanker Company on behalf of both partners until the Iranians could man their 'new' ships. The agreement was negotiated principally by Ronald Ilian. He was to follow up later by putting together a package by which we acquired a major stake in the Stolt Nielsen Company which owned chemical and special product tankers and had financial problems. We also re-negotiated a contract with Mitsubishi for two VLCCs which Rob Horton managed to convert into a new contract for three semi-container ships to be bare-boated to Ocean Transport & Trading for their Barber Blue Sea Service. These deals seemed right at the time since they enabled us to redeploy our resources, human and material, more profitably. But they were expedients and my heart was never in joint enterprises. Invited to speak at an international shipping conference in Hong Kong on the subject of the tanker crisis in 1975 my Cassandra-like analysis of the tanker crisis suggested that it might be 1982-3 before equilibrium between tanker demand and supply could be expected. This was scorned by Y K Pao – shortly to be Sir Yew Kong Pao – and a charming little fireball of a naturalised Canadian called Papachristides. In the event, 1983 was to come and go with little improvement and many famous names expunged from the roll. In November, 1975 the queen inaugurated BP's Forties Field in the North Sea, a great triumph for our exploration and engineering colleagues, a vast source of short-haul crude oil - and another potent reason why the demand for tankers, particularly by our own group, would dwindle further. But the international ship-building programme seemed to be possessed of its own momentum. Cath and I had already made another trip to Japan with Lord and Lady Carrington and Sir Eri and Lady Drake when Iona Carrington named the *British Reliance* On that occasion we returned home by way of Alaska to visit the new port at Valdez. We were also flown up to the North Slope where the almost-completed Trans-Alaska pipeline started it journey from Prudhoe Bay in the north to Valdez in the south. A few months later Cath herself was invited by the chairman of the Swedish Salen Group to name a new 320,000-ton ULCC in Malmo The ship was to be called *Sea Serenade*, a romantic name for what turned out to be one of a class of six rather splendid, Rolls Royce standard ships. Salen sent over their executive jet for our party of seven and my father-in-law was pleased to look down upon the city of Hamburg from 33,000ft, reflecting that it had figured often as a target for the RAF when he was being bombed out of his douce bungalow in the west of Scotland. The *Sea Serenade* was complete and lying alongside the fitting-out jetty, immense even by big ship standards. Cath had suggested, rather diffidently, to Salen's managing director, Clarence Dybeck, that she might name the ship in Swedish. Clarence, whom I knew well, looked at her with alarm, sucked in his breath and asked if he might hear what she proposed to say, just in case. She had been coached by Hervo Pahlsson, wife of our Gothenburg agent and a great personal friend. Her accent may not have been perfect but Clarence's face broke into a broad grin and he encouraged her to go ahead. On the day, she did the deed in Swedish and, for good measure incorporated a sentence or two of Swedish in her thank-you speech at the banquet that night. The following day the Lear Je returned us home having added a third of a million tons to the 100 million-ton surplus looking for work. Tragically, less than ten years later, the *Sea Serenade's* career was ended by an Iraqi Exocet

Rob Horton, after barely 18 months of the shipping world moved on to take charge of group central planning through which many of the more cerebral of the up-and-coming tended to pass He had not been long in the tanker company but he blew through it like a refreshing wind and his influence was enormous. He was succeeded by Ronald Ilian, 'primus inter pares' of the original four fleet managers, later AGM (Operations) and, more recently, AGM (Commercial) when Gordon Bissett left to go to the Thyssen Group. At that time Ralph Maybourn had taken over as AGM (Operations), Frank Broad becoming chief marine superintendent

274

n his place.   With the massive reduction in ship numbers the fleets had been consolidated from four into two groups, but the control methods adopted earlier remained unaltered.

The company was changing.   Eric Drake had retired to be succeeded by David Steel.   Christopher Laidlaw was on the main board, his place on the executive committee of the BP Trading board taken by Geoffrey Butcher, a supply man.   Peter Walters, later to be joint deputy chairman with Laidlaw and ultimately chairman of the group, was now the main board director with shipping in his portfolio so that the chain of command passed through a different cast of characters.   Our corporate planning in the tanker company – started originally by Ernest Colley, a logical realist who reminded me of Enoch Powell – operated smoothly enough, but planning mainly concerned retrenchment.   The cycle started in the spring with the managing director, general manager and four AGMs hiding away in some country hotel for a weekend to chew over the facts and figures presented by our own in-house planning team.   When further refined by the planners to our satisfaction we spent another weekend at a group conference centre, a pleasant country house in Hertfordshire, with our full team of 24 senior managers, explaining the battle plan, discussing it with them and further adjusting it before presenting it to the main BP board in early summer.   Once the plan had gained board approval it became the operating blueprint for the coming year Sadly, and no matter how clever we thought we had become at operating ships, the plan always incorporated cut-backs.

But life was not all despondency.   The *British Dragoon*, a 50,000-ton crude carrier was taken out of service and outfitted for lightering.   That is to say she went alongside deeply-laden VLCCs in some convenient place like Lyme Bay and took off 50,000 tons of cargo to lighten a big ship's draft by several feet thus extending her range of discharge ports.   The *British Kiwi*, a Bird-class products carrier of 20,000 tons was fitted out as a fire-fighting and rescue ship to cover the Forties Field where she remained for many years. Fitted with four Schottle propellers she was almost as manoueverable as a small warship. Her fire-fighting capacity was impressive and she had extensive workshops and accommodation for contractors' staff working in the field. Her conversion was a great success. Later we fitted out the *British Resolution* as a VLCC depot ship into which big ships from Alaska could off-load their cargo for transfer into smaller ships capable of transiting the

Panama Canal. For more than a year this became an important link in the distribution of Alaskan crude because of the difficulties of discharging at Californian ports and pumping through the landward pipeline system which did not extend into the Mid-west where a significant market for the crude existed. We had an inauguration of the service in Panama Bay because the government asked for one. Bill Barker, my young shipmate from the *British Cavalier* 20 years before, now chief marine superintendent since Broad's retirement, and I travelled out together and were on hand for an informal visit by General Trujillo, the President. Trujillo, every inch the macho soldier, was intrigued by the size of the ship, by the operation itself but most of all by the captain, Douglas Buckley, whom he immediately recognized as another buccaneer in his own mould. Later Trujillo insisted on taking Douglas with him in the presidential helicopter for a weekend at his hunting lodge up-country. They departed with a case of Black Label and I was convinced we would get Douglas's head back in a canvas bag on Monday. But he returned in good order, perfectly sober and complaining only that, at one stage, he had had to follow the general through a raging mountain torrent with a rifle over his head. The general also insisted that Douglas telephone his wife in Devon from the hunting lodge. She told him he must be drunk - and, at that time on a Saturday night in up-country Panama, he probably was.

The major event of that summer was the queen's jubilee and, for BP Tankers in particular, participation in the Spithead naval review. Twelve months before we had been asked by the General Council of British Shipping, an amalgamation of the Chamber of Shipping and the British Shipping Federation the previous year, whether we would nominate a ship for the review. At the Coronation Review the *British Sailor*, then flag-ship, had been in the line. In jubilee year BP intended to make its contribution to the celebrations and a ship at Spithead was fitting. We offered the General Council a VLCC and had the offer turned down by the Ministry of Defence who claimed that they did not have an anchorage with water sufficiently deep to accommodate such a large ship. We persevered: VLCC or nothing at one stage. It was easier, in the prevailing market, to use a VLCC when there was a surplus of that class than to take out a products carrier then at a premium. Besides, the VLCC would be more impressive! Perseverance won in the end.

The *British Respect*, in which Commodore Alan Davies flew his flag, was nominated and so programmed that she arrived spick, span and freshly painted on the appointed day the week before the review. She occupied the most westerly position in the anchorage seven miles from the *Ark Royal* and the *Hermes*, and we thought her impressive. We had arranged At Home days throughout the *Respect's* time at Spithead. Staff from every corner of the group drew lots for places for a day. Tuesday, Review Day, was reserved for the board, ministers and opposition and the Establishment generally. Saturday and Monday were designated for the group's 'lottery' winners and Sunday reserved for our own tanker company office people who had also drawn lots. On each day 200 visitors arrived at Southampton by train around 1000 and were taken on a cruise through the fleet in a chartered tender to arrive alongside the *British Respect* at 1130. After a tour of the ship the guests were given a cordon bleu luncheon to show what our own catering people could do on a big occasion. In anticipation of the days ahead Cath and I boarded the ship on Friday evening and occupied the owner's suite, quite as comfortable as any cruise liner. Ralph Maybourn, the AGM (Operations) and the mastermind behind the arrangements, was also there. Saturday and Monday were a great success. But Sunday, for our own tribe, was much the best fun.

On Monday I had to attend a meeting in London and was chagrined, on my return, to be told that, after that afternoon's Practice Review, when Admiral Sir Henry Leach, C in C Fleet, had steamed the review ships round the anchored ships, the *British*

• *British Respect at the Jubilee Review, 1977*

Respect had received a crisp telling-off in a signal from the admiral. Noting that she was the only ship which had not manned the side he had signalled to Davies, 'Hope the *British Respect* will show more respect to Her Majesty tomorrow.'

'Length overall 1,200ft, crew 40.   Can man the side at 30ft intervals but Her Majesty would not see' might have explained it, but no reply had been sent.   I was even more furious when the story got into the morning papers, the gossip columns gleeful at this addition to telling naval signals.   I wrote to Sir Henry, a greatly respected naval officer, but I cannot recall that I ever received a reply. We had never intended to try and ape the capital ships – it would have taken an imported ship's company of 400 to have achieved that.   Instead, on the day, we had 250 worthy folk assembled on the bridges as *Britannia* swung round our bow to start back through the anchorage.   In 1953 officers and guests on board the *British Sailor* had put their signatures somewhere on a large photograph of the ship.   In 1977 we repeated the exercise in the *Respect*.   Somewhere in a comfortable bungalow near Lyme Regis, Frank Broad, chief officer of the *Sailor* at the Coronation Review and recently-retired chief marine superintendent, in the *Respect* at the Jubilee Review, has both pictures on his walls.

Construction of the first Mitsubishi semi-container ships to replace the VLCCs we no longer required was nearing completion. In August Cath and I returned to Japan as guests of Sir Lindsay and Lady Alexander for the naming of the *Memnon*.   Sir Lindsay was chairman of Ocean Fleets, a non-executive director of BP and a formidable member of the BP Tanker Company executive committee consisting of one or two non-executive members from other shipping companies together with BP Tanker directors.   In my time the non-executives were Sir Frederic Harmer, deputy chairman of P & O, Sir Lindsay Alexander, Sir Frederick Bolton and Sir Robert Ropner, although they did not all serve at the same time.   The executive committee must have seemed a good idea to Eric Drake, whose brain-child it was, and to Peter Walters who inherited it.   Certainly it sharpened up the office bearers and each month we had to be ready for a penetrating examination of what we were doing.   Preparation for the meetings took time, of course, and there was no reciprocity.   None of us was ever invited to join their boards until Peter Cazalet became a non-executive director of P & O years later.

Sir Lindsay Alexander was a sharp-witted man.   I do not believe he had a high regard for BP Tanker's managerial style but he was always the soul of courtesy to me. It was kind of him to invite Cath and me to Nagasaki where Trish, wife of the deputy chairman, Peter Walters, named the *Memnon*. I found the ceremony particularly poignant. *Memnon* had been the name of an *Ajax*-class Blue Funnel ship torpedoed off the West African coast in early 1941 when Conrad Hopkins was serving in her as a midshipman. From him I had heard the details of the sinking and the subsequent harrowing boat trip. My recollections of him were ineradicably associated with the name Memnon – King of Ethiopia, slain by proud Achilles after an heroic struggle.

To add to the misery of surplus tonnage Cath named her third and final VLCC at Scott Lithgow's yard in Greenock. The *World Score* had been built for the Niarchos Group whose London managing director, Nollie Zervudachi, entertained us generously. Cath and her party flew from London in a chartered aircraft: I arrived at Prestwick from New York, independently, at 0530 on the day of the launch to be greeted at the aircraft door by my brother-in-law, George Porter, who was the British Airways station manager. If a smattering of Dutch and Swedish had been called for at the previous two namings straightforward English was all that was required for the *World Score*. Cath, a native but from further up the river, made mileage out of the 'local girl' theme.

The head of BP's international affairs unit at that time was an ex-Foreign Office man, Robert Belgrave, who also farmed the family acres at Piddle Hinchcombe in Dorset. His brother-in-law, recently-promoted Rear Admiral William Sturdee Staveley, I had been introduced to at the time of the naval review when he was Admiral in command of Aircraft Carriers and Assault Ships with a substantial part of his command anchored in Spithead. He expressed an interest in the way big merchant ships were operated and I reciprocated by showing a similar interest in warships. There was some sense in this because for some time I had been a General Council of British Shipping nominee on a Joint Defence Committee with representatives from the MoD, the Department of Transport and the General Council. On two occasions I had attended conferences at Annapolis where the naval arms of the NATO powers discussed maritime warfare and trade protection. The list of speakers was always impressive but it was sometimes difficult for commercial shipping people to reconcile military

● *From left to right, Admiral Staveley, the author, Robert Belgrave and Captain Anson aboard the Ark Royal, 1978*

aspirations and expectations with the cold world of reality as we perceived it. This did not surprise me because for years my colleagues and I on the Joint Defence Committee had been frustrated in trying to get the civil servants from MoD and their colleagues from Transport – not all inspiring – to come clean and tell us more about the kind of war they were thinking of fighting. Much of our discussion had seemed a waste of time although years later, in the Falklands War, I had to concede that the years of talking had not been entirely in vain. But in 1977 this seemed unlikely although trips to Annapolis every second year were important for the contacts made and for the intellectual stimulus of the arguments. Anyway, William Staveley and I did a deal. If I arranged for him to make a passage through the Dover Strait in a fully-laden, deep-draft VLCC he would take me to sea in a warship. As it happened the warship came first and, in March, 1978 Robert Belgrave and I, accompanying Admiral Staveley, flew from Leuchars to the *Ark Royal* working up her Phantom, Buccaneer and Gannet squadrons in the North Sea prior to a goodwill voyage to the USA which turned out to be her last commission. It was exhilarating. The captain was a naval airman called Ted Anson who retired some years later as Vice Admiral Sir Edward

Anson, a brilliant thought on someone's part to appoint an airman to command the *Ark Royal* during her final commission.

The ship fascinated me. By that time she was well over 20 years old. Below decks, I was struck by the old-fashioned nature of her design and construction. It was like being back on board a pre-war Blue Funnel ship. But she had a young ship's company of 2,500 who thought they were the navy's best and that atmosphere pervaded the ship. Before dinner on our first evening Belgrave and I were taken up to the flying control bridge which stuck out from the port side of the bridge house proper and gave an uninterrupted view over the flight deck. A Gannet was airborne and Phantoms were taking off from both catapults. The activity on deck, prior to a take-off, was like a ballet dance derived from 'The Inferno' – controlled, brilliantly-choreographed and fantastically-lit until the last second when the whine of twin jets rose to an immense crescendo and an arm bearing a light signal dropped. With an explosive report, the aeroplane hurtled down the deck and over the bow to disappear into the night sky, the jets looking like two glowing cigarette ends disappearing into the distance. After completing their exercise the aircraft began landing on again. Standing behind a group of professionals talking them down, one could feel, palpably, the willing down safely by every soul on deck of the young men in the cockpit. Commander Flying or his deputy would mutter a few words into his microphone. The pilot, lining himself up with the deck-landing lights, seemed to hang for a second just above the stern and then, in an immense rush, sweep over the after end onto the flight deck, wheels on with a great thud and hurtle forward until checked ferociously by the arrestor wire. Unhooked, the aeroplane taxied forward, the canopy rose and two slim figures in green denims would climb down and stroll aft removing their helmets as they came. They all looked about 18 and their courage and competence humbled me.

Afterwards, a dozen of us had a simple shipboard dinner in the admiral's quarters with William Staveley at the head of the table and Captain Anson at the other end. The Commander, Weatherall, must have been there too. Years later he commanded the new *Ark Royal* and afterwards became an admiral in his turn. Next day we toured the ship from bow to stern and truck to keel. Walter Mitty-like, I learned to fly sitting in the cockpit, first of a Phantom and then of a Buccaneer, until William Staveley whisked Belgrave and me off in a Sea King to visit the ships of the support group.

Back in London the world seemed rather flat.

The return match took place later in the year when Staveley and I flew from Portsmouth to the *British Promise* inward-bound for Rotterdam. She was larger than the *Ark Royal*, but her crew numbered barely 40. The admiral, I think, was taken aback. Captain Paul Dimmock was relieving a more senior master on leave. Dimmock was in his early 30s, young for command of a ship like the *Promise*; but he and his ship's company put on a brave show, although he whispered to me at the beginning that they had no idea how to deal with an admiral being quite unaccustomed to such an exotic sort of chap. Dimmock need not have worried because this particular admiral proved to be an exemplary guest. I have always admired Staveley for being one of the few senior naval officers to discover how merchant ships worked – which had nothing to do with his promotion to first sea lord, of course.

Throughout a lifetime spent in and around merchant ships I have always been intrigued by the ways of warships. Many years before the *Ark Royal* interlude I was invited to spend a day on board *HMS Totem*, a T-class submarine. My companion, Roderick Symon, himself Commander RNR was a marine superintendent in Britannic House. He and I joined *Totem* at Gosport early one cold but brilliant January morning. It was obvious, at once, that we were the oldest people on board, the captain himself a lieutenant in his late 20s. As we cast off and throbbed out through the harbour entrance a signalman came round and noted down our next-of-kin, with addresses, so that the appropriate 'blood' signal could be sent before the boat dived. Ominous, I thought. South of the Owers we reached deeper water and the klaxon sounded for diving stations. With the others I scrambled down the vertical ladder of the conning tower, second last to leave the bridge. Looking up as the descending officer-of-the-watch pulled the hatch down behind him I was just in time to see a crescent of pale blue winter sky before the steel lid clanged shut. Whatever was a claustrophobic like me doing in a place like this? My admiration for the courage of submariners, of whatever nationality, was notched up another point. For a little while I was decidedly uncomfortable at being in a small steel tube stuffed to overflowing with machinery, gadgetry and piping. Moving about fore and aft was possible only if great care was taken to avoid the protuberances. Gradually, however, the excitement of being inside an expertly-controlled piece of machinery took over.

282

It didn't take long to become accustomed to variations in the boat's attitude. One could feel a 'bow down' or a 'bow up' alignment instantly and it soon became evident that being submerged in the shallow waters off the Isle of Wight presented the submariner with formidable problems. The morning's exercise was to avoid the attentions of anti-submarine aircraft and it was much too esoteric a game of chess for amateurs to understand. Whoever won, it was the RAF who broke off the engagement first and went home to lunch leaving us 30 minutes or so for our midday meal in the wardroom. Halfway through lunch, with the CO explaining his intention to make dummy torpedo runs on handy merchant ships during the afternoon, the ward-room curtains tilted forward as the now-familiar bow-down attitude developed. 'Cook on the wheel!' said the captain as he fled towards the control room. Submarines are no place for the nervous, but I was fascinated to see how the hunter stalked his prey when we did a submerged 'attack' on an east-bound American Victory ship that afternoon. Looking at the target through the periscope it appeared to occupy most of the western horizon as it bore down silently in our direction at an approach angle of perhaps 45° to the line of sight. The size and proximity of the merchant ship was an optical illusion created by the periscope's magnification, but it made one wonder how a torpedo could miss. Nevertheless, after the first run the captain, in the simulator, confessed that he had so missed. A target speed of 20 knots was excessive, he decided, and would account for his 'phantom' torpedoes passing well ahead of the Victory ship. It was sheer theatre and I was impressed by the level of training and commitment on board. Returning to harbour the navigator controlled the passage up Spithead blind, from the control platform in the depths of the submarine, a work of art and applied science by a young man of 25. I thought of Dierksen and U176 a lot that day. I still think of him and his crew from time to time and, however harshly they dealt with the *Polydorus* in an inglorious cause, they were the bravest of the brave.

My final brush with a warship was in the *Leander*-class frigate *Baccchante* exercising from Portland when I spent a fine summer day watching young men manoeuvering their narrow, thin-skinned weapons platform at 30 knots, and loved every minute of it. I cherished those opportunities to see the navy at work. In his working life a merchant seaman puts in much more sea time than his RN counterpart, but it is seafaring of a different dimension.

In London the depressed state of the tanker market continued to haunt us.   It was ironic that massive retrenchment should be necessary now that we had more effective control over our own operations than ever before.   In the politics of this industry in recession a number of us, in particular Ilian, Maybourn and myself, were deeply involved through the General Council of Shipping. It had changed remarkably from its days, prior to 1975, as the Chamber of Shipping of the United Kingdom.   In that year the Chamber had amalgamated with the British Shipping Federation, the industry organisation concerned with manpower and industrial relations.   The merger was masterminded by Tim Bolton and Lindsay Alexander, both of whom were on the BP Tanker board. At the time I shared the majority view that it was the proper thing to do, that personnel matters were central to the industry and that it was logical that there be only one body. I lived to change my mind for one of the results, which we should have anticipated but did not, was that wrangling with the trades unions and indifferent industrial relations inhibited commercial and technical considerations in ways not previously experienced when personnel matters had been kept well clear of business.   At that time the trades unions, however badly led, were in the ascendant. In the shipping industry the employers' organisation – the Shipping Federation – and the trade association – the Chamber of Shipping - became uneasy bedfellows in a situation where shipowners lacked the clout, or the stomach, to handle the unions.   The headquarters of the General Council in St Mary Axe had been modernised and the council chamber no longer consisted of a semi-circle of seats looking to the dais but was like any other boardroom, comfortable in a modern, anonymous and uninspiring way and certainly without the charisma of former days. Whatever else the liner knights might have been, most had been larger than life: the meritocrats lacked their colour.

Our oil industry organisations, OCIMF, TOVALOP and CRISTAL, thrived and did much quiet, effective work seeking operational improvements, oil pollution control and promoting improved safety practices. Because these groups were international our meetings tended to take place either in the USA, London or Bermuda with an occasional sortie to Tokyo. Over the years I saw a great deal of the world through the small windows of jet aeroplanes. For my sins, and certainly not for a bet, I have flown from Heathrow on the 0900 Concorde, arrived in Manhattan by

1000 Eastern Standard Time, conducted a day's business and been on board the 2200 Red Eye Special the same evening to be back at Heathrow early the following morning. Jetting about the world sounds glamorous, and it has its compensations; but it leaves no time for awareness of one's surroundings. My peregrinations were controlled by Margaret Reilly, my secretary since the late 60s. Outstandingly good at everything she touched she was also a thoroughly nice girl. Only child of a British soldier who had arrived in a tank outside a house in Nijmegen in 1945 and wooed one of the daughters, she was born three days before our own son, Geoffrey. She came to me on a temporary posting at the age of 18 and never went back again. She made life smoother because I did not have to look over my shoulder – I knew the shop was properly tended.

The British, I think, are good at crisis management. They think so too. Perhaps it is because they let themselves become involved in too many crises. Certainly, their generally phlegmatic, not to say bovine, temperament enables them to deal with disaster coolly. The tanker trade had suffered its own share of setbacks throughout the post-war years, some the result of the phenomenal growth in the industry and in the size of the ships. But, when a 58,000-ton Greek tanker, the *Christos Bitas*, on charter to BP, struck the Hat and Barrels Rocks near the Smalls on the Pembrokeshire coast in October 1978 it had nothing directly to do with industrial growth. It appeared to be old-fashioned bad navigation and incompetence compounded when the ship's master, finding her still afloat, elected to steam into the Irish Sea spewing crude oil from the ruptured side. Soon the *Christos Bitas* was listing heavily and frantically transmitting a distress call. Our operations group in London knew at once that they had a major incident on their hands although, strictly speaking, it was none of their business. The ship was under the Greek flag and independent. It was the responsibility of her master and owners to sort out their own problems. But the cargo was consigned to BP and there was no question of our standing idly by while another *Torrey Canyon* or *Amoco Cadiz* developed. Overnight Captain Stuart Le Fevre, a London-based marine superintendent who happened to be in-specting a ship at Angle Bay, managed to get himself on board the *Christos Bitas* by helicopter. His report called for immediate assistance to lighter the cargo out of the stricken ship. The *Esso York*, a ship fitted like our own *British Dragoon* with the proper

285

equipment for lightering VLCCs, was close at hand in Angle Bay and was released at once by Esso to go to the *Christos Bitas*. By the time she arrived alongside Bill Barker, the chief marine superintendent, Stewart Speed, the chief engineer superintendent, and Fred Day, my friend from the *British Skill* experiments, had already joined Le Fevre on board. In the meantime, Smits, the Dutch salvage company had been engaged by the owners; but even Smits did not have the resources to get the cargo out. What was required was a large lightering ship like the *Esso York* or the bigger *British Dragoon*, now on her way from Rotterdam at full speed. Our own team in co-operation with the salvage company put together a plan for pressurising some of the *Christos Bitas* cargo tanks and transferring the crude oil to a receiving ship using portable pumps. On the day after the accident the *Esso York* took 1,800 tons but was released on the arrival of the *British Dragoon* which, over the next 10 days, transferred the entire cargo under conditions of extreme hazard and the close scrutiny of the television cameras. Half way through, Ralph Maybourn took Stanley Clinton Davies, the responsible minister, for a visit which encouraged the team. Operational control of our part of the action – the transfer of the oil from the *Christos Bitas* into the *British*

• *British Dragoon alongside the stricken Christos Bitas*

Dragoon – was maintained day and night from our Britannic House operations room. This went excellently, but the public relations were less successful as the salvage company attracted most of the kudos once success was within sight. If this was rather hard on the BP people involved, their efforts and courage were recognized where it matters most. A month or two later Barker, Speed and Le Fevre were presented with substantial mementoes by the Department of Trade. Meanwhile the owners and salvors had failed to find a port of refuge willing to accommodate the severely damaged *Christos Bitas*. Eventually she was towed out to the west of Ireland and sunk in deep water.

Early in the following year a much bigger ship, the *Andros Patria*, homeward bound and fully laden with more than 200,000 tons of crude oil suffered a devastating explosion in a ballast tank while steaming off the Spanish coast. There was no danger of the ship sinking, but obviously she had to be lightered. Again, she was on a voyage charter to BP and we were forced to transfer the cargo. Such a formidable task demanded a safe anchorage; but no country in Europe or Africa wanted to know about the *Andros Patria*. Perhaps it was too much to expect any government to accept such a potential hazard off its coast. In the end, the ship was emptied completely at sea while steaming at dead slow speed. The *British Dragoon*, again pressed into emergency service, took the cargo, 35,000 tons at a time, and transferred it to the *British Promise*, a VLCC of the same size as the Greek but unable to go alongside herself since she was not fitted with the pneumatic fendering essential to carry out the operation safely. This convoy of three ships steamed almost 2,000 miles, for four weeks in the Eastern Atlantic following good weather until the task was accomplished. Little of that incident saw the light of day on television or in the British press but it was, if anything, an even greater technical triumph than the salving of the *Christos Bitas'* cargo. It presented no local threat or the prospect of violent death so was not news.

Perhaps once a year Cath accompanied me on a foreign journey if there was a company or social justification. In the spring of 1980 we were in San Diego together and had to be in New York 10 days later. I took a week's leave on the spot and we flew up to Las Vegas, we stayed a night in Caesar's Palace – and didn't place a bet – then took off next morning to drive to Denver. Our route took us by way of the Grand Canyon, Monument Valley, Mesa Verde

287

National Park, through the Rocky Mountains and a number o
Colorado towns where people from Lunnonengland might b
thought to have two heads, but where the hospitality was warn
indeed. The Grand Canyon must surely be one of the few natura
phenomena which surpasses even its own reputation; the journey
was a joy, including the Navaho Indian who arrived, on cue, in
pick-up the morning I could not start the Oldsmobile at 7,000f
elevation. The Navaho have an affinity for machinery and are said
to lurk behind cactus bushes waiting for an opportunity to bea
some sense into the paleface's automobile. This one did. And
ever since we saw the sunrise in Monument Valley, I have been
unable to look at an old John Wayne film without recognizing the
Eagle Mesa and the Rabbit, outcrops of limestone sticking out o
the desert like fingers.

In August I was one of an eight-man delegation from the British

- *George King CBE with Cath and Geoffrey outside Buckingham
  Palace, March 20, 1979*

shipping industry on a mission to the People's Republic of China, led by Adrian Swire, then president of the General Council of British Shipping, and Patrick Shovelton, its director general. Since the mission was government-sponsored we had to fly the flag. British Airways, at that time, did not operate a direct London-Beijing service so we flew to Hong Kong where we caught a People's Republic train for Canton. There we boarded the first Chinese National Airlines Boeing 747 to come into service. At 2200 we reached Beijing, 30 hours out from London and somewhat jaded. Protocol, nevertheless, had to be observed and there was an appropriate welcoming ceremony throughout which we and our Chinese hosts sat in arm chairs placed round three sides of a square, conversing politely through interpreters, sipping green tea and sponging hands and faces with hot towels delivered by young women wearing simple white blouses and plain black skirts. We got to bed in the Beijing Hotel – in those days still the Peking Hotel – about midnight only to be roused at 0630 next morning to be driven 70-odd miles for the ritual visit to the Great Wall and the Ming Tombs. That surely wiped the sleep from our eyes. Our stay in Beijing lasted six days talking at length to different government departments morning and afternoon. Every evening we attended banquets either as guests or hosts. From the capital we travelled to Shanghai. A trip down the Yangtse convinced me that I knew where all the second-hand European ships had ended up. The most memorable experience in that dynamic city was an evening at the Chinese opera. It promised to be horrendous but I remembered a theatre in Amsterdam so many years before when, against our will, the chief engineer and I had been persuaded to accompany Tommy Govan to what turned out to be a virtuoso performance of flamenco dancing and were captivated. So it was with the Chinese opera. The music was certainly different but the actions and acrobats, were world class.

Our next stop was a government rest centre at Hangzhou where Mao Tse Tung was reputed to have spent many week-ends. It was a beautiful place and Mao had been well-advised to seek sanctuary there. Bustling Canton where our tour ended almost two weeks after our arrival was vastly different but we had little time left in which to make comparisons. On Sunday we flew to Hong Kong less than an hour away and at lunch it was uncanny how, after two weeks of superb Chinese food, we all ordered steak. By evening the party had broken up and the team gone their separate ways. I was on the BA flight to London later that night, but I cherish the memory of our short, intense, overpowering experience in China. I had always thought of the Chinese as clever, astute and devious, with a banana-skin sense of humour. Although that view had been partly confirmed they are, of course, far more complex than any such simplification suggests. The people in charge were serious, publicly humourless and committed to the Revolution. The workers seemed industrious, curious and good-natured; but there were so many of them. Even miles from the cities the landscape never seemed to be empty of figures. I had always thought England a green and pleasant land, and much of France and Germany looks manicured; but southern China appeared even more ordered and geometric. Only close inspection revealed the myriad straw hats dotted about every field, each shading a peasant on his or her knees. Little wonder the land looked orderly. If the Yellow Peril was one of the bogeys of the middle years of this century I came away with the impression that the Chinese have enough problems of their own, feeding and controlling a billion clever, industrious and probably independent-minded citizens to bother about the rest of the world. What contribution our mission made to their future welfare I know not. Whether it did any good or no, I would not have missed that Chinese journey for a fortune.

But time was drawing in. I had already told Peter Walters that I would like to retire two years hence by which time I should have put in 40 years since climbing the *Asphalion's* gangway. Had the state of the industry been different, had I not been acutely aware of the likelihood of further retrenchment, had it not been clear that shipping was changing rapidly away from the style which I recognized, concerned with the bottom line almost to the exclusion of things I thought important and worthwhile, I would have carried on for three or four years longer. But to what end? Like Canute I could not staunch the tide. In any case, a new kind of man with a different outlook was going to be needed. I was surrounded by able people as entitled to their opportunities as I had been privileged to enjoy mine. Walters, a man of the future, knew this well. I did not yet think of myself as a man of the past, but I knew it was time to hand over the baton.

Early 1981 was devoted to tying up ends. Margaret Reilly, now married to a young BP accountant, had transferred to a prestigious staff job and thus she would not be left without a role when

I disappeared – always a danger for a brigand chief's secretary in a big organisation – her place taken by Ellen Morrison whose husband was approaching retirement. She would be leaving about the same time as I. Ellen was efficient but, from January onwards I was rarely in the office. I attended a final series of OCIMF, TOVALOP and CRISTAL meetings in San Francisco, accompanied by Cath. It had long been the custom, when one of the 'circuit' retired, to accord him the dubious honour of a 'roast' at the end of the conference dinner. This American invention consists of a number of short but extravagantly insulting valedictory speeches by the victim's closest colleagues and the bestowal of many small, and often vulgar, gifts. Having taken part in many such tribal rituals it was unlikely that I should escape exposure of my own inadequacies. After a superb dinner hosted by Bill Banks, executive vice president of Chevron Transportation, my West Coast opposite number, I was well and truly cooked. Amongst a number of oddities was a beautiful piece of Steuben glass in the shape of a crown. It seemed appropriate, but surprising coming from a group of republicans! There were tears behind my eyes when I said my last official goodbye to America.

Time now seemed divided between handing over to Ronald Ilian who was succeeding me and the retiring executive's lap of honour. In February Cath and I flew to Dyce and transferred to a helicopter bound for the Forties Field. Safety rules required us to wear survival suits and inflatable life waistcoats which included Cath and her lady companion, secretary to George Buckenham the head of the local off-shore marine department and with whom I had served in the *British Resource*. His secretary turned out to be the daughter of a man who had been on George Irvine's staff in the Singer Company and was making the trip because a woman was not permitted on the Forties unless accompanied by another. Few ladies had visited the field so Cath was being accorded a great privilege, of which I was well aware. I was proud of her as she clambered over the Forties Charlie platform, dressed in a high-visibility survival suit, heavy half-boots two sizes too large and a white safety helmet, asking questions and not looking through the open steel ladders at the cold grey-green North Sea boiling 30ft below, because of her dread of heights and fear of moving water. It took courage just to be there.

We had a wonderful day – at least so I thought. But it was essential that the shipping man should eat on board his own ship so we were helicoptered from the platform to the guard ship, *Forties Kiwi*. Her crew had laid on a gargantuan lunch which, sadly, the ladies were unable to enjoy. Cath, a veteran of the seaways, managed to retain what little she ate, but the young lady from the office was less fortunate. After we had been shown all the tricks the *Kiwi* could perform, we took off for Aberdeen, an hour's flying time away. It was noisy and cold in the Sikorsky but, on arrival, the local head of PR, a marvellous woman called Sheila Black, met the ladies with large brandies and led them to a warm changing room. We returned to the field manager's house, Cath soaked in a hot bath for half-an-hour, had a blissful sleep until 1800 and that evening our hosts, the Williamsons, gave a small dinner party for one or two couples we knew well – a tremendous contrast to the raw, real-life day we had just spent on the North Sea. Next day I was taken to sea in the Aberdeen lifeboat, a 54ft *Arun*-class craft – a great treat arranged by my local colleagues in order to get the old man seasick. Alas, I disappointed them although I nearly dislocated both shoulders as the boat pounded into heavy seas crossing the bar. That evening we attended the mariners' annual dinner dance and said our farewells. A week later we paid our last visit to Shetland and were on our way south again as March slid towards April.

On Sunday March 29, 1981, accompanied by Cath and her father, I walked up the gangway of the last ship with which I was to be involved while in office. The flag-ship, *British Respect*, now under the command of a new commodore, John Wharrie, was lying at the Isle of Grain where we were bidden for lunch. John and his wife Margaret came from Glasgow and were a cheerful and friendly couple. They had brought together a large group of our friends from fleet and office, together with their wives and husbands, and we had a splendid and convivial lunch. The leave-taking afterwards I found unbearably moving because I was saying goodbye to the life Cath and I had lived for so many years and to the ships at the very heart of it. As I walked the length of the *British Respect's* great maindeck and over the gangway my thoughts went back to that more modest gangway I had climbed at Conrad Hopkins' heels to board the *Asphalion* so many years before. The romp over sunlit uplands had ended. The future would be another country.

Index

293